The **Season** of **Creation**
A Preaching Commentary

Norman C. Habel, David Rhoads,
and H. Paul Santmire
Editors

Fortress Press
Minneapolis

THE SEASON OF CREATION
A Preaching Commentary

Unless otherwise noted, scripture quotations are the author's own translation or from the New Revised Standard Version Bible, copyright © 1989 by the Division of Christian Education of the National Council of Churches of Christ in the USA, and are used with permission.

Scripture is from the Revised Standard Version of the Bible, copyright © 1952 [2nd edition, 1971] by the Division of Christian Education of the National Council of the Churches of Christ in the United States of America. Used by permission. All rights reserved.

Scripture is taken from *The New King James Version*, copyright © 1979, 1980, 1982 Thomas Nelson, Inc. Used by permission. All rights reserved.

Excerpts from *The New Jerusalem Bible*, copyright © 1985 by Darton, Longman & Todd, Ltd. and Doubleday, a division of Bantam Doubleday Dell Publishing Group, Inc. Reprinted by permission.

Excerpts from the *Jewish Study Bible*, Jewish Publication Society Tanakh translation © 1985, 1999 by the Jewish Publication Society.

The poem "God's Teardrop Exploded" (p. 200) is copyright © Sarfraz Ahmed and used by permission of the author.

"Blessing the Animals: A Sermon" by David Rhoads was originally published in *Earth and Word: Classic Sermons on Saving the Planet*, ed. David Rhoads, 238–43, copyright © 2007, and is reproduced with permission of Continuum Publishing Company in the format Tradebook via Copyright Clearance Center.

Cover design: Laurie Ingram
Cover illustration: Brian Jensen
Book design: James Korsmo / Timothy W. Larson

Library of Congress Cataloging-in-Publication Data

The season of creation : a preaching commentary / Norman C. Habel, David Rhoads,
    and H. Paul Santmire, editors.
    p. cm.
Includes bibliographical references.
ISBN 978–0–8006–9657–3 (alk. paper)
1. Ecotheology. 2. Human ecology—Religious aspects—Christianity. 3. Ecotheology—
Sermons. 4. Human ecology—Religious aspects—Christianity—Sermons. 5. Church year.
I. Habel, Norman C. II. Rhoads, David M. III. Santmire, H. Paul.
BT695.5.S34 2011
261.8'8—dc22   2011015026

Manufactured in the U.S.A.
15   14   13   12   11   1   2   3   4   5   6   7   8   9   10

Contents

Part Two
SPIRIT, WORD, WISDOM
ENGAGING THE SUNDAYS AND READINGS

Preface

About a decade ago, Norman C. Habel contacted me about being the U.S. point person for the new Season of Creation that he and a team of people from the Uniting Church had developed for use in Australia (www.seasonofcreation.com). I was delighted to adapt and promote the materials on our Web of Creation Web site (www.webofcreation.org). The first task was to "translate" the liturgies from Australian into North American English by changing some titles (Outback Sunday to Wilderness Sunday) and many of the specific references in the liturgies (robins for cockatoos). In this effort, I asked my good friend and theologian Paul Santmire to review the liturgies and add his suggestions. Thus began the work of this trio of collaborators.

About five years later, the three of us found ourselves having dinner together at the Society of Biblical Literature meeting in Boston. We shared the meaningful experiences that each of us had had from celebrating the Season of Creation in our respective congregations. We agreed that it would be important to find ways to promote this optional season in the church year and to provide resources to support the celebrations. So we hatched the idea of editing a commentary on the lectionary lessons for the Season of Creation. Norman had already written a theological reflection on worship and some guidelines for reading the Bible. Paul and I eventually edited and added to these materials so that they became a truly collaborative representation of our thinking. These became the introductory materials for the volume. At that time, we also decided to ask people from around the world to do a commentary on the lessons for one of the twelve Sundays in the three-year cycle of the Season of Creation (four Sundays each year). Paul and Norman each agreed to write one of the commentaries. I agreed to contact other writers and edit their commentaries. We were absolutely delighted by the response and the reflections submitted by each contributor. Meanwhile, we secured a commitment from Fortress Press to publish the book and we were off and running. Our gratitude goes to Michael West, who guided the project at Fortress, and to David Lott, who edited it so carefully.

Norman and Paul and I believe the urgency of the environmental crises of our time and the neglect we as Christians have paid to God's relationship to the rest of nature and our relationship to the rest of nature merits a special season of worship to draw us in dramatic ways into the full orbit of God's gracious love for creation and into the fullness of our human vocation before God as brother-keepers, sister-keepers, and Earth-keepers. We hope that by means of this resource you also will find rich experiences and deeper meaning through your celebrations of the Season of Creation.

PART ONE

THEOLOGY, LITURGY, BIBLE
ENGAGING THE SEASON

One

Introducing the
Season of Creation

A Special Season of the Church Year

The Season of Creation is an optional season for the church year. For the most part, the seasons of the church year follow the life of Jesus: Advent, Christmas, Epiphany, Lent, and Easter. The remainder of the church year encompasses Pentecost season (or Ordinary Time), which celebrates life in the Holy Spirit. Of course, there are many special days and occasional services throughout the calendar of the church year, such as Christ the King Sunday and Rogation Day. God is celebrated throughout the entire church year. And God the Creator, Christ the Redeemer of creation, and the Holy Spirit as Sustainer of life are integral to worship throughout the church year. We hope that caring for creation is a vital dimension of every worship service.

There is no focus in the church year on God the Creator, however, no opportunity to reflect in a concentrated way on the foundation of redemption and sanctification, namely, the very creation itself that is redeemed and sanctified. For centuries, our theology, our ethics, and our worship have been oriented in two dimensions: our relationship with God and our human relationships with one another. Now it is time to turn our attention to God's relationship with all creation and with our relationship with creation (and with God through creation). The experience of a Season of Creation through four Sundays in the church year alone will not bring the transformation in consciousness we need to address the ecological problems we face today in God's creation. Yet unless we can see what

3

worship can be like in a season devoted fully to Creator and creation, we will probably not adequately incorporate care for creation into worship throughout the rest of the year. A Season of Creation has proven to be valuable in its own right. Yet we also need the Season of Creation to wake us up and show us another way to do worship *all the time.*

For four Sundays in the church year, you can join in a wholehearted experience of celebrating the mysteries and wonders of creation with God, Christ, and the Holy Spirit. In a special way, the Season of Creation follows the lead of the psalmists who exhort us to celebrate together *with* creation—with the forest, the rivers, and the fields who praise the Creator in their own way. We celebrate Earth, the garden planet God has chosen as God's sanctuary and as our home. We celebrate with the creatures God has created as our kin on this blue-green planet. As we celebrate, we are conscious of the crisis that creation faces because of human greed, exploitation, and neglect. As we celebrate, we empathize with those parts of creation—human and nonhuman—that are groaning because of human crimes against creation. And, especially, we celebrate the Christ, whose death brings forgiveness for our sins against creation and whose risen presence is the cosmic power at work in reconciling and restoring creation.

The Season of Creation is a relatively new season of the church year, a season that is also known in the church bodies of some countries as "Creation Time." As an optional season, the Season of Creation can be celebrated at different points in the church year. Most commonly it has been celebrated between Creation Day on September 1 and St. Francis of Assisi Day on October 4. In this scenario, the four Sundays in September are the core Sundays of the Season of Creation. Nevertheless, the Season of Creation can be celebrated appropriately in the Easter Season or at other times in the Pentecost Season. Some congregations have spread the celebration of the four Sundays throughout the church year.

The Season of Creation is not simply a harvest thanksgiving festival writ large nor a four-week affirmation of the wonders of creation, though these themes do indeed play a role. Nor is the Season of Creation primarily designed to redress the relative lack of emphasis contemporary Christians have placed on the first article of the Apostles' Creed in their worship, though surely this deficiency needs to be overcome. Moreover, the Season of Creation is not introduced first and foremost as an ecclesiastical program to encourage Christian engagement in the current environmental movement, though this may indeed be a significant outcome of participation in this Creation Season.

In response to the ecological crisis, many congregations throughout the world quite appropriately celebrate a secular occasion such as Earth Day or World Environment Day with Christian worship. We applaud these occasions for worship. At the same time, the Season of Creation goes further. It brings the celebration of Earth fully into the orbit of Christian worship as a natural and integral part of the church year. And it extends over a period of four Sundays as a means to enable a much richer and deeper expression of worship.

Fundamentally, the Season of Creation recognizes that our relationship with the rest of nature is a religious and spiritual matter that views life as "creation." The Season of Creation challenges us to reorient our relationship with creation, with the Creator, with Christ, and with the Holy Spirit. While this challenge may have been provoked, in part, by the current ecological crisis and a growing awareness of our place in the web of life, the origins of our reorientation lie deep in our Christian tradition, both in our biblical roots and in our theological heritage. We are challenged to return to our biblical and theological traditions to rediscover our intimate connections with creation and with Christ and the Holy Spirit in creation. We return to see ourselves again as part of the very Earth from which we are made.

The Season of Creation is part of the heritage of mainstream Christian worship. There is no break from the gospel at the core of our faith. Christ is at the heart of our celebrations. The incarnate Christ connects us with Earth. The cosmic Christ is the new life at the core of creation. In the Season of Creation we celebrate Christ together with creation, we face the ecological crisis with Christ, and we serve Christ in the healing of creation.

Why a Season of Creation?

There are many reasons! Here are seven of them:

First, *because God is first and foremost the Creator of all of life.* To fail to focus adequately on this dimension of God's reality in worship is to fail to appreciate the fullness God's work, and it is to narrow and diminish our relationship with God. Our own fullness of life depends upon our relationship with God as Creator.

Second, *because we were created with the rest of nature.* We came from Earth and we cannot survive without all that Earth provides. Just as Earth has creative powers, so Earth itself has restorative powers. Unless we have centered opportunities to express awareness of and gratitude for our dependence upon Earth and our relationship with other creatures, we will not be whole as human beings.

Third, *because God has given us a creation to celebrate with*! In recent years, much of humanity has viewed creation as a resource to be exploited rather than a mystery to be celebrated and sustained. The time has come not only to celebrate creation but to transform our human relationship to creation by worshiping in solidarity with creation

Fourth, *because through worship we have an opportunity to come to terms with the current ecological crises in a spiritual way so as to empathize with a groaning creation.* Worship provides a viable and meaningful way not only to include creation's praise of God but also to engender a deep relationship with the suffering of a groaning creation.

Fifth, *because a fresh focus on the wonders and wounds of creation will help us in positive ways to love creation and so care for creation as our personal vocation and our congregational ministry.* Worshiping with this new awareness may well provide the impetus for a new mission for the church, a mission to creation.

Sixth, *because this season enables us to celebrate the many ways in which Christ is connected with creation.* From the mystery of the incarnation to the mystery of a cosmic Christ who reconciles all things in heaven and Earth, we celebrate the connection of Christ with creation. And we seek to identify with Earth in solidarity with Christ.

Seventh, *because this season enables us to deepen our understanding and experience of the Holy Spirit in relationship with creation.* As the "Giver of life" and the "Sustainer of life," the Holy Spirit is the source of our empowerment, inspiration, and guidance as we seek to live in a way sustainable for all God's creation. Being "in the unity of the Holy Spirit" encompasses our relationship with all of life. This is foundational for our worship.

Church leaders have called for a richer spiritual connection with creation. Many Christians are searching for ways to promote a ministry to care for Earth. Our precious planet is at risk. Because worship is so central to the Christian life, it behooves us to provide foundational experiences in worship to foster a deep transformation in our relationship with the rest of creation. By concentrating our worship on God's creation and our relationship with Christ in creation, we can seek ways to heal rather than exploit creation, to care for our planet home rather than destroy it. And, as we learn what it means to celebrate God the Creator and to worship with creation in a Season of Creation, we may also come to worship God as Creator more meaningfully throughout the entire church year.

Origins and Growth

In a sense, the origins of the Season of Creation can be traced back to the very beginnings of creation. On the seventh day, according to the Genesis 1 account, God celebrated the completion of creation by resting and by blessing that day. The blessing of God, therefore, was not confined to creation as such, but also included a specific time for affirming and restoring creation. The psalmist calls on God to continue that celebration so that God can "rejoice in all his works" (Ps. 104:31). Surely, we can rejoice with God!

The Season of Creation that serves as a basis for this book originated in Australia and has been adapted for use in North America. At the same time, there are many different expressions of a Season of Creation or Creation Time in the church year celebrated in different denominations and diverse countries. Today, the celebration of a Season of Creation is truly a worldwide movement with origins in several simultaneous movements.

In 1999, the Ecumenical Patriarch Dimitrios I of Constantinople declared September 1 to be Creation Day, a time to offer "prayers and supplications to the Maker of all, both as thanksgiving for the great gift of creation and as a petition for its protection and salvation."[1]

In Europe, the European Christian Environmental Network chose the four Sundays of September as an appropriate time to celebrate creation and to come to terms with the current environmental crisis. They designated September as Creation Time, a season recently endorsed by the Third European Ecumenical Assembly and celebrated, for example, by the Bishop of London at St. Paul's Cathedral.

This season has also been widely promoted in the Philippines and endorsed by their Catholic Bishops Conference. In their Calendar Statement of 2003, they wrote: "During this special period of 'Creation Time' we urge that 'our different liturgies celebrate the beauty and pain of our world, our connectedness to the natural world and the ongoing struggle for social justice.'"[2]

In the Episcopal Church in the United States, the Season of Creation was inaugurated in the mid-1990s at the Church of the Redeemer in Morristown, New Jersey. The season has been widely adapted and celebrated among Episcopal congregations. In 2005, the Episcopal Diocese of Minnesota called for its congregations to observe a Creation Season of four to eight weeks during Pentecost. The Episcopal Church provides many resources for celebrating this season.

Without any knowledge of developments in other countries, the spontaneous movement upon which our work is based arose in Australia, initiated primarily by Norman C. Habel. In 2000, St. Stephen Lutheran Church in Adelaide, South Australia, celebrated the first Season of Creation in Australia. For four weeks, adults and children relived the great creation stories in the Bible. The members confessed what humanity has done to creation and how God is working to renew creation.

From 2001 to 2003, Habel worked with the Uniting Church Commission for Mission in Melbourne, Victoria. After a series of workshops, their leaders agreed to explore the idea of a specific Season of Creation. In 2003 and 2004, the Uniting Church in Melbourne provided the funds to develop the resources needed to celebrate the Season of Creation. In 2005, after being tested in about fifty congregations in Melbourne and Adelaide, the Season of Creation was announced as an optional season for congregations across Australia.

In the United States, David Rhoads began to adapt and promote the Australian Season of Creation for use in the United States through the Green Congregation Program and the Web of Creation Web site (see below, p. 14). Since that time, congregations of various denominations in the United States have incorporated the Season of Creation in creative ways with new hymns, anthems, and liturgies.

Since 2005, the Season of Creation has been celebrated by congregations of various denominations in other countries as well. For example, in a 2008 newsletter of the Network of Earthkeeping Christian Communities of South Africa (NECCSA), the Anglican Archbishop of Cape Town, South Africa, wrote, "In adopting 'The Season of Creation' we are affirming that we are choosing the option of flourishing humanity with flourishing creation. . . . My prayer is that this may enhance our worship of God, deepen our comprehension of God as Creator, and broaden our understanding of what it means to be stewards of creation."[3]

In 2009, the United Church of Canada passed a resolution urging churches to celebrate Creation Time during five Sundays in the Pentecost season. The Sundays are organized around the theme "What Is Creation Saying to Us?" The weekly celebrations focus on such messages as "Share My Abundance," "Delight in Me," and "Walk Lightly on Me." The United Church provides extensive liturgical resources. In addition, they have chosen the color orange and designed a stole for the celebration of Creation Time.

The movement for a Season of Creation or Creation Time will continue to spread as more and more denominations and congregations recognize the importance of worshiping our Creator together with creation in this time when we are so acutely aware of the problems and possibilities of our human relationship with the rest of nature.

Features of the Season of Creation

THE LITURGIES

Historically, the various seasons of the church year evolved over time in the early church, as did the basic structure of the eucharistic liturgy itself. The Season of Creation also evolved as an ecumenical form of worship. The team involved in the production of the basic liturgy, readings, and resources for the Season of Creation (on the Web site and in this volume) reflect a process to which a range of traditional denominations have contributed.

The underlying structure of the Season of Creation liturgy found in these resources is basically the same as that found in most churches. The distinctive feature of this liturgy, however, is the fact that a biblical theology of creation informs the several major components of the Season of Creation liturgy and worship resources. As a result, there is a coherent theological progression that informs the sequence of worship. The Season of Creation is not intended to be simply a traditional liturgy with creation motifs included at appropriate points, but a worship sequence that involves creation in a specific progression based on biblical theology. This new theology of "worshiping with creation" is developed in the next chapter.

THE DOMAINS

Traditionally, the names and focuses of the various Sundays of any given season center on specific themes and significant times in the life of Christ. We remember Sundays called Transfiguration or Septuagesima. We celebrate Sundays such as Palm Sunday and Easter Sunday. Other days such as Epiphany and Good Friday are associated with other days of the week. In the Season of Creation, we seek to connect the Sundays of the season with specific domains of God's work of creation. Thus, for example, we celebrate Forest Sunday, Ocean Sunday, and Earth Sunday.

The final Sunday in the three-year cycle is, appropriately, Cosmos or Universe Sunday.

By connecting the Sundays to domains of creation, we hope to achieve four things: (a) to engender an awareness that we are worshiping *with* this domain of creation on a given Sunday; (b) to make a connection with these particular domains in the biblical readings for the day; (c) to foster a realization that each of these domains requires healing because of our environmental sins against creation; and (d) to provide an opportunity for God to bring about reconciliation with this domain of creation.

By highlighting these very concrete dimensions of the domains of creation, visual and tactile experiences can also be readily represented in our worship experience. These can be achieved not only through the language of the liturgy but also through incorporating relevant images and expressions of nature inside the worship space of the church. In this way, members of a congregation can use their artistic abilities and imaginations to turn the sanctuary into the vibrant part of the domain of creation being celebrated.

FLEXIBILITY OF USE

While there is an established structure and progression in the liturgy, different congregations and diverse denominations will modify the language to fit their traditions, depending on whether they are more formal or more free-flowing than the pattern provided by the Season of Creation liturgies found on the Web site. The liturgies were developed originally by a team that included a variety of denominations. Two versions, one more formal than the other, are located on the Web site. The liturgies may be downloaded free from the site and adapted to meet the needs and commitments of the congregation. This season also provides an opportunity for congregations and church groups to create new liturgies, hymns, anthems, confessions, prayers, and blessings.

The language of liturgy varies from country to country. For example, regional flora and fauna will vary. What was originally Outback Sunday in Australia is obviously more appropriately named Wilderness Sunday in most parts of the world. In the invitation to worship, Australians may invite kangaroos and cockatoos to praise the Creator, whereas in Alaska an invitation to polar bears and seal pups may be more appropriate. Locally, some congregations have also chosen to vary the titles of the Sundays to take into account specific issues or needs. In the face of global warming, for example, some congregations have chosen Solar Sunday as the specific designation of Sky Sunday and worshiped with these contemporary issues in mind. The readings for a given Sunday are chosen to suit the original designation of a Sunday within a sequence of Sundays, a factor that should be taken into account in modifying the domain names of the Sundays. And, as mentioned above, the whole Season of Creation is in some places referred to as "Creation Time," which may be organized around Christian commitments and practices more than domains of creation.

READING THE BIBLE

The Season of Creation has incorporated a sequence of readings appropriate to the domain name used for each Sunday. Just as we seek to worship with creation and our kin in creation, so, too, we are interested in how we should read, study, and preach from the readings in this context. Accordingly, we are seeking to read the relevant Bible texts also from the perspective of Earth and of members of the Earth community. We have become aware that in the past most interpretations of texts about creation—Earth or our kin on this planet—have been read from an anthropocentric perspective, focusing on the interests of humans. The task before us is to begin reading also from the perspective of creation.

In chapter 3, this approach to reading the Bible is outlined in detail, with principles and examples for interpreting the Bible. Furthermore, the commentators on the lessons for the Season of Creation, featured in the textual commentaries of this volume, take into account the anthropocentric dimensions of the text and its interpreters and then seek to read the text with empathy for Earth, identifying with the various domains and nonhuman characters in the reading. In so doing, we seek not only to worship with creation but to join with creation in the task of healing and sustaining our planet.

Readings for the Season of Creation

The Season of Creation is celebrated during four Sundays in each of the three years of the Revised Common Lectionary. The sequence of four readings for the Season of Creation creates a liturgical pattern similar to that in the season of Advent. The readings covering the three-year cycle correspond broadly to the years of Matthew, Mark, and Luke in the Revised Common Lectionary. The sequence of readings in each series follows a broad structure of creation, alienation, passion, and new creation. The readings also pay special attention to the story of Earth in the Scriptures, a story that completes the story of God and the story of humanity in the Scriptures.

YEAR I—SERIES A: THE SPIRIT SERIES (YEAR OF MATTHEW)

This series concentrates on those texts where the Spirit is breathing life into creation, suffering with creation, and renewing all creation.

First Sunday in Creation: Forest Sunday

Old Testament	Genesis 2:4b-22
Psalm	Psalm 139:13-16
Epistle	Acts 17:22-28
Gospel	John 3:1-16

Second Sunday in Creation: Land Sunday

Old Testament	Genesis 3:14-19; 4:8-16
Psalm	Psalm 139:7-12
Epistle	Romans 5:12-17
Gospel	Matthew 12:38-40

Third Sunday in Creation: Outback/Wilderness Sunday

Old Testament	Joel 1:8-10, 17-20
Psalm	Psalm 18:6-19
Epistle	Romans 8:18-27
Gospel	Matthew 3:13—4:2 or Mark 1:9-13

Fourth Sunday in Creation: River Sunday

Old Testament	Genesis 8:20-22; 9:12-17
Psalm	Psalm 104:27-33
Epistle	Revelation 22:1-5
Gospel	Matthew 28:1-10

YEAR 2—SERIES B: THE WORD SERIES (YEAR OF MARK)

The second series focuses on those texts where the Word is the impulse that summons forth creation, evokes praise from creation, and stirs life in creation.

First Sunday in Creation: Earth Sunday

Old Testament	Genesis 1:1-25
Psalm	Psalm 33:1-9
Epistle	Romans 1:18-23
Gospel	John 1:1-14

Second Sunday in Creation: Humanity Sunday

Old Testament	Genesis 1:26-28
Psalm	Psalm 8
Epistle	Philippians 2:1-8
Gospel	Mark 10:41-45

Third Sunday in Creation: Sky Sunday

Old Testament	Jeremiah 4:23-28
Psalm	Psalm 19:1-6
Epistle	Philippians 2:14-18
Gospel	Mark 15:33-39

Fourth Sunday in Creation: Mountain Sunday

Old Testament	Isaiah 65:17-25
Psalm	Psalm 48:1-11
Epistle	Romans 8:28-39
Gospel	Mark 16:14-18

YEAR 3—SERIES C: THE WISDOM SERIES (YEAR OF LUKE)

The third series includes those texts where Wisdom is the designing force behind creation and the impulse that enables the parts of creation to fulfill their roles.

First Sunday in Creation: Ocean Sunday

Old Testament	Job 38:1-18
Psalm	Psalm 104:1-9, 24-26
Epistle	Ephesians 1:3-10
Gospel	Luke 5:1-11

Second Sunday in Creation: Fauna Sunday

Old Testament	Job 39:1-8, 26-30
Psalm	Psalm 104:14-23

| Epistle | 1 Corinthians 1:10-19 |
| Gospel | Luke 12:22-31 |

Third Sunday in Creation: Storm Sunday

Old Testament	Job 28:20-27
Psalm	Psalm 29
Epistle	1 Corinthians 1:20-31
Gospel	Luke 8:22-25

Fourth Sunday in Creation: Cosmos Sunday

Old Testament	Proverbs 8:22-31
Psalm	Psalm 148
Epistle	Colossians 1:15-20
Gospel	John 6:41-51

The Season of Creation Web Site and Logo

The Season of Creation Web site (http://www.seasonofcreation.com) includes, among other things, a set of liturgies for each of the Sundays in the three-year cycle, visuals that may be used during worship on these Sundays, sermon themes, brief Bible studies on the readings for a given Sunday, and suggestions for Earth care that congregations may wish to consider as part of their mission. In addition, news and documents relating to the expansion of the Season of Creation around the world are also included. This volume is designed to supplement and interpret the resources found on the Web site and to provide a more comprehensive analysis of the biblical readings for preaching and for Bible study in general.

The Season of Creation has a logo that is displayed on the back cover of this volume. The orb of the logo is planet Earth filled with the waves of God's Spirit. The veins of the leaf suggest the web of creation. The leaf forms a tree of life that is also the cross of Christ. Leaves from the tree of life are for healing the nations (Rev. 22:2).

NOTES

1. "Message of His All Holiness the Ecumenical Patriarch Dimitrios I on the day of the protection of the Environment (1st September 1989)," http://www.ec-patr.org/docdisplay .php?lang=en&id=464&tla=en, accessed March 7, 2011.

2. "Celebrating Creation Day and Creation Time," A Pastoral Statement of the CBCP Permanent Council, September 1, 2003, http://www.cbcponline.net/documents/2000s/ html/2003-creation.html, accessed March 7, 2011.

3. This statement is not currently available at the NECCSA Web site, but see their 2007 statement, "A South African Season of Creation, " at http://www.neccsa.org.za/Season% 20of%20creation.htm, accessed March 7, 2011.

Two

A Theology
of Liturgy in a New Key
Worshiping with Creation

Worship is the central recurring event in the life of a Christian community. Christian worship is a ritual in which God sets us in right relationship with Godself, with ourselves, and with our fellow creatures. Now it is time to integrate God's creation explicitly and comprehensively into the dynamics of worship so that we can be much more aware of how God sets us in right relationship with the natural world.

Worship is a symbiotic relationship between God and the worshiping community. God is giving and acting, and worshipers are responding in faith. Although the word *worship* implies that it is predominantly about what we do, worship is really preeminently about what God is doing.[1] God is actively present in all of God's trinitarian fullness—forgiving; offering God's self in the proclamation of the Word through Scripture and preaching; healing and restoring through the sacramental bread and wine; blessing the community; and commissioning worshipers to carry out God's work in the world.

In the past, our worship has focused mainly on the relationship between God and humans. In recent years, however, we have become more attuned to the extraordinary number of references throughout our worship traditions to God as the Creator and to a concern for the well-being of other creatures. We have begun to lift up these traditions and to give them prominence. In addition, new editions of hymnals and weekly resources for worship in many denominations are bringing to the fore God's relationship with all creation and our relationship with the rest of creation. We now are on the cusp of articulating theologies of worship that fully integrate creation and of developing even more liturgical resources to bring fundamental change to the worshipers' relationship with God and with the rest of nature.

The Season of Creation is intended to highlight and strengthen this movement. It offers us an opportunity to turn our full attention toward God the Creator and toward our relationship with the whole creation. The experience of worship during the Season of Creation has been exhilarating for many congregations. However, God's relationship with creation and our relationship with the rest of creation must become integral and common to *all* worship, not just the Season of Creation. Hence, this theological reflection on worship is meant for more than the Season of Creation. It is an expression of theology in a new key for our worship in every time and place.

Worship as Reorientation

Worship is about being reinstated to our proper place in relation to God, ourselves, our fellow humans, and all other creatures. It is like being lost in the woods and stopping to orient ourselves by means of a compass, and then finding our way home. It is like being lost at sea and stopping to locate ourselves by means of the constellations in the sky, and then returning to solid ground. It is like using a global positioning locator to know just where we are in relation to everything else. Worship is a matter of getting our godly bearings and being situated in our true and rightful place in the universe. In this process, it is not we who set ourselves right, however. Rather, when we worship we put ourselves in a position to allow God to give us our bearings, to reorient us, to restore us to our rightful relationships.[2]

We find our relationships restored through the specific portions of the liturgy. For example, by praising God, we restore God to God's rightful place in our lives as the one who creates and sustains us. By thanksgiving, we recognize our human dependence on God for life and health. By confession and forgiveness, we position ourselves to overcome our self-alienation and the brokenness of our relationships with one another and all creation. By hearing the word, we rediscover a proper sense of direction and purpose in life. Through the offering, we dedicate ourselves and our resources as gifts of God to this renewed vocation. Through prayer, we express a longing for all who are lost or broken to be restored to a place of wholeness in relationship. By communing together, we return from alienation to a harmonious connection with others of the human community and the rest of creation. With blessing and commission, we go out with a renewed sense of who we are, where we are, and where we are going. We have found our bearings, and we have reaffirmed who we truly are and whose we truly are—and, in so doing, we have found our home, our place of belonging. And we know what we are called to be and to do in our life in the world.

It is important to grasp clearly that the relationship with God in worship—God's action and our response in faith—is not simply a matter of moving into a relationship. It is not just a reconnection. It is a deep inter-relationship of participation in the life of God. The Gospel of John refers to it as a relationship of "abiding in" (John 15:1-11, 17:20-24). In worship, we are not just merely working our way through a rite; we are enacting a drama of personal and communal transformation. And it is not just our thoughts and ideas that are being transformed, but our whole selves in relation to God and to creation. God is really present, not just revealing knowledge about God but revealing God's very own self to us and for us and the entire creation. In worship, we are called into intimate communion with the God who has created us and all things. We are called into relationship with the Christ who redeems us and the whole creation. And we are called to share in the life of the Holy Spirit who empowers and sustains us and all creatures.

In practice, however, our restoration/reorientation through worship has tended to leave out an important, indeed crucial, relationship. We are reoriented to God, self, and the human community, but often we have experienced that reorientation without a self-conscious reorientation of our relationship with the rest of creation, which is the matrix in which we live and move and have our being. We are a part of nature. Along with all other living beings and nonliving things, we *are* nature. Creation is one reality.

If God created the world as a place in which human life is inextricably woven into the rest of creation, then we need to make the natural world self-consciously an integral part of our worshiping experience. If worship means being restored to our proper place in the world in order to reorient us, to recall who we are, where we have come from, the things upon which we depend, and that for which we are responsible, then worship must be a celebration of all of creation and a reorientation of ourselves to our proper place within it. Just as human health and well-being, peace and justice, are dependent on our right relationships with each other, so also they are dependent on our relationships with the rest of creation. According to the creation story in Genesis 1, this is what we are called to do: love God, love our neighbors, care for creation.

A Theology of Worship

Why is it important to articulate a "theology" of worship? There has always been a close relationship between theology and worship, as indeed there should be. Worship expresses what we believe. It embodies the theologies we espouse, for better or for worse. It manifests in the gathered community the most significant views we embrace about God, Christ, and the Holy Spirit. Therefore, as we change our theology, so we must change our worship in order to reflect what we most ardently believe. Indeed, throughout history, theologies have changed and expanded. And they are changing again today in relation to the ecological challenges of planet Earth and of our increased awareness of the natural world and our human relationship to it.

It is no longer possible to do a serious constructive or systematic theology without encompassing the centrality of God the Creator and of creation itself. Nor is it any longer viable to do a theology of the Old Testament or the New Testament without shifting the weight of the study to embrace God's relationship with all of creation. We see the Bible with new eyes and understand God's redeeming work in fresh ways.[3] So also, our theology of worship should reflect the same shift. Our worship needs to embody these developments as we discern more fully the dimensions of God's word and work.[4]

Consider the changes that took place in the sixteenth-century Protestant Reformation: theology was conceived in new ways; the Bible was interpreted with new eyes; ethical commitments were reconfigured; and worship was transformed. The same could be said of the Roman Catholic Church after Vatican II. Due to changing times and fresh challenges, the church has always risen to the occasion. Now we are facing ecological threats to the very existence of life as we have known it on Earth. Is there any doubt that this defining issue of the twenty-first century represents a challenge to the church? We are called to rise to this challenge and to address our human relationship with the rest of nature.

Given this new understanding of the challenges of our time, we must reshape and enhance our worship so that our relationship with the whole creation is writ large across our liturgies, our lectionaries, and our church year—not just with a few phrases here and there, not just with an occasional hymn, not just with a few special days in the church calendar. Our relationship with all creation must now become as central and as obvious in worship as are our relationships with God and with each other. God's love of creation, God's desire to redeem creation, and God's action in reorienting our human relationship with the rest of creation ought to be so present in all we do in worship that they claim our hearts and minds with enthusiasm. This involves recognizing God as the Creator and creation itself as an integral part of everything we do in worship.

Celebrating the Season of Creation gives us a vision of what that kind of worship could be like in every liturgical season—as we celebrate the role of Christ in redeeming creation and the work of the Holy Spirit in sustaining creation. The Season of Creation can be the basis for transforming all of our worship in a new key.

WORSHIPING TOGETHER WITH ALL OF NATURE

Perhaps the most important thing we can say about a new theology of liturgy is that we are called to worship and praise God *with* nature. Remember that Scripture calls for the hills to clap their hands and the trees to sing for joy, along with animals and sea creatures, the seas and the soils, the fields and the grain. Psalm 148 commands every aspect of creation to glorify God and, in sum, calls out: "All creation, praise the LORD!" (Psalm 148; cf. also 1 Chron. 16:29-34, as well as Psalms 104 and 148, among others). Hence, nature itself is to be experienced as part of our worshiping community, as our partner in praise.

WORSHIP AS NEW CREATION

We have emphasized worship as two-dimensional: the actions of God orienting us to right relationships, and our faithful responses to God's actions. The reorientation to the natural world brought about by God in worship represents a fundamental change of direction for us. It is not just a matter of accommodating a few new ideas or practices. Further, restoration to relationship with God, others, and nature is by no means the same as assimilation into the society and culture around us. Reconciled relationships with God will orient us to values, actions, and structures that may go against the grain of the world around us. They can be fundamentally countercultural.

Reconciled relationships with other humans will set us at odds with the injustices, oppressions, neglect, and discrimination by groups and individuals not sharing the church's values. Being reoriented to a love of nature and the care for creation may likewise lead us to resist and oppose the practices of local and national governments, businesses, corporations, and others who contribute to the flagrant degradation of Earth's natural systems and life.

Worship can be subversive of the culture and an expression of countercultural thinking and acting. Worship can lead us to counter the consumer mentality and practices of our time that treat people and Earth as commodities to be exploited. It can lead us to advocate for public policies and laws that foster love of neighbor and care for creation. At the same time, our reorientation in worship may lead us to affirm many movements and actions in the culture around us that further the kinds of values and behaviors fostered by Christian ways of being in the world.

By drawing us into a reorientation of relationships, worship is meant to give us a taste of new creation—creation redeemed and reconciled. For this brief period of time, we celebrate our communion with God, with each other, and with all creation so that we get a glimpse of God's vision for the whole world. We are placed on the trajectory that God is moving along in order to bring creation to fulfillment. We have suspended the claims of the world around us, yet brought that world with us into worship, seen it and ourselves transformed, and then revisioned that world as God's creation. With this experience of transformation, we reenter our ordinary lives as changed people, ready to remake the world as God would have it made anew, in whatever ways, modest or visionary, that the Spirit of God inspires us to follow.

In this comprehensive sense, then, worship is a radical reorientation. It is resocialization at a primary level. It challenges our culture's core values, which we sometimes assume to be fixed. It invites us into a way of being in the world that is healing and wholesome, that fosters justice and peace, that bears reverence for life, that enhances care for people and nature, and that serves rather than dominates.

Care for Creation in the Seasons and Days of the Church Year

Again, worship in solidarity with all creation is a goal for more than the Season of Creation. It is the kind of worship we are called to practice all year and in every season. Each season of the church year lends itself to the thematic development of our relationship with all creation:

- *Advent*: all creation groans together as we await redemption and restoration of all of life. Advent is a time to repent in preparation for a new age in which the leaves of the trees, as John the Seer depicts it in his vision of the new Jerusalem, will be "for healing of the nations" (Rev. 22:2).
- *Christmas*: We celebrate the Word made flesh, God become incarnate as human being in solidarity with all other humans and in solidarity with all of life. We acknowledge the ways in which the embodiment of the incarnation affirms the realities of God's creation.
- *Epiphany*: Here we celebrate the manifestation and glory of God not only in the arrival of the Christ child but also in the light and glory of God present in the beautiful works of human creativity, in the magnificence of the whole Earth, and indeed in the resplendent vastness of the whole cosmos.
- *Lent*: During Lent, we recognize our complicity in sin, not only against God and against one another, but also against the rest of nature, which has been degraded by our individual and corporate actions. We grieve losses to God's good Earth and reflect on the sacrifices we must make to stop our sins against creation even as we seek to hear, with new ears, the voice of every suffering creature.
- *Easter*: We celebrate the resurrection of human life and envision the restoration/regeneration of the entire cosmos as a new creation.
- *Pentecost or Ordinary Time*: We reflect on the spiritual wisdom we need and the actions we can take—as individuals, as congregations, and as a society—to live in a world where human and nonhuman creation can thrive together in the full flourishing that only the Spirit can give.
- *Season of Creation*: We focus on God as Creator and the wonders of creation, all designed to help us love creation as God does and commit ourselves to care for it and rejoice in it.
- *Special Days*: There are many special occasions in the year when it is especially appropriate that care for creation becomes the focus of the whole service, such as St. Francis Day and Rogation Day. There are also days in the lives of many cultures that are opportunities for celebrating creation, such as Thanksgiving Day and Earth Day Sunday. Special services might include a blessing of the animals, tree-planting ceremonies, and a greening of the cross service, among others.

In all of these seasons and days, there is the opportunity to encompass all of God's creation in our observances and celebrations. Seasonal decorations, banners, and sayings can keep this message before the congregation throughout the year. Further, we can enhance the experience of worship by bringing signs of living nature into the sanctuary: placing greenery and flowering plants or trees in the church; giving people seeds or seedlings to plant; decorating the sanctuary with natural art; opening the sanctuary to natural light through windows and skylights; and worshiping outside. We can also employ special colors (Earth tones!), paraments, banners, and other decorative appointments for the Season of Creation. Green is beautiful! And so are all colors, as we know from the witness of the rainbow.

Earth-friendly practices can also contribute to the integrity and witness of the worship: beeswax candles instead of oil-based candles; home-grown plants or flowers instead of commercially produced products transported from a distance (the latter may bring with them the stain of injustice); local wine and organic, whole-grain bread; postconsumer paper; baskets at exits to recycle bulletins; minimized paper and energy use; communion practices that limit waste (for example, glass drinking cups instead of disposable plastic cups); worship vessels cleaned in an Earth-safe detergent; fair-trade palms purchased for Palm Sunday, and so on.

In all these ways, we can create an ethos in the congregation that will pervade worship with care for creation and with an experience of the God-given integrity of nature itself.

In sum, in order for us to be truly reoriented by God in our worship, we should incorporate love for, celebration of, concern for, prayer for, and a commitment to care for all creation into every dimension of our worship experience. Just as we cannot imagine worship without praise of God and expressions of love for others, especially those in need, so, too, we should not be able to imagine worship without expressions of our love for and our commitment to God's creation.

A Theology of the Liturgy

We now turn to explore essential elements of the liturgy that help us to worship in this new key. Each element of the liturgy needs to be reconceived so as to embrace all of creation in our worship. Below you will see the distinct theologies that best articulate the different dynamics of each part of the liturgy in relation to caring for creation. Our purpose here is to integrate fully all relationships in worship: God and humans; humans and humans; God and all creation; humans and the rest of creation.

The Invocation: The God of All Creation and a Theology of Earth Sanctuary

The reorientation generated by worship begins by emphasizing the image of the God who is depicted in the first article of the Christian creeds. The God whose active presence we invoke in worship is the Creator of the immense universe through all time and space. This God is not only a personal God and a God of human beings. This God is also the one who created and continues to create the heavens and the Earth. From beginning to end, the work of God has to do with all creation. The following invocation seems appropriate.

> We invoke the active presence of God the Creator who formed all creation, God the Word who redeems all creation, and God the Spirit who sustains all creation and brings it to fulfillment.

When we lift up this image of God as Creator, then we also need to rethink the dimensions of the sanctuary within which we worship; for example, "In communion with all the Earth, we gather to worship God the Creator of all things, God the Redeemer of all things, and God the Sustainer of all things." Only a sanctuary the size of Earth itself is adequate for our worship. Only then do we begin adequately to honor God as Creator. Only then are we able to embrace fully all the living creatures and nonliving realities of the Earth community upon which humans depend and with whom we share this creation. We enter into an awareness of this all-encompassing sanctuary of Earth when we acknowledge and invoke the active presence of the one who fills all creation with glory.

DOWN-TO-EARTH WORSHIP

A fundamental way to allow God to reorient us in worship, then, is to see Earth, rather than the walls of our own church building, as our sanctuary. In this respect, as we worship, Earth is for us a sacred space, a place where God is active and where God encounters us. Scriptures reveal God's presence permeating all creation and making it sacred. Consider Isaiah's spectacular vision (6:3), incorporated in many eucharistic prayers:

> Holy, holy, holy is the LORD of hosts!
> The whole Earth is full of God's glory.

The apostle Paul also makes it quite clear that the invisible power and presence of God can be known to all people on Earth, so that we have no excuse for not knowing there is a Creator (Rom. 1:19-20).[5]

When we take seriously the presence of God in the whole creation, moreover, we are called to rethink our idea of God so as to look to God not only above us in the heavens but also in "deep down things."[6] In the past, we tended to accept the traditional cosmology of ancient peoples, the view of the cosmos that heaven is up and Earth is down, and so we prayed "up" as if God were only above in heaven. Now we have a new view of the universe and planet Earth so that we may think of God as everywhere in all things. This actually turns out to be closer to the biblical view in the sense that God is filling Earth with God's glory. Also, the Bible presents the view that the impulse of our Creator is to move down into this world. While we do pray, "Our Father who art in heaven," all the more so we also pray, "Your kingdom come . . . on Earth . . ." (Matt. 6:9-10). So we confess that God is vitally present in all creatures, human and nonhuman.

This biblical revelation of how the glory of God fills Earth—and indeed all of creation—does not claim that creation itself is God. We do not worship creation. God's presence is "in, with, and under" every aspect of this world, as Martin Luther teaches us.[7] Of course, the most powerful and definitive revelation of God's glory is seen in the person of Jesus Christ. And it is from God's presence and activity in Jesus that we know that God's holiness and glory are everywhere in creation. Seeing God made flesh in Christ, we can then "lift up our eyes to the hills," as the psalmist says (Ps. 121:1), and indeed contemplate the whole creation and the glory of God the Creator.

Call this the resacralization of creation. When we see God in Christ and then also in, with, and under the whole Earth, and indeed the whole cosmos, then for us all things are sacred. Closer at hand, too, is this: if God is so intimately and immediately present in all things, God is not only in the bread and wine of the Eucharist and in all people as the body of Christ; God is also present in the paraments and the banners, in the flowers and in the candles, in the altar and in the symbols, in the organ and in the pews, in the actions and in the gestures, in the speaking and in the song, in the light and in the dark.[8] All of these have the effect of connecting us with their root and source in the larger sanctuary of Earth, because all of these derive from living and nonliving realities in creation. When this discernment happens, we have succeeded in breaking down the barrier between church and world, between insiders and outsiders, between worshipers and nature. Whether in the church building or outside, the ground upon which we stand is "holy ground." All of our worship reflects the glorious presence of God permeating all things.

Many of us have had experiences in which God encounters us in our relationship with the natural world. In seeing Earth as God's sanctuary, we are honoring those experiences and we are acknowledging that God actively seeks us through nature, just as God seeks us through other people. As Martin Luther has written, "Our home, field, garden, and everything, is full of Bible, where God through his wondrous works not only preaches, but also knocks on our eyes, touches our senses, and somehow enlightens our hearts."[9] By worshiping with Earth as our sanctuary, we build on those sacred experiences of nature and make ourselves open to God reaching us through nature all the more.

A SANCTUARY FOR ALL OF LIFE

When we commence worship by invoking the presence of the Creator God in God's entire sanctuary of Earth, we are acutely aware that this Earth is an endangered planet—in large part due to our own desecration of the air, the land, and the waters of Earth. How can we treat Earth differently? We humans sometimes designate certain areas of land, air, and water as natural "sanctuaries" that offer protection to a variety of animals, species of plants, and whole ecosystems. Can we not think of all of Earth as God's sanctuary for the benefit of the whole Earth community that God has created? Can we not think of this Earth sanctuary as a place of safety and well-being for all creatures great and small?

This is the challenge we have right at the beginning of our worship—to broaden our horizon so that we have a vision of God writ large over creation and so that we are reoriented in relationship not only with one another and with all humanity but also with God's whole creation.

The Invitation and Gloria:
A Theology of Kinship with Creation

Our reorientation in worship continues with the call to worship or invitation—as we affirm our solidarity with the rest of creation by inviting all creation to join in worship. In this process, we not only praise God for creation, we also worship God with creation.

> We invite the birds and the insects, the animals on land and the fish of the sea, the rocks and the trees, the soil and the air, the mountains and the valleys, the oceans and the rivers, the sun, the moon, and all stars to join in communion with us this day in bringing glory and praise to the God who has created us and who sustains us forever.

We might include the other members of Earth community who live together with us on our church property:

> Today we invite as our partners in worship the pine trees that live on our property, the plants in our garden, the lush grass and the bright bushes, the cardinals and the crows that feed on the worms, the beetles and the bees, the rabbits and the raccoons who share this space with us. Join us in praise of our Creator.

We might state this invitation in an inverse way, namely, that we are calling ourselves to join the rest of creation in worship already taking place everywhere:

> Today we call ourselves to join in the hymn of all creation—with the wrens and the robins, the otters and the owls, the baboons and the butterflies, the elm trees and the pine trees, the rice and the snow peas, the grass and the grasshoppers, the lava and the lakes, the mountains and the seas, and all created things everywhere.

We are invited to "join the communion of all creation," to "let heaven and nature sing" and to "let all creation join as one, to praise [God's] holy name." All together, the choir of creation acknowledges God as the inexhaustible source of life and goodness.

CONVERSION TO EARTH

To consider worshiping *with* our kin in creation may require something of a conversion. The fundamental problem that this new theology of worship addresses is our human alienation from the rest of God's creation and our consequent misuse of God's creation. In worship, God is restoring us to our relationship to Earth by broadening our worship experience to encompass all that God loves and by connecting us to all that Christ seeks to redeem and reconcile, by the life-giving power of the Holy Spirit.

In order to worship with creation, we first need to recognize our kinship with the rest of creation—including Earth as our primal parent. As Genesis 2 teaches us, living things have all commonly emerged from the soil. So we are all kin. To view Earth as other than mere matter and to know all creatures as our kin may, as we have suggested, require a radical change of consciousness. But this is the truth we now confess with new enthusiasm. God is reorienting us to a relationship with Earth so that we can now experience all creatures as our kin, as we join all creation in praise.

Likewise, the concept of evolution teaches us that humans have a biological connection with other creatures and a common origin in Earth. Humans are born of Earth, and so "we are creatures of the Earth."[10] We are comprised of the same elements that make up the planet and the same stardust of which the galaxies are composed. The cells of our bodies are composed of 65 to 90 percent water. We share DNA in common with other creatures. Hence, we are all kin biologically. We are "natural" creatures through and through.

As such, the scientific construct of evolution helps us to understand much more concretely what Genesis 2 means when it says that humans are "of the soil." This is how the Bible sees our kinship with the larger world of nature. When Job said, "Naked I came from my mother's womb, and naked shall I return there!" (Job 1:21), he meant a coming from and a return to Earth as his mother. In Genesis 2, Earth is the common source of all living beings. God molds the first human, Adam (*adam*), from the soil (*adamah*) of Earth. Adam's name means "Earth-man." Similarly, in Genesis 1, all animal life comes from the *adamah* of Earth. God says, "Let the earth bring forth living creatures of every kind" (Gen. 1:24). And God says, "Let Earth put forth vegetation" (Gen. 1:11). All humans and all fauna and flora share the same origin and the same ground, Earth. Kinship among the living creatures in this garden world extends particularly to breath. According to the Bible, all living things are commonly animated by God's breath.

THE CHOIR OF ALL CREATION

To grasp how it is that creation is to praise God, we need to understand that Earth and members of Earth community are not treated as "it" in the Bible. Earth is often personalized—as a subject who can hear the voice of God (Isa. 1:2, 34:1, 49:13; Jer. 6:19, 22:29; Joel 2:21-22), as having emotions, as capable of suffering and mourning (Isa. 24:4, 33:9; Jer. 4:28, 12:4, 11, 14:4, 23:10; Joel 1:18-20), and as obeying God's commands. As such, we can view Earth in personal relationship with God and with us as a worshiping community.

And indeed, like humans, this entire created order is called to praise God. Just listen to these acclamations from 1 Chronicles 16:29b, 31-33:

> Worship the LORD in holy splendor:
> tremble before him, all the earth . . .
> Let the heavens be glad, and let the earth rejoice,
> and let them say among the nations, "The LORD is king."
> Let the sea roar and all that fills it;
> let the field exalt and everything in it.
> Then shall the trees of the forest sing for joy
> before the LORD . . .

In Psalm 148, everything from sun and moon to sea monsters and snow are called upon to praise God—along with all rulers and peoples of Earth. Our invitation bids us to join with the whole choir of creation. Our call to worship is to "let all creation praise the Lord."

Of course, we need not assume that plants and animals have special voices for praise. Rather, they praise God simply by being who they were created to be and by thriving in that life. But God has ears to hear this "music of the spheres" all the more. This understanding of praise means that when we humans behave in ways that harm or destroy other living things, we diminish their capacity to praise God! Then the land languishes, the grapevines dry up, and the wheat withers. Then their voice is one of lament. Being in solidarity with the rest of nature makes us acutely aware of the ways in which plants and animals suffer, often as a result of human activity. Can we then also worship in ways that enable us to lament with other creatures as well as to celebrate with them, and to express our responsibility toward them? If we will do so, only then will we truly join them in worship with integrity, as the God we know in the Bible intends us to do.

We need to find ways in worship to make this common voice a reality. We need to use our imaginations to consider how our worship might change so that we praise God with creation. As we have suggested, we can begin by inviting otherkind to join humankind in our worship. And we can so fill our liturgies with references to fellow creatures that our kinship with them permeates all we do in our worship. Also, can we be aware of the natural surroundings of our worship center? Can we bring life into the sanctuary, such as trees and plants and flowers, and even living things like fish and birds and gerbils? Can we use the service of the Blessing of the Animals (human and nonhuman animals alike!) as an opportunity to strengthen our kinship with nature and to be more aware of our common worship with these and all living things? Some congregations have even experimented with projecting images of the galaxies and their myriad stars on the worship-center walls. In this way, in our mind's eye, our sanctuary for worship can become not just a building, and not even just the Earth itself, but the entire universe. We can see the entire creation in our worship, in John Calvin's words, as "the theater of God's glory."[11]

The Confession:
A Theology of Alienation and Reconciliation

Confession and absolution in worship are based on a theology of alienation and reconciliation. Traditionally, we have confessed the sins we have committed—both individually and collectively—against God and other humans. Our reorientation in worship means that we will now also confess our sins against the rest of nature, against God's creation. In the case of sins against Earth, our confession is rooted in the fact that we humans have become alienated from Earth and need to be deeply reconnected to Earth as our home and restored to a proper and life-giving relationship with God's creation. In response to our confession, we hear the word of Christ that our sins against creation are forgiven and our alienation from Earth is healed. We hear the invitation of Christ to return to a new relationship with Earth as our home—with a vocation of service to Earth rather than a relationship of domination and exploitation.

SINS AGAINST CREATION

It is appropriate in our worship that we make confession of our sins against creation. Having invoked the presence of God the Creator, having seen Earth as the sanctuary of our worship, having established our human solidarity with all creation, and having invited the whole Earth community into a chorus of praise, we must now acknowledge our broken relationship with creation. How have we polluted and desecrated this sanctuary called Earth? What crimes have we committed against creation?

How have we, individually and collectively, contributed to endangering life on our planet?

The point is that the ecological crisis is not just an environmental issue. Fundamentally, it is a religious and spiritual issue, resulting from the fact that we humans have become alienated from the rest of nature.[12] Only recently have churches recognized that environmental devastation is a sin against creation, even a blasphemy against God. Our sins against creation are many and longstanding. We commit them in our personal behavior; we commit them together as a dimension of our way of life in the economic and social systems of which we are a part.

EARTH AS DISPOSABLE; HEAVENISM AS SIN

One reason we have sinned against creation is that we have focused on an other-worldly religion to the detriment of Earth. We have relegated God to heaven and to a life after death, seeing this world merely as a place of pilgrimage or even just as a place for human mastery. This view may be termed "heavenism"—a belief that ultimately heaven above is our only and true home and Earth is but a stopover on the road to eternity. After death, we leave our bodies, and our souls go to heaven. The body is disposable, like some ill-begotten plastic bottle. However, this view ignores the biblical emphasis on our life together in this world and the ultimate affirmation of the resurrection of the body.

A similar image is that Earth itself is disposable. According to some popular views, Earth will continue to deteriorate until its final destruction at the hands of God. Before that day of wrath, however, the faithful will be caught up in the rapture to escape the final conflagration. Earth itself is destined for destruction, as if God would slough off creation for some spiritual reality alone.[13] These negative religious attitudes toward Earth reinforce the secular view of a disposable world, a society in which everything can be used and thrown away—somewhere. However, none of these views accounts for the biblical expectation that Jesus is returning—here! Nor does it account for the world-affirming vision in the book of Revelation of a renewed heaven and a renewed Earth *here*—where God will dwell!

EARTH AS INFERIOR; DOMINATION AS SIN

Many of us in the Western/Northern world have been conditioned by our religious traditions and by our cultures to believe that human beings are superior to the rest of creation in a way that gives us the right to dominate nature. This attitude is reinforced by some interpretations of Genesis 1, which maintain that this passage gives humans the right to "dominate" nature and to "subdue" it, in God's image no less. This view has engendered a deep-seated belief in some Christian circles that God has commissioned human beings to rule over all creatures and that we are therefore free to exploit Earth for our own purposes.

However, recent interpretations of Genesis 1 suggest a different reading. The need to "subdue" nature was rooted in the constant threats to humans from nature at that time. People had to control nature in those days in order to protect cities from floods and themselves from attacks by wild animals. Furthermore, as we know from some of the Bible's Wisdom writings, the word *dominion* did not necessarily mean to "dominate" but, rather, to "exercise responsibility for," as a good king would protect and care for those in the realm. This understanding is more in keeping with God's image in the Genesis creation stories, according to which God creates things as good in their own right, commands animals to multiply and fill the Earth, and creates humans last of all in order to take care of creation. Later, God instructs Noah to be responsible for preserving all species of animals.

Also of considerable import, the first creation story is set side-by-side with the second creation story in Genesis 2, according to which humans are mandated, as many Christians have been taught for generations, "to till and to keep" the land. But that familiar translation is probably better rendered in a different way. We now know that the term for "till" means to "serve" and that the term for "keep" means to "protect" or to "preserve." Humans are "to serve and to preserve" Earth, a relationship that is the exact opposite of a mandate to dominate. Finally, we have the teaching of Jesus, who told his disciples not to "dominate" or to "rule over" anyone, but to be a servant in all things (Mark 10:41-45). Also, strikingly, Jesus called his disciples to "behold the beauties of the lilies of the fields" (Matt. 6:28). Jesus thereby affirmed the faith of his forebears, that "the Earth is the LORD's and the fulness thereof" (Ps. 24:1, RSV).

Only as we understand that our human vocation is to serve and preserve God's good Earth will we see clearly how we have sinned in our disregard, our abuse, and our arrogance. As individuals and as a whole society, we have been curved in upon ourselves—having nature serve us like a slave rather than having us serve nature as beloved by God. When we see how we have been alienated from creation, we discover a desire to confess our sin in order to be restored to a healthy relationship of solidarity with the rest of nature.

CONFESSION AND RECONCILIATION

Our confessions can enumerate the long list of destructive deeds humans have committed, especially in our time. The list seems endless— pollution, poisoning with toxic waste, nuclear radiation, deforestation, excessive land clearance, breaching the ozone layer, extinction of species, and so on. We need to acknowledge them. And it is critical that we name them in worship, that we be specific—even about the ways we in our personal lives and in our local practices degrade creation.

Then we hear an absolution and a word of assurance from Christ. This assurance is a word of forgiveness for our sins. In light of this liberation from sin, we can recommit ourselves to our vocation to serve and to preserve—to rectify the wrongs we have done and to take actions to create a world in which all creation thrives together.

Just as we are reconciled with other humans by confession and forgiveness, so also we are reconciled with all creation. The reorientation of our worship calls us to see Earth as God's good creation, to confess our violations of creation, and to respond to God's call to care for it and to use it wisely, according to the mandates of God's justice. But this will not be easy. Conversion never is. For us to return to Earth, to overcome our separation from it, and to celebrate this garden planet as our home is a daunting task of reorientation.

The Scripture Readings: A Theology of Listening

Throughout the liturgical year, we listen to God's word through the reading of Scripture. In so doing, our ears may typically be attuned to hear the voice of the poor. Now they also need to be attuned to the voice of Earth itself, as it groans in travail. And in all of this we can hear the gospel message that the cosmic Christ reconciles all creation to God. These voices reorient us through our listening.

WE HEAR THE VOICE OF GOD

We are familiar with God's good news for humans. Now we also hear the good news of what God has done, is doing, and will do for the whole creation (including humans): God created the world and declared it to be good; God continues to make known God's glory everywhere in the world; Jesus announces the kingdom of God as restoration for all creation; God redeems the fallen world through Jesus; Jesus' death reconciles all things and brings about new creation; and God reveals a renewed heaven and a renewed Earth where God will dwell with people in peace and justice and will finally be "all in all" (1 Cor. 15:28).

God's words in Scripture bear the reality of which they speak. They bear not just ideas about God, but the active presence of God's reality. The active presence of God makes the announcements of good news "performative words," words that carry out the blessings and the forgiveness and the healings and the love that they announce. So we need to listen carefully not only for words bringing redemption and liberation for humans but also for words announcing restoration for the land and the waters and the nourishment and provision for all living creatures.

WE HEAR THE VOICE OF THE POOR

Scripture makes clear that God's love gravitates to the most vulnerable in society: the poor, the oppressed, the abandoned, and the marginalized. In most societies, such people do not have a voice. Scripture gives them a voice. The Old Testament is filled with prophets who speak on behalf of the poor, the hungry, the orphans, and the widows. Jesus himself speaks on behalf of the "least of these" when he declares that the final judgment is based on goodness toward them. Jesus announces the year of the Lord's favor on behalf of the captives, the blind, and the oppressed (Luke 4:18-19). Jesus "came to seek out and to save the lost" (Luke 19:10). Paul also advocates on behalf of the weak. And James condemns any favoritism toward the rich when he asks: "Has not God chosen the poor?" (Jas. 2:5). Scripture thus gives a powerful voice to the vulnerable.

WE HEAR THE VOICE OF EARTH

We also need to hear in Scripture the voice of suffering nature itself. Leonardo Boff has said that we need to listen to "the cry of the poor" and also to "the cry of the Earth."[14] This is critical to reorientation in worship, namely, that we attune our ears to hear in Scripture the voice of Earth. If God knows the fall of every sparrow, then "who will speak for the sparrow?"[15] Clearly, Scripture does. And having been brought in worship to a sense of solidarity with creation, having been forgiven our sins against Earth, and having become reconciled to creation, we can listen closely to the voice of Earth in the proclamation of the Word.

Voices of praise are not the only sounds of Earth. When the capacity of creation to praise God is diminished, then we hear another voice from Earth, a voice of suffering and languishing, sounds of mourning and lament. Prophets, whose spirits were especially sensitive to the voices of the natural world, announce that Earth mourns and fields lament. As noted above, Earth and Earth community suffer and mourn. Earth may tremble or quake in response to human or divine deeds (Jer. 8:16, 10:10, 49:21). At the very end of his oath of innocence, Job swears that he will let his land become thorns and weeds if the land has "cried out" against him and its furrows have "wept together" (Job 31:38-40). Job is sensitive to more than the need for human justice in his community; he also knows the cry of injustice that can rise from Earth (cf. Joel 1:10, 18, 20).

In other texts, Earth suffers grievous harm, but no cry is heard. Jeremiah's vision of this devastation of Earth reaches cosmic proportions: "I looked on Earth, and lo, it was waste and void! I looked to the heavens and they had no light!" (4:23). In Jeremiah's vision, Earth returns to the lifeless and empty state that existed before creation (Gen. 1:2): the birds flee, the mountains shake, and the farmlands become deserts. After railing about human injustice and the prosperity of the wicked, Jeremiah declares, "How long will Earth mourn, and the grass of every field wither? For of the wickedness of those who live in it, the animals and the birds are swept away" (Jer. 12:4). In this portrayal, Earth itself has empathy for humans who are suffering at the hands of the wealthy and the powerful. Earth mourns because of human injustice.

GROANING IN TRAVAIL

Perhaps the most powerful expression of Earth suffering is found in Romans 8:18-27. All creation is groaning because of the forces of destruction and the crimes against creation that reach back to the very first curse imposed on Earth because of the sins of humanity.

> For the creation waits with eager longing for the revealing of the children of God; for the creation was subjected to futility, not of its own will but by the will of the one who subjected it, in hope that the creation itself will be set free from its bondage to decay and will obtain the freedom of the glory of the children of God. We know that the whole creation has been groaning in labor pains until now; and not only the creation, but we ourselves, who have the first fruits of the Spirit, groan inwardly while we wait for adoption, the redemption of our bodies. (Rom. 8:19-23)

Paul's view of creation is that of a subject with an inner longing, with deep empathy. Indeed, humans and nature groan together.

Here the groaning of creation, however, is not one of resignation. Paul discerns that the suffering of creation has creative potential. Creation is waiting for renewal and liberation. The groans of creation are not the last gasps of a dying cosmos. Far from it! The Greek term used here refers to "labor pains," the groaning of a woman in childbirth. Paul is signaling that creation is an active participant in God's plan for redemption and restoration. Earth is waiting for the revealing of children of God who will live together in justice and who will care for Earth.

HEARING THE VOICE OF EARTH TODAY

Clearly the suffering of creation today is far more extensive and serious than ever before. The cries of the fallen forests, the dying deserts, and the polluted air rise daily from Earth. It is an axiom of social justice that the true depth and force of any injustice can only be understood by those experiencing that injustice. Their voice must be heard and taken with utmost seriousness—and made an integral part of our human quest for justice!

Many people throughout the world have heard the cry of creation, especially people who live close to the land. Native peoples who live their lives in interrelationship with the land hear the voice of Earth: Native Americans, the Rainbow people of Australia, and many others. The words of Galarrwuy Yunupingu reflect their pain:

> I understand that Mother earth is suffering because there is so much devastation. Trees are dying and have to be cleared away, lands are cut by floodwaters and many other types of environmental destruction are taking place. That is when you experience the suffering of the Spirit of the Land.[16]

How we hear the voices of nature in worship is something we need to explore. In addition to naming the cries of creation, we can listen to the voice of Earth in Scripture. We can include readings in worship by contemporary poets and prophets who have a genuine spirit of empathy for Earth. We might even compose and read "Epistles from Earth" so as to give Earth a voice. We could write lamentations of the Spirit, reflecting the groaning of the Spirit of God empathizing with Earth.

Creation is groaning aloud for those with ears sensitive enough to hear—from Scripture, from those who speak on Earth's behalf, and from creation itself. Can we hear them? And if we can, how should we respond?

Proclaiming the Gospel: A Theology of Incarnation and Reconciliation

Central to our proclamation in preaching is the gospel of Jesus Christ. The good news of Christ is based on a theology of the incarnation. In Christ, God is manifest in the biological web of life in a profound and definitive way. We accept the full weight of this affirmation, namely, that this Word emerged in flesh and "dwelt among us, full of grace and truth; we have beheld his glory . . ." (John 1:14, RSV). God emerges enfleshed as a human being; the Creator is manifest as clay; the Word is born in the flesh as Mary's child. Jesus was not a fleeting docetic visitor, not a ghostly bearer of some Gnostic truth, but a mortal, a truly human being, flesh and blood.

Jesus was a very specific human being in time and place: a Jewish male born to Mary and Joseph in first-century Palestine in the eastern Mediterranean world under the Roman Empire; an Israelite raised in Nazareth of Galilee; a carpenter by trade; publically active in Galilee and surrounding areas; recognized as a prophet and teacher with disciples and followers; at odds with the leaders of Israel; and executed in Jerusalem.

Furthermore, insofar as Jesus belongs fully to Earth, God becomes incarnate in Earth. All the natural biological processes of human flesh are true of Jesus. Jesus smells, tastes, and feels as all humans do. Jesus breathes the same air with all other living creatures on Earth, eats food grown from the same ground, and drinks water from the same wells. In Jesus, God is manifested in the web of life. God becomes part of Earth's biology. Jesus was fully rooted in creation as all human beings are rooted in nature. Put in contemporary terms, Jesus was a mammal, a *homo sapien,* a higher primate, in the gene pool, with human DNA. This claim represents the contemporary affirmation of the full humanity of Jesus.

Christian theology has sometimes emphasized Jesus' humanity in a way that has diminished the role of Christ in the original creation and eclipsed the ongoing relationship of Christ with creation. The risen Christ has been seen as a spiritual being who is detached from Earth, who resides in heaven, and who is liberated from the burden of the material world. In contrast to this point of view, our proclamation recognizes that the good news of Jesus Christ encompasses all of creation. We affirm a theology in which Christ is rooted in creation, redeems creation, and fulfills creation.

CHRIST ACTIVE IN CREATION

So we proclaim that Christ was active in creation from the very beginning. The Gospel of John affirms that the Word existed in the beginning and that "all things came into being through him" (John 1:3). As such, the cosmos has a christic imprint. Hence, when the Word became flesh in Jesus, he did not do so as a stranger to flesh. As Paul Collins writes, "Christ comes to all things, not as a stranger, for he is the first born of all creation, and in him all things were created."[17] Furthermore, God raised the crucified Jesus to be the cosmic Christ who reconciles and restores all things in creation.[18]

CHRIST PRESENT IN CREATION

The Gospel of John affirms that the glory of God that was manifest in Christ is the very glory that fills all of Earth. This insight is critical: the God we see manifest as the Christ reveals to us the God who is present but hidden in all creation. Hence, the activity we see in Jesus becomes the lens through which we discern God in all things. As Paul says, "We know that in everything God works for good . . ." (Rom. 8:28, RSV).

Hence, as Collins writes, "Christ is not only the matrix and prius of all things: he is the intention, the fullness, and the integrity of all things. . . . Nor are all things a tumbled multitude of facts in an unrelated mass, for in him all things hold together."[19] Jesus is the Wisdom of God. God has gathered up "all things in him" (Eph. 1:10) and has made him the "head over all things" (1:22) and "the fullness of him who is all in all" (1:23). "In him all things in heaven and on earth were created" (Col. 1:16). "He himself is before all things and in him all things hold together" (Col. 1:17). "Through him God was pleased to reconcile all things to himself" (Col. 1:20). Christ is "the heir of all things" (Heb. 1:2), and he "sustains all things" (Heb. 1:3).

THROUGH HIS LIFE AND DEATH, CHRIST REDEEMS CREATION

Jesus proclaimed a kingdom that restores not just humanity but all creation, including humanity, as one reality. Jesus calmed storms, provided bread for the hungry in the desert, liberated people from demonic powers in nature, made common cause with the most vulnerable in society, healed the sick, preached good news to the poor, told parables using examples of nature, forgave sinners, welcomed the outcasts, and blessed the children. And he called others to join him in this mission to proclaim the good news of this kingdom.

God's incarnation in creation is especially revealed in the cross. We tend to think of God in relation to nature as present in nature's grandeur, its wondrous and awesome manifestations. In the shame and ignominy of the cross, we become aware of God's presence in the tragic, the violent, and the ugly dimensions of nature. If God is present in such a gruesome reality as the cross, then God is surely everywhere in life. Just as the cross shows God to be in solidarity with suffering humanity, so also the cross shows God to be in solidarity with the tragic and suffering places in all nature as well. The cross keeps us from romanticizing nature or idealizing it. The cross enables us to face the terrible aspects of creation and to know that God is there, too, just as God is hidden in the event of the cross.

The cross is the supreme revelation of who God is and what God is about. As Larry Rasmussen says, "The cross is the indecent exposure and scandal of God. . . . God is concealed in a vilified and broken human being, Jesus is God made poor and abused."[20] The God of suffering love revealed in Jesus Christ lives as a servant and dies a shameful death on a cross. Yet this is the very God whose presence fills Earth. Or, as Niels Gregersen writes, "the death of Christ becomes an icon of God's redemptive co-suffering with all sentient life as well as the victims of social competition."[21]

CHRIST RECONCILES ALL CREATION

The God whose presence fills Earth and who suffers with creation is also the God who through Christ is restoring creation and reconciling alienated dimensions of the creation. The resurrection is more than the rising of an individual human from the grave; it is the rising of the Lord of the whole creation who will one day consummate that whole creation. The incarnate Christ became the risen Christ—the "cosmic Christ" who is already at work transforming the cosmos, restoring creation, reconciling all things. There is no separation of creation and redemption here. There is seamless continuity. Redemption can even be considered God's ongoing creative activity in a restorative mode. Already in the prophet Second Isaiah, the terms *creation* and *salvation* began to be used to identify the same works of God, sometimes interchangeably.

This reconciliation overcomes all forms of alienation. Not only are humans alienated from each other by violence, war, enmity, and neglect, but also the integrity of creation has been violated by invasive acts of human domination and greed. The sins that Christ overcomes are not merely the personal wrongs of individual humans, but the massive corporate environmental injustices perpetrated against creation.[22] These destructive forces not only separate humans from Earth as their home, they also lead to the disintegration of those bonds that hold together the intricate ecosystems in God's creation. Christ is the "Lamb of God" who takes away not only my sins but also "the sins of the whole world." And as the cosmic Christ, he continues to be the power of reconciliation for bringing into communion the alienated forces and the disconnected pieces of God's world.

This reconciliation brings peace between God and humans (2 Cor. 5:18) as well as between human communities in conflict (Eph. 2:14-16). Of special significance here is the message of Colossians and Ephesians that this reconciliation extends to "all things." God reconciles "all things" to God's self whether in heaven or on Earth (Col. 1:20). All alienation in creation is being overcome by Christ. The incarnation of God makes possible a "cosmic reconciliation"—the work of God that bears a radical healing, reaching into all corners of the cosmos. How? By a spectacular cosmic conquest? No! Rather, this cosmic peace is effected through the God who suffers on the cross with a suffering humanity and with a suffering creation. We are called to preach and proclaim this good news for all creation!

GOOD NEWS IN WORD AND DEED

The proclamation of good news in worship impresses upon us that God's creative and redemptive work is for all creation, such that we can see our relationship with God and our response to God's saving activity within this larger orbit. But more, the good news is not only directed to humans *about* creation, the gospel is also to be directed *to* creation itself. In the so-called lost ending of Mark's Gospel, Jesus exhorts his followers to go into all the world and proclaim the Gospel to "the whole creation" (Mark 16:15).

How do we proclaim good news to all creation? Our words of good news to nonhuman creation and our blessings on Earth can have a greater effect than we might think. But our good news is also conveyed by our actions of love and care, as we ourselves become agents of reconciliation with the rest of creation, as we let our actions speak louder than our words. God's wounded planet will not be healed by God waving some grand cosmic wand that removes all ills and immediately turns people into friends of the Earth. Only as humans take up the cross will the suffering for others, all others, turn into healing for the weak and into mending for the broken. This message in word and deed is surely good news for the whole creation!

Prayer and Offering:
A Theology of Creation as Gift

Offerings and prayers belong together as presentations of ourselves and the world around us as gifts from God given back to God. Our offerings back to God are tokens of the fact that we recognize all of life as gifted to us from God. Our prayers of thanksgiving are spoken with this awareness. Our prayers of petition match these in the sense that we pray for realities that are now broken and need restoration as re-creation from the One who created them in the first place. Prayers involves God's power to heal humans, nonhumans, and all Earth community.

PRAYER AS THANKSGIVING

Prayers of thanksgiving are critical, because they prevent us from taking for granted what has been provided by God—not just family and loved ones and coworkers and neighbors and companions in the faith, but also the entire created world of which we are a part and upon which we depend as human beings. Unless we are specific about that for which we are thankful, we will tend to neglect it. We commonly pray for people for whom we are grateful. Now we will want to expand our prayers of thanksgiving to include deer and dolphins, woodpeckers and whip-poor-wills, lions and ladybugs, whales and worms. More particularly, it will be important for us to give thanks for specific plants and animals of Earth community that share our church land and that are found in our neighborhoods.

To be sure, thanksgiving can reinforce our focus on ourselves alone when we assume that all of life is a gift just to us. However, if we dislodge ourselves from the center, we can give thanks that animals and plants exist and have life in their own right. And we can be grateful that the grass is created for the cattle, the trees are given as nesting places for birds, the mountain crags provide a dwelling for the goats, as Psalm 104:27 puts it—grateful that "all receive their food in due season." Hence, in solidarity with other life forms, we can give thanks to God both for ourselves and on behalf of other living things. We all live together. We all share Earth together. God created us all together. God redeems us all together. God will bring all creatures to fulfillment together. Hence, our gratitude will fittingly be expressed together.

PRAYER AS PETITION

Prayer petitions also affirm the giftedness of life. When we pray for those who are sick or injured or in trouble or for those whose life is diminished, we are turning for help and healing to the very one who gave us life. Now we will also want to offer supplication for nature around us. We pray in solidarity and empathy with those for whom we offer petitions. Again, it is important to be specific—about global, regional, and local threatened species, endangered animals, air quality, clean water, food security, and removal of toxins on land and in the oceans, among others.

The letter to the Hebrews teaches us how to pray in solidarity with creation: "Remember [in your prayers] those who are in prison as though you were in prison with them. Remember [in your prayers] those being mistreated as though you yourselves were being mistreated" (Heb. 13:3). If we pray for fellow humans with this kind of solidarity, can we not also express the same empathy for endangered plants and polluted waterways and marine animals harmed in oil spills? Can we not remember, in prayer, the animals facing extinction as though we ourselves were facing extinction? Can we not remember, in prayer, the fish ingesting mercury in the water as though we ourselves were exposed to mercury?

As with thanksgiving, prayers of petition will as a matter of course acknowledge the interdependence of our world. We can pray for the healing of those who have cancer at the same time that we pray for the removal from our food of cancer-inducing toxins. We can pray for the relief of those with lung disease along with the purifying of the air. We can pray for the restoration of a whole ecosystem—human and nonhuman life together—that has been devastated by environmental disasters. As we pray, we will recognize not only the brokenness of our personal lives but also the systemic human degradation of the ecosystems that support life in general.

OFFERINGS

Our offerings are usually monetary, representative of the possessions we have, a portion of all that we own and all that we receive as income. They are, of course, a sign that all we have and use and receive are from the abundance of God's Earth. Everything belongs to God and we benefit from it. That is the foundational theology of what is addressed in our "stewardship" commitments.[23]

So how can we make this giftedness of all things real to us? Could we offer at worship some portion of *everything* we have? Some food? Some home products to share? Some tools of our trade? Some clothes? Shoes? Some papers from school or work? Some food or flowers from a garden? Some examples of the fruits of our labor to dedicate before the altar? Could we offer so many of our things, even out of our need, that we see how all things belong to God and all things are to be shared? Would this perhaps lead us to see our food and clothing, our homes and yards, our pets and persons as fully part of God's world, and not as "our property"?

Offering the gifts from God as gifts to others in worship is directly countercultural to the consumer mentality that governs so much of our common life together. Our consumer mentality leads us to define ourselves by the things we have. We own property. We claim property rights to do with what we own as we please. We claim a right to accumulate any and all things we can. We freely dispose of things. The "market economy" is based on unlimited goods and unlimited disposal. It is based on competition. We allow our identities to be determined by productivity—how much we possess, how much our labor is worth—by whether we work or not. The market gives everything a monetary value, treating people as resources and the rest of nature as commodities to be bought and sold.

The offering of ourselves and our possessions to God counters all this and baptizes our economic practices in grace. We see things as gifts to be shared. We value living things in their own right. We treat life with reverence. We express gratitude for it. We know our limits as humans. We walk softly on the Earth. We seek to use what we have for the common good. We find a place for giftedness in an economy of grace. We seek cooperation and collaboration more than competition. The astounding experience of gathering for worship in order to offer ourselves and our belongings back to God places us in a different relationship with one another, with all living things, and with the blessings of Earth. It challenges our culture and calls us into a new creation.

ETHICAL IMPLICATIONS

All of our worship from beginning to end has ethical implications. This has been true from the time of the Hebrew prophets, who declared that

God wanted nothing to do with worship unless there was justice in the land. All elements of worship have moral mandates. We highlight this point here because offerings and prayers are especially obvious in their ethical implications. Offerings and prayers can reinforce our solidarity with the rest of nature so that we will want to make a commitment to do what we can on behalf of those for whom we pray and on behalf of the offerings we dedicate to God.

Our prayers and offerings take us out of a human-centered mentality as we share our gifts and as we pray for others. We are drawn away from ourselves to focus on God's relationship to the whole creation. Often we decide what we are going to do and ask God to bless it. Now in prayer and offering, as we present God's world back to God, we are led to think about what God is doing in the world and to ask, What can we do to be part of God's larger purposes? What part do we play in this new creation?

The Sacraments: A Theology of Presence

In the reorientation that God accomplishes among us in worship, the eucharistic meal is the moment when it all comes together. Here, the community participates in the new creation as concrete and real. The community participates in that new reality with each other as a communion of saints. In our reorientation in worship, we now become aware that the Eucharist is also an expression of our communion with all creation— because God's presence in bread and wine connects us with God's presence in creation. In this sense, the Eucharist is a healing experience of restoration and reconciliation for all of life.

THE PRESENCE OF CHRIST IN THE SACRAMENTS AND IN ALL CREATION

We have affirmed that Christ is "in, with, and under" all creation. The sacrament makes it clear that this is not just a generic statement about God's presence. Rather, Christ is concretely in, with, and under each thing in creation. We know that Christ is present in the worshipers, who are the body of Christ. The Eucharist affirms that Christ is also present in the bread and in the wine as we receive the "body of Christ" and the "blood of Christ." The elements bear Christ to us. The words of the Eucharist do not put the presence of Christ into the bread and wine. That presence is already there, as it is in all things. Rather, the words of the Eucharist reveal in a clear and definitive way that we can count on God's presence in these elements. This meal is sacramental, because it is paradigmatic for God's presence everywhere. And we faithfully receive the bread and wine as representative of all the gifts of God's creation, all of which bear Christ's presence.

One key to the sacraments, then, is not that Christ is present only in the elements of the sacrament as we eat and drink "in remembrance" of him. Rather, the presence of Christ in those elements assures us of the presence of Christ everywhere and in everything.[24] If Christ is present in such ordinary elements as grapes and grain, such daily realities as bread and wine, then we can be assured that Christ is in every other element of creation. Martin Luther said that the entire reality of God, without reserve, is present in every single grain of wheat and in every single leaf of the vine.[25] As such, our transcendent God is not floating loose somewhere beyond, but is bound to creation. In this sense, creation is God's home, even as we can think of it as our sanctuary. Hence, as we have said, all creation is sacral, not just the eucharistic meal. In a sense, then, this eucharistic meal is linked with every other meal, every eating and every drinking. If all things are God's, then every meal is a sacral event in which we are offered life from God.

The sacraments assure us that finite realities can bear infinite realities. We partake of the power of the invisible risen and ascended Christ through his presence in the visible elements of the bread and wine. The specific life-giving impulses that are mediated through this sacred meal include forgiveness, bonding, and healing. There is no dualism here. Material reality is worthy to bear spiritual reality. The Eucharist is thus an extraordinary expression of the affirmation of all creation. All creation is good and it is well worth redeeming. Matter is good and it can be wedded to the spiritual. Bread and wine do not have to be changed into something else in order to become Christ's body and blood. The bread and wine remain the same, and at the same time they are the body and blood of Christ. Christ is present in, with, and under the elements, the worshipers, and the whole creation.

THE EUCHARIST ENCOMPASSES SPACE AND TIME

The God of the eucharistic meal is a God who fills all creation with the divine presence, from the most distant stardust to the bread and wine on the table. The God who is present in Holy Communion is the cosmic Christ who gathers all things to himself. Given this cosmic perspective, the eucharistic table becomes a symbol of the center of the cosmos.

Not only does the Eucharist witness to God in all space, it also witnesses to God in all time. The Eucharist recalls for us the past. It recalls the meal that Christ had with his disciples, the moment when Christ offered himself for the life of the world, in word and then in act. It recalls for us the resurrection of Jesus and Jesus' risen presence among us. The Eucharist also anticipates the final meal, the messianic banquet. Hence, by recollection and anticipation, the Eucharist brings the past and the future into the present time.

In these ways, the Eucharist is an event where space and time come together—all creation reaching back to Christ, the Alpha of all things, and straining forward to Christ, who is to come again, the Omega of all things. All of this is given to us *in the present*, in the compassion and goodness and forgiveness we encounter in Christ through the breaking of the bread and the sharing of the wine.

DISCERNING THE BODY

Paul said that if we partake of this meal "without discerning the body," we eat in an "unworthy manner" (1 Cor. 11:29, 27). Discerning the body here does not refer to a belief that the risen body of Christ is really present in the bread and wine. That affirmation is taken for granted. Rather, by "the body," Paul here means the body of Christ as the gathered community. In this context, he meant that in the meal, some participants were eating their fill while others were going hungry. To eat without sensitivity to the body of Christ, that is, to those among them who were hungry, is to eat and drink in an unworthy way. As such, sharing in the communion of saints without discerning the needs of the world's weak and vulnerable is to partake unworthily. Which is a sobering thought, since the "Eucharist is today celebrated in a world where over one thousand million people are regularly hungry."[26]

And more: if we are to take the mandate to "discern the body" seriously, we will want to see ourselves in the context of the cosmic Christ, who fills sanctuary Earth and indeed the whole creation. Paul says that all creation eagerly anticipates the revealing of children of God who will care for this creation in ways that will enable creation to thrive. Eucharist today is celebrated in a world where species face extinction, waterways are degraded, and natural habitats are being destroyed. If we see that the whole creation is groaning, then we are called to eat and drink in a way that is mindful not only of our fellow humans everywhere who are vulnerable but also of our animal and plant kin that are endangered.

Can we embrace in the moment of this sacrament a transforming experience of new creation? Can we so encounter Christ in the sacrament that we can also contemplate Christ's glorious presence in the whole creation? Can we enter into a vision of the Eucharist in which we are in communion with all Earth community? Can we commit ourselves to Earth community in a way that enables us to partake in a manner that is worthy of the Lord?

The Commission and Blessing: A Theology of Ministry

The commission and blessing for worshiping with creation are based on a theology of ministry to Earth. We hear the call of Christ to serve by caring for Earth. We are ready to consider our commitment to serve and protect Earth as followers of Christ. We announce our intent to love nature and nurture Earth as nature has long nurtured us.

> May the God of all creation bless you and keep you.
> May the God of all people bless your dedication to care
>   for the poor.
> May the God whose glory fills the world bless your
>   commitment to serve Earth.
> "Go in peace," the leader says, "Remember the poor.
>   Care for the Earth."
> And the people say, "Thanks be to God."

THE THIRD MISSION OF THE CHURCH

A theology of Earth ministry requires a heightened awareness of mission to creation, what may be called the "third mission" of the church.[27] Traditionally, the first mission of the church, grounded in Matthew 28:19, is to go into the world and to preach the gospel to the greater human community and to disciple all nations for Christ. The second mission, grounded in Luke 4:18-19, extends the saving power of Christ to liberate human beings from the systemic forces that oppress them so that they can embrace God's work in the world.

The third mission of the church goes beyond the first two and embraces the whole Earth (Mark 16:15). This mission brings the message that there is good news for Earth. It involves participating in the ministry of the cosmic Christ and being claimed by the works of the groaning Spirit, as we find ways to halt the destructive forces at work against creation and as we identify, wherever possible, the often-obscured, God-given forces of renewal in the life of creation itself.

A VOCATION TO SERVE AND TO PROTECT EARTH

We are here reminded of Genesis 2 and the announcement of the commission from God for humans to serve and to preserve the Earth. According to the Genesis account, then, Earth keeping is the foundational vocation of all humans. And, as we have seen, both God and Earth are partners with humans in our Earth-keeping vocation. After the first human being was created, God placed him in a fertile garden of trees to serve and to protect it. Christ's teaching affirms this vocation. Disciples of Christ are called to be servants of all. By implication, the "all" includes "all things" in creation. Our mission, then, includes a vocation to minister to Earth and to serve our kin in creation. This role implies that we stand in solidarity with creation and that we cooperate with God and with nature in restoring Earth.

EARTH AS PARTNER IN HEALING

It is common today to hear expressions like "saving Earth," "sustaining Earth," "preserving this planet," and "healing Earth." Unfortunately, the language of healing can too easily be subsumed under a medical model where Earth is the patient and humans are the experts, the scientists with all the technological answers. Clearly, the contribution of science and technology are absolutely critical. Nevertheless, there is sometimes an inherent arrogance in that kind of medical model. By contrast, we seek a medical model in which the patient is partner in the healing process. As children of Earth, we seek to relate to Earth as a partner.[28] If we are to be involved in restoring nature, then, we need to begin with openness to the healing capacities inherent in nature and to discern how creation heals itself and us. Healing begins with recognizing that we are working *with* our kin in creation and *with* Earth.

The process of mutual healing and nurture extends to all aspects of life on Earth and indeed to Earth itself. This impulse to nurture comes from God's Spirit moving through creation. David Suzuki and Amanda McConnell call this spiritual impulse to nurture the "law of love" in nature. They write:

When we observe the care with which a mud dauber prepares a mud enclosure, inserts a paralyzed victim as food, and deposits an egg, can we be so anthropocentric as to deny this the name of love? How else can we interpret the male sea horse's protective act of accepting babies into his pouch, the months-long incubation of an emperor penguin's egg on the feet of its vigilant parent, or the epic journey of Pacific salmon returning from their natal stream to mate and die in the creation of the next generation? If these are innate actions dictated by genetically encoded instructions, all the more reason to conclude that love in its many manifestations is fashioned into the very blueprint of life.[29]

The spiritual impulse to nurture or to love that is deep within Earth and within the creatures of Earth is a force we need to recognize as vital to our connection with Earth. We need to return to Earth and discover again ways to experience these nurturing impulses and to live in harmony with them. For our God is a God whose healing Spirit renews the very ground from which it emerges (Ps. 104:30).

At the same time, as the Scriptures teach us, and as the book of Job in particular makes undeniably clear, we also need to be very much aware of this disturbing truth: there is much in nature that is strange and alien to us, a sobering fact that we already have had occasion to notice. In this respect, nature is not our friend, nor a source of healing. Stars are swept into black holes. Tsunami waves swallow ships and demolish islands. Rats spread plagues in cities, and mosquitoes swarm over children in rural areas, bringing the scourges of smallpox or malaria. The Bible knows this alien side of nature well.[30] Recognition of this dimension of the natural world will instill a spirit of humility in us and give us occasion to ponder all the more the mysteries of God's providence, how in this era of God's history with the whole creation, "under the sign of the cross," we walk by faith, not by sight. We can contemplate the healing that is sometimes apparent in natural processes, to be sure. But when we do, we always see "in a mirror, dimly" (1 Cor. 13:12).

THE LOVE OF GOD AND OUR MINISTRY TO CREATION

This nurture and healing power at work in creation, under the sign of the cross, is ultimately grounded in God's love for creation. Creation exists because God chose to create and continues to do so, in spite of what we have done to creation. The continuing love of God sustains all creation (Ps. 136:1-9). God rejoices in all things that God has made (Ps. 104:31). And God invites us to do the same: to love Earth, to nurture our kin, to

embrace our home. We are called to love creation. We may "take care" of
our possessions, but we "love" our children. We will not restore what we
do not love.

Pursuing ecological justice for all Earth community—human and
nonhuman life alike—is the very definition of our healing ministry to
creation. Many ecologists argue that nature and the diverse parts of nature
have an inherent right to survive and a right to justice. All of the natural
world has intrinsic value and therefore ought to be accorded appropriate
respect and God-given rights. Where the rights and integrity of creation
have been violated, especially by human beings, Earth cries out for justice.
But that cry is often not heard by those who are abusing Earth. We in the
church are called to be prophets, like the prophets of old. We are called to
hear the cries of Earth and the cries of the poor and to speak against the
injustices done to them. As Paul Santmire writes,

> We Christians will be a voice for the voiceless, for the sake of the creatures
> of nature who have no voice in human affairs. We will listen to the plaintiff
> cries of the great whales and hear the groaning of the forest, and we will be
> their advocates in the village square and in the courts of power, by the grace
> of God. All the more so we will hear the bitter wailing of little children who
> live on the trash mountains and who wear clothes that have been washed in
> streams overflowing with heinous poisons and who sometimes drink these
> very waters.[31]

Ours is a prophetic mission, a call for justice and peace on Earth and for
Earth. As advocates of justice, we recognize that social justice and ecological justice are interrelated needs. It is the oppressed who suffer most from
the exploitation of forests and the pollution of our waters. It is people
from poorer countries that suffer most from ecological disaster and degradation, people with the least protection and the fewest resources with
which to respond. It is people of color who are faced with environmental
racism, perpetrated by many governments and corporations who dump
toxic waste—including nuclear waste—and other toxins on communities
of color and on indigenous peoples.[32]

Whatever the injustice, this is our ministry. We are called to listen to
and to speak on behalf of the people and the lands of Earth—to expose
the injustices and to right the wrongs. We assume this role as those who
know Christ the crucified, who suffered with creation and for creation,
with the oppressed and for the oppressed. The cross leads us to stand with
the victims in their suffering.[33]

We leave the service of worship reoriented by God to a right relationship with the whole creation. As we do, we commit ourselves to be part of this third mission of the church to Earth, especially this freshly configured vision of our co-mission *with* nature, to love and nurture all creatures and all things—for God's sake!

RESOURCES

In addition to the titles cited in the notes, please see the following:

Brown, William P. *The Ethos of the Cosmos: The Genesis of Moral Imagination in the Bible.* Grand Rapids: Eerdmans, 1999.

Edwards, Denis. *Jesus the Wisdom of God: An Ecological Theology.* Homebush, NSW: St. Paul Publications, 1991.

Habel, Norman C. *An Inconvenient Text: Is a Green Reading of the Bible Possible?* Adelaide: ATF, 2009.

Hiebert, Theodore. *The Yahwist's Landscape: Nature and Religion in Early Israel.* Minneapolis: Fortress Press, 2008 (1996).

McDonagh, Sean. *To Care for the Earth: A Call to a New Theology.* London: Geoffrey Chapman, 1986.

Moltmann, Jürgen. *God in Creation: A New Theology of Creation and the Spirit of God.* Trans. Margaret Kohl. Minneapolis: Fortress Press, 1993 (1985).

Nash, James. *Loving Nature: Ecological Integrity and Christian Responsibility.* Nashville: Abingdon, 1991.

Rasmussen, Larry. *Earth Community, Earth Ethics.* Maryknoll, N.Y.: Orbis, 1997.

Senn, Frank C. *New Creation: A Liturgical Worldview.* Minneapolis: Fortress Press, 2000.

Sittler, Joseph. *Evocations of Grace: Writings on Ecology, Theology, and Ethics,* eds. Steven Bouma-Prediger and Peter Bakken. Grand Rapids: Eerdmans, 2000.

Stewart, Benjamin M. *A Watered Garden: Christian Worship and Earth's Ecology.* Worship Matters. Minneapolis: Augsburg Fortress, 2011.

Vajta, Vilmos. *Luther on Worship: An Interpretation.* Trans. U. S. Leupold. Philadelphia: Muhlenburg, 1958.

NOTES

1. On this point, see, for example, Craig Satterlee, *When God Speaks through Worship: Stories Congregations Live By* (Herndon, Va.: Alban Institute, 2009).

2. For a theology of liturgy that also treats worship as reorientation, albeit in a different way, see Gordon Lathrop, *Holy Ground: A Liturgical Cosmology* (Minneapolis: Fortress Press, 2003).

3. For an instructive exploration of biblical creation theology, see Terence E. Fretheim, *God and World in the Old Testament: A Relational Theology of Creation* (Nashville: Abingdon, 2006).

4. For further development of this theme, see Lathrop, *Holy Ground*, and H. Paul Sant-mire, *Ritualizing Nature: Renewing Christian Liturgy in a Time of Crisis, Theology and the Sciences* (Minneapolis: Fortress Press, 2008).

5. On Paul, see David Horrell, Cherryl Hunt, and Christopher Southgate, eds., *Greening Paul: Rereading the Apostle in a Time of Ecological Crisis* (Waco: Baylor University Press, 2010).

6. From the poem, "God's Grandeur," in *The Poems of Gerard Manley Hopkins*, ed. W. H. Gardner, and N. H. MacKensie (New York: Oxford University Press, 1970), 66.

7. For a review of Luther's theology of divine immanence, see H. Paul Santmire, *The Travail of Nature: The Ambiguous Ecological Promise of Christian Theology*, Theology and the Sciences (Minneapolis: Fortress Press, 2000), 128–32.

8. For a more detailed discussion of these ideas, see Santmire, *Ritualizing Nature*, 154–74.

9. Martin Luther, *Werke* (Weimarer Ausgabe), 49:434, cited by Niels Henrik Gregersen, "Grace in Nature and History: Luther's Doctrine of Creation Revisited," Dialog 44, no.1 (Spring 2005): 58.

10. David Suzuki and Amanda McConnell, *The Sacred Balance: Rediscovering Our Place in Nature* (New York: Bantam, 1999), 38.

11. Calvin uses this expression often. For references and explication of this theme, see Susan Schreiner, *The Theater of His Glory: Nature and the Natural Order in the Thought of John Calvin* (Grand Rapids: Baker, 1991), esp. 145–46 n.40.

12. See also the introduction to *Earth and Word: Classic Sermons on Saving the Planet*, ed. David Rhoads (New York: Continuum, 2007), xiii–xx.

13. For a careful critique of such views, see Barbara R. Rossing, *The Rapture Exposed: The Message of Hope in the Book of Revelation* (Boulder: Westview, 2004).

14. Leonardo Boff, *Cry of the Earth, Cry of the Poor* (Maryknoll, N.Y.: Orbis, 1997), 104.

15. David Rhoads, "Who Will Speak for the Sparrow? Eco-Justice Criticism and the New Testament," in *Literary Encounters with the Reign of God: Festschrift for Robert Tannehill* (London: T & T Clark, 2003), 64–86.

16. Galarrwuy Yunupingu, "Concepts of Land and Spirituality," in *Aboriginal Spirituality, Past, Present and Future*, ed. Anne Pattel-Gray (Melbourne: HarperCollins, 1996), 9–10.

17. Paul Collins, *God's Earth: Religion as if It Really Mattered* (Melbourne: Dove, 1995), 82.

18. On the "cosmic Christ," see Denis Edwards, *Jesus and the Cosmos* (Homebush, NSW: St. Paul Publications, 1991), and Santmire, *Ritualizing Nature*, 111–15, 195–98, and 201–203.

19. Collins, *God's Earth*, 82.

20. Larry Rasmussen, "Returning to our Senses: The Theology of the Cross as a Theology of Ecojustice," in *After Nature's Revolt: Ecojustice and Theology*, ed. Dieter Hessel (Minneapolis: Fortress Press, 1992), 47.

21. Niels Gregersen, "The Cross of Christ in an Evolutionary World," *Dialog: A Journal of Theology* 40 (2001): 205.

22. On this point, see Norman C. Habel, "The Crucified Land: Towards Our Reconciliation with Earth," *Colloquium* 28 (1996): 15.

23. On the ambiguities of the concept of "stewardship," see Santmire, *Ritualizing Nature*, 252–58.

24. For this extended reading of the "real presence" of Christ in the Eucharist, see ibid., 167–71. This view of the Eucharist does not preclude traditions with diverse views of the Eucharist that also affirm the presence of Christ in all things.

25. For an explication of Luther's thought in this respect, see Santmire, *The Travail of Nature*, 129ff.

26. Sean McDonagh, *To Care for the Earth: A Call to a New Theology* (London: Geoffrey Chapman, 1986), 171.

27. See Norman C. Habel, "The Third Mission of the Church; Good News for the Earth," *Trinity Occasional Papers* 17, no. 1 (1998): 31–43; and David Rhoads and Barbara R. Rossing, "A Beloved Earth Community: Christian Mission in an Ecological Age," in Peter Vethanayagamony, ed., *Mission After Christendom: Emergent Themes in Contemporary Mission* (Louisville: Westminster John Knox, 2010), 128–43.

28. See Santmire, *Ritualizing Nature*, 216–44.

29. Suzuki and McConnell, The Sacred Balance, 173.

30. See also Terence E. Fretheim, *Creation Untamed: The Bible, God, and Natural Disasters* (Grand Rapids: Baker Academic, 2010).

31. H. Paul Santmire, *Nature Reborn: The Ecological and Cosmic Promise of Christian Theology, Theology and the Sciences* (Minneapolis: Fortress Press, 2000), 121.

32. See Robert Bullard, *Confronting Environmental Racism: Voices from the Grassroots* (Atlanta: South End, 1996).

33. Rasmussen, "Returning to Our Senses," 54.

Three

Engaging the Bible in a New Key
Reading and Preaching with Creation

During each of the seasons of the church year we approach the Bible from a specific perspective and with specific concerns. During the season of Advent we anticipate the coming of the Messiah and the birth of the Christ child. We identify with the people of God who lived in hope. We read and preach with that same hope in our hearts. We hear the voices of the prophets announcing the coming Prince of Peace and the voice of heavenly host proclaiming peace on Earth.

During the season of Lent we walk with Jesus of Nazareth on his way to the cross. We empathize with disciples like Peter and Mary as they share Jesus' journey. We identify with Jesus, who suffers and dies on the cross for us. And we hear the voice of Jesus crying: *Why have you forsaken me?*

During the season of Easter we experience the risen Christ anew. We empathize with Thomas the Twin and celebrate with Peter in his boat when he sees Jesus walking on the shore of Galilee. We hear the voices of angels announcing that Jesus has risen, and we hear the risen Jesus speak the name, "Mary!"

So also in the Season of Creation, we see the skies open for the descending Spirit, and we experience Jesus baptized in the waters of the Jordan River. We empathize with Nicodemus, and we join Paul's longing on behalf of the "groaning" creation. We hear the risen Jesus commission his disciples to "preach the gospel to the whole creation."

Through the centuries, we have heard and read these messages in ways that are appropriate to various times and diverse cultures. Each season has a context and a set of concerns that provide an atmosphere in which that season is celebrated and in which the stories and teachings of the Bible are interpreted and made relevant. The Season of Creation has its own context and set of concerns. Here we seek to name these as a basis for unpacking the biblical texts for our time.

Conscious of the Creation Context

For each of the Sundays of the Season of Creation there is a specific domain of creation that is the focus of that Sunday—rivers, sky, wilderness, and so on. Each of these domains has been affected to some degree by the way humanity has used or abused that domain. The clearing of forests and the consequent displacement of human communities cannot be ignored on Forest Sunday. The rising seas and the refugees that result from inundation into low-lying regions provide a context for Ocean Sunday. And so on.

This focus on the creation context relates to at least two aspects of the Season of Creation liturgy analyzed in the previous chapter. First, in this season we come with an awareness that we are preaching in a sanctuary called Earth, filled with the visible presence of God pulsing through creation. Second, that presence or glory is with us not only in the specific domain of creation but also in the sanctuary of the building where we celebrate and in which we worship. In this season, we do not simply preach from a pulpit in a sacred building. In art and imagination, we can take the opportunity to decorate the sanctuary or project pictures of a forest or of our planet. In this way, we can preach beside a river, on a mountaintop, or in an ocean filled with God's presence. This imaginative liturgical artwork will assist us to read, preach, and worship in a relationship with a specific domain of creation.

A crucial context within which we read and interpret texts selected for the Season of Creation is the current environmental context. Interpreting the text in the context of the current ecological crisis connects us with particular acts of confession in the Season of Creation liturgy. Whatever domain of creation that is the focus of our worship on a given Sunday is also a realm that has been exploited and polluted by human hands. We are present with God in a creation violated by human folly and sin. We read with an awareness of this creation context: a suffering, sacred planet.

The first question we may ask when we read a text is: How does our presence in a specific domain of creation, filled with God's presence and violated by human sin, prepare us to interpret the texts and to preach about a given text in the Season of Creation?

Example: Assume that we are reading Genesis 1 to prepare a sermon for Earth Sunday. We recognize from the outset that we belong to the space age and know planet Earth as a precious piece of stardust. We no longer reflect the ancient worldview of Genesis where Earth was viewed as a body of land surrounded by sea and covered by a solid canopy called sky.

Not only does our worldview reflect the space-age mind-set in which we have been educated; we are also becoming more and more conscious that we belong to a greenhouse age. This planet is undergoing radical climate changes due especially to the greenhouse gases being pumped into the atmosphere. As we preach, the planet that is the context of our sermon is being transformed by the greed of humanity.

We might point to a specific example in Australia where the environment is suffering at the local level. Due to an extended drought, climate change, and excessive irrigation, not one drop of water from the Murray-Darling river system—a system comparable to the Mississippi-Missouri in the United States—reached the sea between 2000 and 2010. This is a tragedy for the life of the river itself. And it has had devastating effects on the human communities and on the communities of flora and fauna that have depended on this river for life and health.

Then, in 2011, the same area experienced abnormal downpours with flash floods described as inland tsunamis. They covered an area equivalent to France and Germany combined. Once again, this region was faced with violent forces because of the imbalance of the weather systems. Once again, all members of Earth community suffered with a groaning Earth.

Suspecting a Human Bias

Over the centuries we have read the Bible in a variety of ways using a range of different approaches. Almost all of these approaches have been basically anthropocentric—that is, we have read the text from the perspective of human beings. Human concerns, human interests, and human aspirations have dominated our way of relating to nature. We are human beings, and it is understandable that we read from a human perspective and with a human bias. Just as privileged human beings have read the text in biased ways against the most vulnerable human communities, with tragic consequences, so we have read the text with bias against nature herself.

As we reread biblical texts in the current context of a suffering creation, it is therefore reasonable to inquire as to whether most interpreters still reflect an anthropocentric bias and whether the texts themselves in fact reflect a similar bias. Alternatively, we can reread the texts to ascertain whether Earth, members of Earth community, or given domains of Earth are key characters in the narrative, play a key role in the plot, or represent important realities in the text. Can we discern spiritual, sacred, and meaningful dimensions in elements of the universe other than God or humans?

Before we begin rereading the text, however, it is wise for us to examine the nature of our bias. If we trace the understanding we have of ourselves as humans, especially in the Western world, we become aware of a duality that has evolved and that has been taken for granted as self-evident. This duality separates humans and nature in a variety of ways. Humans are often assumed to be spiritual, superior, rational beings of a higher order than the rest of nature. Humans claim to be closer to God and of much greater value than the rest of nature. The natural world exists for the benefit of humans.

This dualism and the resulting alienation of humans from creation was explored in more detail in the previous chapter. Evoking a consciousness of this alienation is a crucial aspect of repentance in the context of a suffering creation. As we read and preach, we suspect that the bias of dualism also informs our approach and therefore needs to be overcome. We must also examine whether this dualistic orientation may be present not only in the assumptions of later interpreters but also in the texts themselves. As we read we ask: Has an anthropocentric bias prevented us from discerning the unique presence, value, and spiritual significance of nonhuman characters or domains in the text?

Example: A frequent feature of scholarly analyses of Genesis 1 is the identification of the creation of humans in verses 26-28 as the climax of the creation story. This anthropocentric focus often leads interpreters to view humans as the pinnacle of creation. God, it is argued, created the world for the benefit of humans. Just as some nations have used the Bible to justify imperial colonization and domination of other nations, so we have used these texts to justify human domination of nature. This text leads some scholars to discern a dualistic view of creation: humans are godlike and superior to the rest of creation.

If, however, we set aside the preceding assumptions and take a closer look at the opening verses of Genesis, we discover another perspective. Verse 1 presents us with the title for the narrative that follows. Who is the subject first introduced in the text? Earth! How is Earth described? Earth is present in the darkness but without the living form it later assumes! Where is Earth located? Deep in the primal waters that are later separated for Earth to appear! What is the metaphor suggested by this image? An embryo in the primal waters! What happens on the third day? Does God say, "Let there be Earth?" No! God says, "Let the waters separate/burst and let the land appear!" Land emerges from the waters and comes into being. Land is *born*. And what does God name the land? Earth!

In other words, if we set aside the anthropocentric readings of Genesis 1 and focus on Earth as the primary character in the narrative, we gain a rich new understanding of the creation story.

Identifying with Earth

If we, like most interpreters, have viewed ourselves as separate from and superior to the rest of creation, how might we reread the text so that Earth, the wider Earth community, and the various domains of nature are not dismissed and devalued as secondary?

This is perhaps the step that requires the greatest leap of faith on the part of the reader, a step designed to overcome the bias of dualism that we find in ourselves, other readers, and potentially within the text itself. As human beings, we identify, often unconsciously, with the various human characters in the biblical story. We can identify with the experiences of these characters, even if they are not necessarily individuals we admire or emulate.

The challenge we face is to empathize and even identify in solidarity with Earth, domains of Earth, or members of the Earth community—and then read the text from their perspective. Why? In part, because we dwell on a living planet called Earth, where we are an integral part of the web of nature, where we are kin with all creatures on this planet. We are born of Earth, made of Earth, and survive as living expressions of the ecosystem that has emerged on this planet. We are in fact in solidarity with the rest of creation, whether we realize it or not. We are Earth beings and we are here invited to read and preach, as Earth beings, of our relationship with all Earth community. Just as we are called to solidarity with our vulnerable human brothers and sisters, so we are called into solidarity with vulnerable and suffering Earth.

When we empathize with Earth and members of the Earth community we become conscious of the many injustices perpetrated against Earth. It is natural, therefore, that readers in solidarity with Earth may seek to expose the wrongs that Earth itself has suffered and also to discern, where possible, the way Earth has resisted these wrongs. We ask our Lord to make our spirits sensitive to the cries for justice from the soil and the seas, the suffering of lands exploited by human greed, and the groaning of creation in anticipation of a new creation. Empathy with the domains of creation when reading the text translates into empathy with a suffering creation that is our home.

We are acutely aware, however, that we are human beings. We are not trees or mountains or kangaroos or snow leopards. Any attempt to identify or empathize with Earth or members of Earth community will remain less than ideal. That does not mean we should dismiss this step as futile. Far from it! We are part of Earth and can no longer ignore those nonhuman subjects, our kin in creation, who not only have intrinsic value but have a voice to be heard in the text. Just as the vulnerable humans of the Earth need to be heard, so now also vulnerable Earth itself needs to be heard. As we read we ask: What is the message revealed in the text when I identify with Earth, domains of Earth, or members of the wider Earth community and then read from their perspective?

Example: If we now seek to be in solidarity with Earth in Genesis 1, we are privileged to discover a remarkable experience. We begin with Earth as the unformed land mass deep in the primal waters, deep in the darkness, waiting to appear. We have a sense of identifying with an embryo anticipating birth.

We have a new appreciation of the creation of light that will enable Earth to be seen. We may also appreciate anew the creation of a sky beneath which there will be space for plants and animals to appear and come alive. But, especially, we will celebrate the call from God for Earth to emerge from the dark waters and appear. Yes, appear or be revealed! The Hebrew word used here for "appear" is the word normally used for God's appearing. It is the Hebrew word for a theophany. So the appearance of Earth is more than one of a series of acts of creation. Earth is revealed.

The Earth story continues throughout the creation account. Earth comes alive with vegetation. Earth brings forth living creatures. Earth is a co-creator with God, a creative presence for us to celebrate and hold sacred.

Retrieving the Voices of Creation

When we empathize with Earth, we are more likely to hear the voices of Earth, whether explicit or suppressed by the bias of the context. Earth or members of the Earth community may play a key role or be highly valued in the text. Because of the Western interpretative tradition we have inherited, however, that dimension of the text has been ignored or suppressed. Moreover, when we read about nonhuman figures communicating in some way—mourning, praising, or singing—we have tended in the past to dismiss these expressions as poetic license or symbolic language. But these passages may well reflect how nature communicates, even if in its own way.

When we identify with Earth and members of the Earth community, we recognize them as subjects with a voice. The exegetical task is to retrieve that voice. In some contexts, the voice of nonhuman subjects is evident but has been traditionally ignored by exegetes. In other contexts, the voice of Earth or members of Earth community is not explicit, but nevertheless present. These subjects play roles in the text that are more than mere scenery or secondary images. Their voices need to be heard, voices that need not correspond to the language or words we commonly associate with the human voice. Just as we hear the cries of the poor, so now we hear the cries of Earth.

It is the task of the preacher to articulate these voices. This may be done in a variety of ways. In the tradition of narrative preaching, the preacher may play the role of the key domain or nonhuman character in the text and tell the story or message from its perspective. Most of us will have heard the preacher play the role of Peter, Mary Magdalene, or another of the disciples. The task here is to let the voice of Earth, the Red Sea, Mount Sinai, or some other domain of creation be heard.

There is a sense in which this process also involves "reading the silences" of the text, silences that support the status quo, the mainstream anthropocentric thought of the author or reader. Like the awful silencing of an abused child or the suppression of the voice of the oppressed, the silence imposed on Earth or nonhuman members of Earth community ought not to be ignored. Retrieving the voice of Earth is an effort to break the silence. Such a silence need not be devoid of communication; day and night are silent in Psalm 19, yet their voices go throughout all of Earth (vv. 2-4).

The readings and the sermon in the Season of Creation are intended to enable these voices to be heard. There is also a connection here with the mission or ministry to creation at the close of the liturgy. By empathizing with the various domains of creation and enabling their voices to be heard, we may become more conscious of the specific ways in which we might be involved in caring for creation, healing this wounded planet, and engaging in a mission to creation. As we read we ask: How can we articulate the interests and voices of nonhuman beings or domains of creation in the text that have been ignored, devalued, or dismissed by past interpreters?

Example: If we now give Earth a voice in the Genesis 1 account of creation, we may hear the following:

> I am Earth. I was first revealed when God summoned the primal waters to part. I came forth from these waters as a living domain with potential to give birth. This is a great honor and grounds for celebration. I am a valued part of the cosmos.
>
> At the request of God I brought forth, like a mother, all of the flora that cover the land and dwell in the sea. I gave birth to vegetation that has the capacity to reproduce. All flora come from within me, are interconnected with me, and are recycled through me.
>
> At the request of God I also brought forth, like a mother, the fauna that live on Earth. They are my offspring and depend on me for subsistence. All fauna depend on the vegetation I produce for their survival and enjoyment of life. I am Earth, the source of daily life for the flora and fauna that I have generated from within me. All fauna and flora are my children, Earth beings.
>
> May I, as the precious being revealed at the beginning, as the source of all flesh and blood, including your own, and as the one who is God's partner in the continuing creation of life, urge you as Earth beings to treasure, trust, and serve me. Let us unite in celebration and service, in healing and ministry.

Discerning the Restorative Powers of Earth

The Bible makes it quite clear that Earth has creative powers. In Genesis 1, as we have seen, Earth is the fecund reality that brings forth plants and animals. Earth itself is a co-creator with God. This is not a one-time event, of course, but an ongoing reality. In one of his seed parables, Jesus attests to the fact that once a seed is planted, "on its own" the earth produces fruit, first the stalk, then the head, then the ripe grain in the head. Furthermore, Earth provides food and water not only for humans but also for all animals as the way in which God "gives them their food in due season" (Ps. 104:27).

We know well the destructive forces of Earth. The Bible attests to them as well. Yet we can, at the same time, proclaim with the Bible that Earth also has restorative powers. Nature recovers from devastation. Nature can bring forth flowers in the desert. Just as Earth mourns and languishes when humans manifest injustice in the land, so also Earth rejoices when humans are living in the land according to the righteous commandments of God. In the psalms, the praise of creation—hills, fields, forests, seas, all creatures—is celebrated in part because it has the capacity to lift the human spirit and to draw us into its praise. All of this is confirmed by contemporary studies that demonstrate how much the beauty of Earth and the flourishing of nature can contribute to the quality of life and well-being of individuals and communities.

Furthermore, nature has healing powers. The author of the book of Revelation gives his depiction of the New Jerusalem as an expression of the new creation. It is a vision in which humans and nature live in closeness and in harmony with each other. The river of life flows down the middle of the city streets and offers unlimited water free of charge. On either side of the river stand the trees of life, offering fruit twelve months of the year so that no one will go hungry. And, John adds, the "leaves of the trees are for the healing of the nations" (22:2). John understood the healing powers of nature. As they did in antiquity, so today we know and appreciate the incredible medicinal properties of so many plants and animals, many of which are now endangered by human activity. And we also know that an intimate relationship with nature can ease depression, calm fears, and speed recovery from accident and illness.

This is good news about Earth that we need to recover from the Bible and proclaim in our preaching. Just as God's love can encounter us in the faces of family and friends, so also God's love can encounter us through the presence of nature around us. Just as we experience healing through our fellow humans, so also we can receive healing from nature.

Furthermore, Earth's restorative powers assure us that we are not alone in our efforts to help the Earth recover from its devastation at human hands. Earth is a partner. And we can often learn from Earth itself what we need to do to cooperate with Earth to speed the recovery of plants and animals and ecosystems under stress and distress. This is a significant part of the proclamation of the good news, that God has created the world in such a way that Earth can be an instrument for God's healing and restoration. So when we read, we ask: In what ways do the presence and depiction of nature in this passage serve to express creative and restorative powers for humans and other life forms?

Example: When we read the Sermon on the Mount, we learn how humans are to love. They are to love as God does, by treating all people with love, regardless of whether they are just or unjust, good or wicked. In explaining this, Jesus names two ways that God expresses God's love, namely, by having the sun rise over the wicked and the good and by sending rain over the just as well as the unjust (Matt. 5:45). God's love is expressed through natural realities on behalf of the well-being of all humankind, and, we might add, all other living things on the face of the Earth. Thus, when we expand the range of expressions of God's love for people through natural forces, we can see and proclaim, with the Bible, how important is the relationship of Earth to human beings.

Human Justice in Ecological Justice

All that we have dealt with so far assumes that Earth is one interwoven web of creation. Therefore, if we are to connect with all of Earth community, we must see social justice as an integral and foremost dimension of ecological justice. They are one and the same thing, because they are so inextricably related to each other. We cannot separate our abuse of Earth from the abuse of humans against humans. It is the same mentality of domination and exploitation that leads humans to treat both Earth and humans with inhumane behavior.

It is clear that our actions against and neglect of nature are directly related to our abuse of humans. And, equally so, our efforts to restore Earth are directly related to our restoration of humans from environmental deprivation. Pollution of air, water, and land is causing human illnesses, genetic aberrations, and displacement. Climate change is causing more severe and unpredictable weather, a reduction in arable land to desert, migrations of environmental refugees, a loss of vital fresh water reserves, increased risk of fire due to dry conditions, and human conflicts over scarce resources. These changes in Earth are affecting everyone. However, they are affecting most especially the poor of the world who are most dependent upon the land and the water for their lives and livelihoods, and who have the least protection against threats to their health and well-being. It is the task of the preacher to articulate these connections both in the text and in its application to our time.

As we read, we ask: How does the passage show (or not) the connection between human injustice and ecological degradation? How does the passage show a relationship between love of neighbor and care for Earth? How can we find (in the passage or in the Bible as a whole) guidance to care for the most vulnerable and to restore justice to all Earth community?

Example: In analyzing Genesis 1, we see that God creates Earth as a whole, including human beings. The salvation history that follows in the biblical materials is not just human history; it is creation history. All are meant to thrive together. Humans have a responsibility to see that all of life—human and nonhuman—may "be fruitful and multiply." The whole creation story and the rest of the Bible stories that follow display what that responsibility is to be like: humans are to "serve and preserve" garden Earth; Noah preserves all species, humans included; the Sabbath laws call for rest for humans and animals and land together; all creation is to worship God in solidarity; when there is injustice among humans in the land, the Earth withers and does not produce crops; when the future is secured by God, the land will produce abundantly year-round so no one is hungry. Our common fate as creatures of Earth is tied up together; and humans are to exercise dominion in solidarity *with* creation, not above it.

This opening story of creation sets the framework for the rest of the Bible. It calls for human beings to embrace a vocation of responsibility: to be Earth keepers, just as we are to be keepers of our sisters and brothers. The rest of the Bible unfolds the full purpose to act as agents in God's image, namely, to serve rather than to lord over.

Connecting with Christ

In our interpretation of biblical texts, particularly in the New Testament lessons, we need to ask how Christ is involved in creation and in the restoration of creation. We need to explore how Christ is connected with us as creatures and with the rest of creation. We need to consider where the good news is found in the text or in the wider context and where Christ is at work in the origins, suffering, and liberation of all creation. As we read we may ask:

- Does the text point to Christ and the origins of creation or continuing creation?
- Does the text point to Christ suffering with and for creation?
- Does the text connect with Christ forgiving sins, including environmental sins?

- Does the text reveal the presence of the risen and cosmic Christ reconciling all creation?

Example: As we analyze the epistle lesson for Earth Sunday (Rom. 1:18-23), we are made aware that creation is not simply a beautiful work of art. It is also a means of revelation, a vehicle for proclaiming God's presence. The glory of God Paul mentions is the visible presence of the Creator mediated through everything from the sunset to the storm, from the garden frog to the mountain lion.

And, as the Gospel lesson for this Sunday (John 1:1-14) discloses, God's glory is revealed to us even more clearly in Jesus Christ. For that very Word that called Earth to appear from beneath the primal waters is now revealed in Jesus Christ. And in one of the most radical assertions of the Gospels, John declares that "the Word became flesh" (John 1:14). In other words, God "became flesh." And flesh is composed of water, air, and soil—the basic stuff of Earth. So the Word became a part of Earth. In short, Christ and creation are connected from the beginnings of creation, through the incarnation to the birth of a new creation.

Conclusion

We urge you to reread these suggested guidelines from time to time, so that your sensitivities to the presence and voices of all Earth community in the text are maintained and sharpened. For every Sunday in the three-year common lectionary, not just for the Season of Creation, we can explore in creative and insightful ways the words we need to hear and the messages we need to proclaim that will engage us in "the care and redemption of all that God has made."

RESOURCES

Bauckham, Richard. *The Bible and Ecology: Rediscovering the Community of Creation.* Waco: Baylor University Press, 2010.

Bredin, Mark. *The Ecology of the New Testament: Creation, Re-Creation, and the Environment.* Colorado Springs: Biblica, 2010.

Davis, Ellen. *Scripture, Culture, and Agriculture: An Agrarian Reading of the Bible.* Cambridge: Cambridge University Press, 2009.

Fretheim, Terence. *God and World in the Old Testament: A Relational Theology of Creation.* Nashville: Abingdon, 2005.

————. *Creation Untamed: The Bible, God, and Natural Disasters.* Grand Rapids: Baker, 2010.

The Green Bible (NRSV). San Francisco: HarperOne, 2008.

Habel, Norman C. *An Inconvenient Text: Is a Green Reading of the Bible Possible?* Adelaide: ATF, 2009.

————, ed. The Earth Bible series. See the titles, contributors, and tables of contents for the volumes in this series on the Earth Bible pages at http://www.webofcreation.org.

————, and Peter Trudinger, eds. *Exploring Ecological Hermeneutics.* Atlanta: Society of Biblical Literature, 2008.

Hiebert, Theodore. *The Yahwist's Landscape: Nature and Religion in Early Israel.* Minneapolis: Fortress Press, 2008.

Horrell. David. *The Bible and the Environment: Towards a Critical Ecological Biblical Theology.* London: Equinox, 2010.

————, Cherryl Hunt, and Christopher Southgate, eds. *Greening Paul: Reading the Apostle in a Time of Ecological Crisis.* Waco: Baylor University Press, 2010.

————, ————, ————, and Francesca Stavrakopoulou. *Ecological Hermeneutics: Biblical, Historical, and Theological Perspectives.* New York: T & T Clark, 2010.

Marlow, Hillary. *Biblical Prophets and Contemporary Environmental Ethics.* New York: Oxford University Press, 2009.

Rhoads, David. "Who Will Speak for the Sparrow? Eco-Justice Criticism and the New Testament," in Sharon H. Ringe and H. C. Paul Kim, eds., *Literary Encounters with the Reign of God: Festschrift for Robert Tannehill*, 64–86. New York: T & T Clark, 2003.

Rossing, Barbara R. *The Rapture Exposed: The Message of Hope in the Book of Revelation.* Boulder: Westview, 2004.

Walker-Jones, Arthur. *The Green Psalter: Resources for an Ecological Spirituality.* Minneapolis: Fortress Press, 2009.

PART TWO

SPIRIT, WORD, WISDOM
ENGAGING THE SUNDAYS
AND READINGS

YEAR A

THE SPIRIT SERIES

First Sunday in Creation

Forest Sunday

Theodore Hiebert

Genesis 2:4b-22
Psalm 139:13-16
Acts 17:22-28
John 3:1-16

Background: Why Trees Matter

When we think about trees and our environmental responsibilities, the first phrase that may come to mind is the slogan "tree hugger." This has become a popular way to disparage the environmental movement by implying that loving nature and taking it seriously are sentimental acts by fringe elements who are not really in touch with the hard realities of the world. I would not be surprised if there are members of our congregations who, consciously or not, have this phrase and its sentiment in the back of their minds somewhere. But it has also been my experience that the members of our congregations are concerned about the deterioration of their environment, and they are simply overwhelmed by the enormity of the problem and at a loss as to what to do. So I believe that when we are talking about forests, we are facing a community partly skeptical and partly curious and concerned.

One of the best ways to motivate such a community to take responsibility for our forests is to acquaint them with the essential roles that trees play in both our physical and spiritual well-being. Scientists tell us that forests are essential both to our physical health and to the health of the planet. When we actually look at the hard realities of the world, it becomes clear pretty quickly that trees are not just a cute, sentimental attraction, as the "tree hugger" critics would have us believe. Forests contribute to our economic well-being: timber remains the principal material humans use for construction worldwide; paper—even in today's electronic age—is essential for communication and education; and for nearly three billion people in the developing world, wood provides the main energy source for heating and cooking. Forests also provide crucial ecosystem services: they harbor most of the world's biodiversity, sheltering more than half of the world's known plant and animal species; they protect and enrich soils and sustain water quality and quantity; and, by absorbing carbon dioxide and producing oxygen, they give us healthy air to breathe and they reduce global warming. As it turns out, life as we know it is impossible without the world's forests.

The problem is that we are losing our forests, and with them all of the essential benefits they provide for our planet and for ourselves. More forest areas have been cleared from 1850 to the present than in all of previous history. Due to population growth and deforestation, the amount of forest cover available to each person has declined globally by 50 percent since 1960. The results of deforestation are serious. Losing forests means losing the incredible diversity of plant and animal life they shelter. According to present trends, one-quarter of the Earth's species of plants and animals will be lost in the next forty years, a loss that will take nature ten million years to replicate. Furthermore, deforestation is a major contributor to global warming, the most serious environmental threat we face. Tropical deforestation produces more global-warming pollution than the total emissions of every car, truck, plane, ship, and train on Earth. Deforestation accounts for about 20 percent of heat-trapping emissions, an amount equivalent to the emissions from China or the United States.

Forests also play an essential role in our spiritual health. This may be trickier to talk about than about those physical forest facts, because saying that trees are important for religious reasons immediately sounds "pagan" and "new age," and it can evoke the precise eye-rolling and dismissive attitude that leads to the "tree hugger" slogan. This nervousness about the religious significance of trees stems largely from our modern worldview that has made a complete split between spirit and matter and that has reduced the natural world, and trees with it, to merely physical objects. As we have just seen, we need forests for our physical well-being. Yet many of us moderns think that is the end of it: trees are part of a scientific equation for physical survival, but not a part of our faith or our spirituality.

However, our faith traditions and our experiences say otherwise. Christians have always considered the world of nature, together with

Scripture, to be a source of divine revelation. If the world (with its trees) communicates in any way the nature of God, then trees communicate in some way a sense of the mystery and meaning behind the world, a sense of the transcendence and character of God. Most of us know down deep that a core aspect of our spirituality and wholeness is nourished by our connection to the world around us. Many of us have experienced this connection in the presence of nature's magnificent forests and trees, whether it be when hiking in our great old-growth forests or simply admiring the age and beauty of the trees in our neighborhoods. In Homewood, Illinois, my hometown, the public-works department is cutting down 2,582 mature ash trees in the parkways along our streets, 241 in our neighborhood alone, because of damage from the invasive emerald ash borer. Over fifteen thousand ash trees will have to come down in Homewood as a whole. We and our neighbors have experienced this not just as a physical fact but with a real sadness; it is a kind of emotional and psychic loss that affects the quality of life in our neighborhood.

When we look for some guidance from our Scriptures in the biblical texts selected for Forest Sunday about the role of forests in God's world, we will be looking at aspects of these texts that biblical scholars, inspirational writers, and preachers often overlooked in the past. Their focus traditionally has been primarily on God and humanity in isolation from the world of nature in which the divine-human drama is played out. We will see that this traditional way of reading these texts—as if they focused on God and humans alone—missed many aspects that we are only now beginning to see and to understand as essential in the biblical drama. We must do new work to recover something of the foundational role of nature in biblical religion, not just to respond adequately to the environmental crisis, but so we can read the Bible correctly and regain a fuller sense of who God is and of who we are in God's world.

First Reading
GENESIS 2:4B-22: THE BIBLE'S OLDEST IDEAS ABOUT TREES

Since the story of the garden of Eden in Genesis 2:4b-22 is the richest of the four texts for this Sunday in its reflections about forests and their significance, and since it provides the theological foundation for later Jewish and Christian thought in the other texts, it requires more attention than the other texts we will investigate. As we will see, the other lectionary selections for Forest Sunday do not specifically mention trees at all. The story of Eden in Genesis 2–3 is the second account of creation in the Bible, following the seven-day account in Genesis 1:1—2:4a attributed to a Priestly writer. But it is, in fact, the older of the two accounts, giving us Israel's first reflections on the world and its beginnings. This creation story is attributed to an author called the Yahwist, who regularly uses the divine name *Yahweh* for God (rendered as "the LORD" in English translations). Creation stories like this one are important because they are more about the present than about the past. By describing the origins of things, they explain why things are the way they are today. Such stories thus provide a kind of divine authorization for the way the world is. Embedded in it are the deepest values about the world held by its author and its audience.

We customarily direct our attention in this story to its account of the first humans and, in particular, to their disobedience of God's commands and to the consequences of this disobedience for human nature. This is an important theme, but it is part of a larger story about the entire world of creation that we often overlook. In one respect, the Yahwist's creation story is very human centered: the human being is the first thing created, and all of the rest of creation—the plants and animals in the garden—seem to be made for human benefit. Yet, in another respect, the human being is not central at all, but a simple, even subservient, part of God's creation, who is given the task of caring for it.

The human role in creation is, in fact, the Yahwist's primary interest in the story's introduction (vv. 4b-6), which describes the absence of life before creation by singling out key features of the audience's own world that did not yet exist: pasture plants (for the Israelites' flocks of sheep and goats; NRSV: "plant of the field"); field crops (of grain and barley, the staples of the Israelite diet; NRSV: "herb of the field"); rain to water these plants; and a farmer to cultivate them. These four items reflect the ancient Israelites' agrarian economy. The Israelites in the Yahwist's audience were small-scale, subsistence farmers involved in rain-fed agriculture, namely, cultivating grain on arable land and raising flocks on nearby pasturage. Thus, when the Yahwist first mentions humanity in this introduction, he thinks of humans not in isolation, or even in relationship to God, but in their intimate relationship to their unique natural environment.

When the story of creation begins, the Yahwist is still primarily interested in the relationship between the first human being and the world's first plants (vv. 7-17). The human being is not described in isolation from the world, as if creation were a mere stage for the human drama, as we have customarily read this story. Rather, the first human is created in such a way that human nature and vocation are completely interrelated with the plants with which the human being shares the world. Human nature and "plant nature," so to speak, are closely connected in this story because they both originate in the Earth's fertile soil (NRSV: "ground"). God makes the first human (*adam*) from the topsoil (*aphar*; NRSV: "dust") of arable land (*adamah*; NRSV: "ground"), and God grows the first plants from the same arable land (*adamah*; vv. 7, 9). In the next episode of the Yahwist's creation story, when the animals are created, they, too, are made from the same fertile soil (*adamah*) that gave birth to plants and humans (v. 19). For the Yahwist, all of life shares a common origin in, and thus a common identity with, the Earth's fertile soil.

Just as humans are connected to plants by their nature, so they are related to plants by their vocation. The first mission God gives humans, before God gives them any commands to love God or their neighbors, is to care for the world's plants: God put the first human in the garden "to farm it and to take care of it" (v. 15; NRSV: "to till it and keep it"). Thus, the original and most fundamental human work is to care for the world's plants. And we may be even a bit more precise. The terms *farm* and *till* actually translate the Hebrew verb *avad*, which literally means "serve," and it is the common Hebrew term used to describe the service of servants to their masters, subjects to the king, and people to their God. This human occupation depicted in Genesis 2 contrasts with the human occupation in the Priestly account of creation in Genesis 1 where the original human mission is to rule over creation (1:26-28). The Yahwist viewed humanity as creation's servant and caretaker, not its master.

Now we are in a position to talk more specifically about the role of forests in the Yahwist's account of creation in Genesis 2, in his own landscape, and in his theology and ethics. The first thing we notice is that, in describing the creation of the world's plants in the garden of Eden, the Yahwist talks only about trees: "In the fertile land [*adamah*], Yahweh, God, grew every tree, those with a beautiful appearance and those with delicious fruit, and also the tree of life in the middle of the garden and the tree of the knowledge of good and evil" (v. 9; author's translation). Now, both the Priest's and the Yahwist's creation stories are parochial in their own ways, mentioning not all of the world's vegetation but specifically those species with which they were most familiar in their own environments. But for the Yahwist to mention only trees is interesting, and a bit puzzling, since we might have expected Yahweh to populate the garden first with the grains and pasturage mentioned in the introduction as not yet existing (v. 5). Yet here at creation, trees stand in for the entire plant kingdom.

We do not know for sure why the Yahwist chose to focus the creation of the plant kingdom on trees as he does here. It is certainly not because he meant to describe an age of hunting and gathering that preceded agriculture. This is a cultivated garden and the first human is a farmer, just as are the members of the first Israelite audience (v. 15). The Yahwist mentions trees "with delicious fruit," and Israelite farmers did supplement their grain-based agriculture with trees, such as olives, figs (Gen. 3:7), pomegranates, date palms, almonds, and walnuts. Yet there are also trees here that are simply beautiful (v. 9). I suspect that in the Yahwist's picture of paradise, from which his ancestors were eventually expelled to the hard, grain-based, rain-fed agriculture of the Mediterranean mountains (3:17-18, 23), the Yahwist is presenting his ideal natural world, a world with abundant spring-fed water not vulnerable to the vicissitudes of Middle Eastern rainfall (vv. 5-6). In this ideal world, trees stand in for the entire world of plants because of their magnificence, their endurance, their beauty, and their bountiful food.

To sum up thus far, the Yahwist views the world's trees as a kind of archetype of the entire plant kingdom, a kingdom to which humans by nature are closely related and for which humans by vocation are directly responsible, not as its master but as its servant. A further aspect of the Yahwist's perspective on forests can be seen in his description of the trees of paradise in two categories: "those with a beautiful appearance and those with delicious fruit" (v. 9; NRSV: "pleasant to the sight and good for food"). By mentioning trees with delicious fruit, the Yahwist acknowledges the role trees play in our physical well-being. They are of instrumental value to us, just as we recognized their value in the introduction by listing some of the ways—building materials, paper, fuel—that forests benefit humans and their economy. A fundamental reason for caring for trees, then, is their great benefit to us and to our way of life.

When the Yahwist also describes trees as "beautiful in appearance," however, he gives trees a value beyond their importance to our physical well-being. He suggests that trees affect our lives in ways that go beyond their physical usefulness to us, namely, that they affect our psychic or emotional or spiritual well-being. Even more, trees have a majesty, an integrity, a value in their own right, apart from their usefulness to us. This is certainly in line with the Priestly notion in the first creation account in Genesis 1, where God identifies the entire plant kingdom with its trees as "good" (1:11-12)—even before humans appear on the world's landscape (1:26-27).

A sense of the integrity of trees in their own right is also in line with the biblical notion of the sacredness of trees. This idea may sound strange or pagan to the modern Christian, but it is a genuine part of biblical thought. It lies behind the description of the tree of knowledge and the tree of life in the garden as possessing divine qualities that may be acquired by consuming their fruit. It also lies behind the description of particular trees in the ancestral narratives as sites of divine revelation (Gen. 12:6-7, 13:18, 21:33; cf. 26:23-25). And it lies behind the image of the tree of life at the center of the redeemed and restored world in the book of Revelation (22:1-5). We might not speak of trees in quite this way today, but this biblical idea is essentially the same as our modern view that creation is a source of the knowledge of God, that the world—with its majestic trees— communicates in some way a sense of the mystery and meaning behind the world, a sense of the transcendence and character of God.

Psalmody

PSALM 139:13-16: GOD'S PRESENCE IN CREATION

Psalm 139 is a sustained reflection on God's presence with the psalmist, which does not exactly fit into one of the major psalm types. It is not really a hymn praising God in general terms; nor is it a Song of Thanksgiving praising God for a specific act of deliverance. Neither is it a lament asking God for help in a time of distress, although some have seen in it aspects of a lament: the psalmist's sense of being hemmed in by God (v. 5) at the beginning of the poem (vv. 1-11) and the psalmist's appeal to God to destroy evildoers at the end (vv. 19-22). It may fit most naturally into a smaller group of psalms known as Songs of Trust, psalms expressing the poet's confidence in God and his sense of dependence on God's care. The intimacy of the relationship between God and the psalmist in this poem is quite remarkable, and, according to our traditional habits of reading Scripture, we might be inclined to view this as a purely spiritual relation- ship that is limited to God and the psalmist alone. If we take a step back from our human-centered perspective, however, we see that the psalmist has the entire world of creation and its processes in view here.

In the specific section of the psalm selected for this Sunday, verses 13-16, the psalmist describes God as his creator and, by extension, the creator of every individual human being. In one of the most fascinating windows into the ancient notion of conception and birth, the psalm- ist emphasizes God's intimate involvement in the ongoing processes of creation as his inward parts (literally, "kidneys") and skeleton (literally, "bones") are woven together (vv. 13, 15) in the womb. The psalmist's view of God as the creator and sustainer of human life is similar to the view of the Yahwist. As we have seen, the Yahwist describes God as the creator of the first human being (Gen. 2:7), but he also acknowledges divine involvement in the conception of each individual thereafter (Gen. 4:1, 16:2, 18:13-14, and so on). When the psalmist mentions being created in the depths of the Earth (v. 15), he may be reflecting the Yahwist's notion of our origin from within the Earth and our connection to its larger processes.

As a matter of fact, the psalmist's notion of God's intimate involvement in the process of creation of each individual human being is part of a much larger notion: God's presence in creation as a whole. When the psalmist refers to himself as one of God's wonderful works (v. 14), he is using a phrase most often employed for God's amazing deeds in creation in general (Pss. 65:5, 145:6). Indeed, the psalmist describes not just God's presence within himself but God's presence in the cosmos as a whole, so that there is no place—not even the realm above the Earth (heaven) nor the realm below the Earth (Sheol) nor the realm beyond the sea (the farthest regions of the Earth, vv. 8-9)—where God is not present. The psalmist's key insight and the reason for his confidence and trust in God is his belief that the cosmos in its entirety is infused with God's presence. While the world's forests are not mentioned specifically by this psalmist, they, too, are part of this world penetrated and preserved by God.

Second Reading
ACTS 17:22-28: THE CHRISTIAN MESSAGE GROUNDED IN CREATION

The aim of the Acts of the Apostles, as the sequel to the Gospel of Luke, is to chronicle the spread of the gospel throughout the known world as the fulfillment of the great commission (Luke 24:47; Acts 1:8). Acts begins with the preaching of Peter and of the apostles in Jerusalem, but it soon moves out into the larger Roman Empire with Paul on his missionary travels. In Acts 17, Paul arrives in Athens, the center of Greek culture and learning, where he engages the spokesmen of the great philosophical traditions of his day, Epicureanism and Stoicism (v. 18). When he is invited by the Court of Areopagus, an influential body with oversight of education and culture, to describe his religious faith (v. 19), Paul is given the opportunity to speak on one of the ancient world's great stages. So we are especially curious to see how Paul will frame the gospel message for this world audience.

What Paul does is to begin his message of the "good news about Jesus and the resurrection" (v. 18) with God the Creator. Paul's explanation of the gospel starts with "the God who made the world and everything in it" (v. 24). Now, this opening reference to the God of creation may be a strategic move on Paul's part, designed to introduce his remarks with a general truth in order to find common ground with his audience. The author of Luke-Acts certainly wished to present Christianity as a legitimate religion on the world stage of the Roman Empire. Yet the fact that Paul begins his statement of faith with an affirmation of creation has profound theological importance. It shows that Paul, as the author of Luke-Acts presents him here, understands the gospel within the larger context of creation. The incarnation is not just God's encounter with humanity but God's encounter with the world, an event within God's ongoing work in creation as a whole. God's redemption is intended for the world, as we will see more directly in this Sunday's Gospel text, not just for its people.

Christianity, together with Paul in his address to the Athenians, has always understood its faith to be grounded in God and God's creation. New Testament writers consistently refer to God as *Creator* (Mark 13:19; Eph. 3:9; Rev. 4:11). Paul himself, in his own exposition of the gospel in the letter to Rome, begins with God the Creator and with the claim that God's eternal power and divine nature have always been clearly evident in God's creation (Rom. 1:19-20). The great Christian creeds have reaffirmed this New Testament belief that the Christian story begins with creation by starting their statements of faith with God the Creator. The Nicene Creed, a summary of the essentials of the Christian faith drawn up in the fourth century and still used in liturgies today, begins: "We believe in one God, the Father, the Almighty, maker of heaven and earth, of all that is, seen and unseen." In this regard, Christian confessions of faith genuinely reflect biblical theology, since the biblical story itself begins with creation. Starting points are not accidental or convenient or preliminary. They are foundational and defining moments, marking out the identity of the members of a community who remember and recite their beginnings. What Paul in Athens and what our religious traditions have always told us is that God is first and foremost the Creator and that we are first and foremost members of creation.

Gospel
JOHN 3:1-16: REDEMPTION AS THE RENEWAL OF CREATION

The story of Nicodemus's visit to Jesus by night in John 3 appears at first glance to have little to say about creation and our role in it. Moreover, it contains John 3:16, a verse that has been used as much as any other verse in the New Testament to present Christianity as an entirely spiritual affair, a religion of personal faith and belief, a religion of eternal life beyond this world. This story's references to being born again, to flesh and Spirit, and to heaven and earth, might easily be taken to describe a dualistic reality in which earthly things must be replaced with heavenly things. But this traditional way of reading John 3 has more to do with some of our contemporary ideas of salvation than with the theology of the Gospel of John itself. We need to do some genuine investigative work to understand properly John's view of new life.

When we hear Jesus tell Nicodemus that he must be "born again" (v. 7, KJV), most of us likely think only of an interior personal experience. But for the Gospel of John, this new birth refers to new way of living in the world here and now. The Greek phrase *gennethenai anothen* means "born anew" (NRSV) or "from above," that is, by God's power from above. This new birth is one of water, that is, baptism, and Spirit (v. 5); it is thus an entry into the new life one lives after baptism in this world as a member of the Christian community. Eternal life (vv. 15, 16) is not understood by this gospel as immortality in heaven but as experiencing God's presence now and living in that presence (cf. 17:1-3).

This view of the new Christian existence as a transformed life in this world is highlighted in verse 16 when this Gospel affirms that "God so loved the world." The Greek word for "world" is *kosmos*, a very big word that can mean the entire universe or, somewhat more narrowly, the Earth, humankind, or the forces in the world opposed to God's rule. Though scholars are inclined to interpret the *kosmos* that God loves in John 3:16 as humankind in particular, we should ask, given the broad meaning of this term, whether it does not evoke in its listeners an image of the world as a whole. By paraphrasing Genesis 1 in the opening lines of the Gospel of John, the author describes Jesus as co-creating with God the entire *kosmos*, as being present within it, and as revealing God "in the flesh," that is, in the realities of this world here and now (1:1-14). Would not the first listeners have heard echoes of the creation as a whole when this Gospel tells us that God loved the *kosmos* and gave God's only Son, its co-creator, to redeem it?

Such a here-and-nowness about God's redemptive plans actually characterizes the New Testament as a whole. God's redemption of the world through Christ is not the abandonment of Earth for heaven but the renewal of this world itself. This is clear even in the most unlikely of places, the book of Revelation. There, in the great climax of redemption history, God does not lift God's people from the world, as the "Left Behind" book series by Tim LaHaye and Jerry Jenkins claims, but God descends to dwell with them on Earth, on an Earth where all of creation is renewed (Revelation 21–22, esp. 21:1-4). And one of the key symbols of that restored creation is the tree of life, the fruit of which heals the nations (Rev. 22:1-2). Just as in the Eden narrative of creation, where the tree symbolizes all of the world's vegetation, so here, too, at the culmination of history, the tree symbolizes the entire plant kingdom and its role in the world (healing). In the biblical worldview, then, at least in some of these key texts, the world's trees and its forests represent the world's entire plant kingdom. We might even say that our honoring and our protection of God's creation is, therefore, in some way symbolized and measured by our care of its trees.

Reflections

When we first imagine how we might rethink our view of forests and remodel our behavior to preserve and protect them—actually, to renew and restore our relationship to them—we tend to think first about the rainforests in the tropics. This is understandable, since the media has focused on them so much recently and because they make such a huge impact on the health of the global environment. Yet this may not be the best place to begin for us, since rainforests are so unreal and distant and foreign to our own experience. The place to begin may be in our own backyards. In this regard, we might take seriously the wisdom of the great commission that being a disciple and an evangelist means starting at home and working outward to the ends of the Earth.

To honor God's creation and to protect it in our own backyards, we might first think of the trees on our own property. As magnificent parts of God's good creation in their own right, how do they remind us of the larger creation of which we, too, are a part? And have we created an environment around them that enhances both their health and ours, or that endangers it? On its Web site, the Tree Care Industry Association identifies local, reputable tree-care companies that can significantly improve the health of our trees—by pruning and thinning deadwood, by applying organic soil-care products to help trees compete with the ubiquitous American lawn, and by mulching (perhaps the single best thing we can do for our trees). Also, local nurseries that specialize in native species provide native trees for planting that enhance the health of the entire local ecosystem.

After considering the trees closest to us, we might consider the trees in our neighborhoods and in our towns. Are there ways we can support the urban forests in our own hometowns? Homewood, Illinois, my hometown, is a Tree City USA, which means that we have a management structure to supervise our trees, a tree ordinance with a plan of action, a budget that devotes at least two dollars per capita annually to reforestation, and an Arbor Day celebration. We have a shared-cost tree program to encourage the planting of trees throughout the village. We also have a highly qualified arborist who—through the care of trees in the parkways and on city property and through the planting of a new native, diversified forest of trees to replace the thousands of ash trees that are coming down because the emerald ash borer—is ensuring a beautiful and healthy environment for the next generation. Each of us can learn about the urban forests in our own hometowns, discover what kind of commitment our towns make to a healthy tree population, and find ways to get involved in the care of trees and in the enhancement of urban forests in our own municipalities.

Last, and certainly not least, we might consider the great old-growth forests in our country and around the world that contribute so much to the health of the global ecosystem. There are a number of ways in which we, in the choices we make, can help to prevent further losses of these forests, protect the world's biodiversity, and slow climate change. Some of the most important ways to help are provided on the Web page of the Union of Concerned Scientists. They include such simple, practical advice as choosing flooring for one's home that comes from sustainable, well-managed forests or from natural alternatives such as bamboo. Ways to help also include urging U.S. support in international climate treaties for REDD (Reduce Emissions from Deforestation and Forest Degradation in Developing Countries), an affordable set of policies that would save tropical forests while honoring the populations and needs of developing countries. The world's tropical forests are remote from us, but we can do simple, practical things to shape our behavior to protect and preserve these magnificent parts of God's creation, thereby ensuring our own health and the health of the planet.

RESOURCES

Information about the role that forests play in the global ecosystem and economy mentioned in the "Background" and some of the suggestions for responding to deforestation mentioned in the "Reflections" have been taken from the Web site of the Union of Concerned Scientists, http://www.ucsusa.org, accessed March 7, 2011.

More details of the Yahwist's values toward nature in Genesis 2:4b-22 may be found in my work *The Yahwist's Landscape: Nature and Religion in Early Israel* (Minneapolis: Fortress Press, 2008), 30–38, 51–75, and 149–62.

The New Testament view presented here that redemption is not an escape from the world but a renewal of the world is set out clearly in Barbara R. Rossing, *The Rapture Exposed: The Message of Hope in the Book of Revelation* (New York: Basic Books, 2004), chaps. 1, 10, 11, and the epilogue; and in David Rhoads's essay, "Who Will Speak for the Sparrow? Eco-Justice Criticism of the New Testament," in *Literary Encounters with the Reign of God*, eds. Sharon Ringe and Paul Kim (New York: T & T Clark, 2004), 64–86, esp. 71–79.

Information about the local care of trees and reputable tree companies can be found on the Web site of the Tree Care Industry Association, http://www.treecareindustry.org, accessed March 7, 2011.

Information about becoming a Tree City USA can be found on the Web site of the Arbor Day Foundation, http://www.arborday.org, accessed March 7, 2011.

A good treatment of both ethical and legal issues present in the preservation of forests can be found in Christopher Stone, *Should Trees Have Standing? Law, Morality, and the Environment*, 3d ed. (New York: Oxford University Press, 2010).

Second Sunday in Creation

Land Sunday

Ched Myers

Genesis 3:14-19;
4:8-16
Psalm 139:7-12
Romans 5:12-17
Matthew 12:38-40

Background

Most contemporary North Americans have been socialized to see and value the earthy terrain around them in terms of private possession, economic exploitation, and commodification. But in stark contrast to the cosmology of modernity, the Bible does not understand land as "real estate"—*ever*. Instead, we can identify at least four major characteristics of land in the biblical tradition: as mother of life; as abundant sustainer of living beings; as altar for worship of the Creator; and as home place.

Mother. In the second Genesis creation account we are told that the human being (*adam*) is formed from the "topsoil" (*adamah*; Gen. 2:7)—a wordplay that is tellingly preserved in the English "human/humus." Scripture is unembarrassed and straightforward: we are birthed from the earth (as are all flora and fauna; Gen. 2:9, 19). This spiritual and material understanding has been embraced both by old indigenous cultures and the new biological sciences, but ignored by Christians for too long.

Sustainer. In this same creation tale, the Earth (*eretz*; Gen. 2:6), is called a "garden" (*gan*; Gen. 2:8). Elsewhere in the Hebrew Scriptures this term is used to describe not only fertile terrain (Deut. 11:10; Isa. 51:3; Jer. 31:12), but also a woman's pleasures (Song of Solomon 4). This garden (LXX: *paradeisos*) provides everything human beings find "delightful" (Gen. 2:9). The adjective *tov*, according to Richard Lowery, "expresses God's intense pleasure at creation's every detail. It is God's cosmic WOW."[1] This divine assessment appears as an emphatic, ecstatic refrain in the first creation account (Gen. 1:4, 10, 12, 18, 21, 25), *before* humans arrive on the scene (thus undermining the common accusation that the Genesis tradition is overly anthropocentric). Lowery also points out that the verb *bara*, reserved exclusively in the Bible for God's creative activity, can also mean "to be fat" (for example, Gen. 27:28, 41:2-4); the Earth embodies a "rich and lavish overflow of goodness, abundant and life giving at its very core."[2] This contrasts sharply with Enlightenment notions of "natural scarcity" and the presumption that the Earth has no intrinsic value until humans reengineer it into something "useful." Yet, biblically, abundance is contingent upon human beings remaining obedient to their vocation to "serve and preserve" creation (Gen. 2:15).[3] To neglect stewardship and "take too much" of the divine gift is to reckon with disaster (see, for example, Num. 11:31-35; Leviticus 25–26)—a hard word in our own historical moment. At the same time, eschatological redemption is most often imagined in Scripture as the *restoration* of the land, such as the prophetic visions of YHWH's reforesting of the desertified Levant (Isa. 35:1-2, 41:17-20) and, even more remarkably, of wild flora and fauna reinhabiting the ruins of imperial cities (Isa. 13:19-22).

Altar. The land is the primary locus for worship in the earliest traditions of Scripture. Torah's first account of an encounter with God outside Eden occurs upon Abram's defection from empire to the marginal desert lands of Canaan (Gen. 12:6f.). He arrives at an oak, which is described in Hebrew as *elon moreh*—a teacher or oracle giver. It is here under this "tree of life" that God first tells Abram of his future in this land—and here that Abram builds the Bible's first altar (similar encounters take place in Gen. 18:1ff.; Judg. 6:11; and 1 Kgs. 19:4). Of particular significance is the often overlooked "eleventh commandment" of Exodus 20:24-25: "You need make for me only an altar of earth and sacrifice on it . . . your offerings of well-being. . . . If you make for me an altar of stone, do not build it of hewn stones; for if you use a chisel upon it you profane it."

No work of human hands (much less technology) can improve on creation; nature is thus the *most* appropriate setting for worship of YHWH. When the people forget this, "teaching trees" and "listening stones" bear witness against them (see Josh. 24:27). Such Earth-based communion hardly bespeaks of a biblical hostility to nature, as is so often claimed by the tradition's critics.

Home. Genesis 3, as we will see below, narrates how humans abandon their symbiotic relationship with the "garden" (Gen. 3:23f.) for the reengineered landscapes of the city (Gen. 4:17) and eventually of empire (Gen. 11:1-9). The subsequent covenantal narrative of Scripture articulates a dialectical relationship between the *homelessness* brought about by human alienation from the land and attempts by God to bring the people back *home* to it. When in exodus, dispossessed people are promised land; when in exile, they are promised a return (Isaiah 40, 65:19-25).[4] In short, the biblical narrative begins with a myth about a garden-home that is lost, and concludes with a myth of that garden-home's restoration (Rev. 22:1-2).

These four characteristics weave throughout the Hebrew Bible, as well as through the life of Jesus of Nazareth, a prophet of the wilderness tradition. They can also be discerned in each of the texts for Land Sunday. Preaching on these themes invites the audience to remember these ancient lessons about belonging, communion, and responsibility, and to act courageously in the teeth of our historic present ecological crisis.

First Reading
GENESIS 3:14-19; 4:8-16

Origin stories matter. They tell us who we are, how we got this way, and what our responsibilities are. They shape meaning and help us order life, for good or for ill. American origin stories such as Columbus's "discovery" of the "New World" or the landing of the Pilgrims at Plymouth Rock obviously function to legitimate European conquest and settlement of the continent. The modern narrative of evolutionary progress does the same thing on a broader canvas, asserting that human history since the dawn of civilization has been a slow but steady climb out of primitive ignorance toward ever-increasing technological, social, and economic sophistication. It is a nonnegotiable article of faith that our own cosmopolitan complexity is superior to all that has gone before, and that this developmental process was inevitable and is irreversible.

The "primeval history" of Genesis tells a very different origin story, indeed, one that contradicts every key aspect of the "salvation story" of progress. For this reason, it has been widely ridiculed in post-Enlightenment modernity as "mythological," "prescientific," and frankly silly. But there are three reasons to focus on Genesis 1–11 at some length here. First, it is difficult to interpret properly this Sunday's texts apart from that creation story. Second, "Ascent of Man" orthodoxy[5] has been showing significant signs of strain under the weight of our deepening environmental crisis. It also fails to square with recent research into human origins. And third, the "political" reading of Genesis 1–11 offered in brief outline here has profound implications for ecological theology and creation spirituality, not to mention the struggle to save the planet.

The two Genesis accounts of creation, when read as a literary whole, portray "the beginning" as a world that was beneficent and bountiful, in no need of human genius to improve or control it. Human beings were deeply embedded in a living biosphere, with a divine appointment as caretaker, in intimate relationship with the whole of creation: "Whatever *adam* called each living being, that was its name" (Gen. 2:19f.). This same intimacy is signaled (in another Hebrew wordplay) by the creation of "woman" (*ishshah*) from the body of "man" (*ish*)—a relationship of solidarity, not hierarchy (Gen. 2:22f.).

But this symbiosis is shattered in the tragic tale of Genesis 3. The primal equilibrium of Eden suffers an epochal rupture known in Christian tradition as "the fall." The "human being" (*adam*) and the "mother of life" (*ava*; Gen. 3:20) conspire to defy the divine taboo against grasping the fruit of the tree of the knowledge of good and evil (Gen. 3:1-6). This drama has long been read in our churches as a theological morality play (about obedience, freedom, power, and/or sex). But it can also be understood to be a mythological way of explaining the change in consciousness that propelled the rise of civilization. That is, the "forbidden fruit" symbolizes the primal human conceit that we, by employing our ingenuity, our technology, and our social organization, can improve on a creation that may be "good," but not good *enough*.

From this view, the creation and fall story represents an ancient warning tale. It was produced by Israel's sages, working with and editing older, ancient Near Eastern sources, probably during the exilic period. In the aftermath of the failed Israelite monarchy, they were attempting to understand their historic experiences of royal exploitation, civil war, erosion of the wilderness traditions, and eventual conquest and dispossession. But they were also reflecting upon the *etiological origin* of human oppression and violence that had brought their people—and all other tribal peoples—to the brink of extinction. The Genesis story identifies the problem not just as moral or political, but *anthropological*: something had gone fundamentally wrong with the human journey, of which Israel's national trauma was but a symptom. Think of Genesis 1–11, then, as a sort of searching, post-9/11 type of reflection—except that the Hebrew scribes of old had the courage to look at the contradictions of their *own* experiment in civilization, rather than avoiding self-examination by scapegoating their enemies!

It is the "deep anthropology" of Genesis that speaks to our current crisis. Indeed, ours is an interesting moment in the protracted culture war between this ancient wisdom tale and our modern messianic fable of progress—but *not* because of the so-called creationist controversy. For the past four decades, postmodern anthropology has been revisiting the question of human origins. On the one hand, human lifeways prior to the rise of civilization are being radically revised and revalued; on the other hand, modern assumptions about the intrinsic nobility (or inevitability) of the turn toward civilization are being questioned.

Human beings lived for hundreds of thousands of years in widely dispersed, clan-based, hunter/gatherer/horticulturalist cultures that were bioregionally situated and organized. These Pleistocene lifeways, according to Paul Shepard, remained unbroken since "the beginning" (regardless of whether we think the story of *homo sapiens* commenced 100,000 or 2.5 million years ago).[6] Thanks to the work of scholars like Marshall Sahlins[7] and John Gowdy,[8] the anthropological assessment of ancient (and contemporary) hunter-gatherer cultures has shifted almost 180 degrees. "Prehistoric" life (in the still-prevalent pejorative parlance) was *not*, as Thomas Hobbes famously and contemptuously put it in *Leviathan*, "solitary, poor, nasty, brutish, and short."[9] In fact, premodern societies are found to have been healthier, more leisurely, freer, more materially satisfied, less anxious, and demonstrably more ecologically sustainable than modern industrial ones. The Eden story, then, can be interpreted as a mythic memory of this "deep history" when humans dwelled symbiotically with the biosphere, relationally with other living creatures, and intimately with the spirit world.

With the advent of the domestication of plants and animals in the late Neolithic period, around 10,000 B.C.E., a slow but steady transformation in human habitation patterns commenced. Often referred to as "the agricultural revolution," it led to increasingly sedentary village lifestyles and a growing food surplus, which in turn led to population increases. Social organization became steadily more complex and violent, as emerging command economies came under management by new military and political elites. The majority of hunter-gatherers did *not* voluntarily embrace these new ways (any more than Native peoples rushed to join

European colonizers after contact in the Americas). Rather, through loss of habitat and conquest, they were forced into peasant servitude by agricultural societies voracious in their appetite for land and labor. We know this process happened independently in several parts of the world over several millennia; the earliest archaeological evidence for walled cities may be at Catal Huyuk in Turkey (c. 6,000 B.C.E.). But this process appears to have first triumphed in Mesopotamia, where delta waterways were harnessed for irrigated farming. Thus, the Semitic tribes to the west had front-row seats for this unfolding drama, and they were among its first victims, which suggests that the old traditions lying behind the Genesis narrative were perhaps the world's first literature of resistance to civilization.

It is instructive that the main "consequences" of the "fall" according to today's text (3:14-19) are the woman's pain in childbirth and the man's condemnation to agricultural toil. Both imply "forced labor" under farming regimes: the woman must bear more children who are physically larger due to higher caloric intake; and *adam* must now struggle with *adamah* (earth, soil), which is no longer a gift but a curse. There is both political and historical memory operating here about how the "original abundance"[10] of free hunter/gatherer/horticulturalists was lost. Societies that domesticate animals and "subdue" land for maximized production ultimately subdue and domesticate people into serfdom. Those who attempted to survive apart from this process were relegated to marginal lands, just as tribal Israel had been driven into the Palestinian highlands and its dry, rocky soil by the Canaanite allies of imperial Egypt who controlled the fertile lowlands.

The story of the fall thus preserves the perspective of indigenous people toward the "curse" of aggressive, colonizing civilizations: agriculture portends the end of Eden (3:23f.). This is further underlined by the first dramatic scene in Genesis 4: the archetypal story of Cain and Abel. Today's second Genesis reading is preceded by God's warning to the farmer Cain (whose name means "spear"): "Sin is lurking at the door; its desire is for you, but you must master it" (4:7). This is the first use of the word *sin* in Torah; and it implies that there is now a power loose in the world that is predatory and addictive, which humans must recognize and resist (see comments below on Romans 5). Abel, on the other hand, may symbolize the remnant of the older, not yet fully domesticated life; as a pastoralist (nomadic forager?), he lives with animals outside the village. He seems to enjoy God's favor.

The first murder takes place in a "field"—the farmer's domain (4:8). Genesis 4:10 articulates further human alienation from the earth: "The blood [*dam*] of your brother cries out from the ground [*adamah*]." As

Ellen van Wolde puts it, the ground is now "seeded" with blood (v. 11).[11] For a second time, God pronounces that the natural fertility of creation has been/will be compromised by the farmer's presumption over life (v. 12). And again the consequence is exile, now intensified: Cain becomes a "fugitive and wanderer on the earth" (v. 14). Wendell Berry often points out that "industrial agriculture," in contrast to local horticulture, has no sense of home, and it wanders the world eager to exploit its advantage, displacing and destroying people of place.[12]

Cain's survival strategy is to build the "first" city (4:17), which, as Jacques Ellul pointed out a half-century ago, deepens the trajectory of the fall.[13] Tellingly, Cain names it after his son Enoch, whose name means "re-creation/inauguration" (*chanakh*; 4:17). The vocation of the city indeed seeks a new beginning: to reengineer all of life according to the dictates of civilization. Within four generations (4:18), the progeny of this project, Lamech, vows a "politics of vengeance" (4:23f.)—and we are soon told that the Earth is "filled with violence" (6:11). This is, in no small measure, due to the rise of the "Nephilim" (6:4), an untranslatable Hebrew moniker sometimes rendered "giants in the earth," but probably to be identified as "mighty warriors." The strange term appears one other time in Scripture, in the report of the Israelite spies dispatched by Moses to do guerilla reconnaissance on the fortified cities of Canaan (Num. 13:17-19). The land "devours its inhabitants; and all the people that we saw in it are of great size. There we saw the Nephilim . . . and we seemed like grasshoppers . . . to them" (Num. 13:32f.; see Josh. 14:12, 15:14; Judg. 1:10). Thus, the Nephilim—also called *Anakim* or *Rephaim*—are "larger-than-life" military opponents in the land of Canaan (see also Deut. 1:28, 2:10f., 16-21, 9:1f., 11:21f.). Later, a heavily armed Philistine professional warrior (like Goliath; 1 Sam. 17:4-7) is called "one of the descendants of the giants" (2 Sam. 21:16).

The Nephilim of Genesis 6 seem to symbolize the warrior classes that had come to dominate the ancient Near East. Paleoanthropologists surmise that these may first have evolved from specialized hunting groups, who were physically stronger and more calculating than the rest of the clan and had become inured to killing. To put it somewhat simplistically, "professional" hunters became strongmen who, over time, became warrior chiefs, then kings. This is why cities, in the Genesis narrative, are later identified with kingdoms that are *innately predatory*—in the spirit of "Nimrod the hunter" (Gen. 10:8-14)! As Andrew Schmookler concludes: "In a very real sense, 'true' warfare may be viewed as one of the more important social consequences of the agricultural revolution."[14] So began the longest war in history, in which relentlessly expanding civilizations conquer and exploit the Earth and all who live symbiotically with her. It continues to our day.

Throughout this rather depressing narrative of a "descent," God offers strategic countermeasures to mitigate the curse of civilization. One is the "mark" God puts on Cain the murderer (4:15). This "tattoo of taboo" could function in two ways. On the one hand, it warned people of the land to "watch out" for aggressive farming cultures. On the other hand, the mark cautions the reader against thinking that the problem of Cain can be solved by killing Cain. The logic of retributive violence can only beget a spiral of violence, a prospect already embodied by Lamech (4:23f.). The land of "Nod, east of Eden" (4:16) thus becomes the first place of "refuge" for the guilty (see Num. 35:13-15; Deut. 4:41-43). Analogous practices of sanctuary can be found in many other indigenous cultures, which similarly had to face the conundrum of how to contain the violent pathologies generated by civilization.

In the Genesis story, the Creator is keenly cognizant of the deteriorating situation. The same divine "council" that created the human being in Genesis 1:26 must convene twice again to mitigate the damage, vignettes that neatly bookend the trajectory from garden to tower. The council considers the new human determination to reengineer creation and decides upon expulsion from Eden (3:22f.). Then, in the face of Babel's aspiration to omnipotence (11:6), the divine council recommends "deconstruction" of imperial monoculture in favor of the original vision of a dispersed, tribally diverse humanity (11:7-9).[15] We will look at other divine countermeasures below in the commentary on the epistle lesson.

The account of the fall concludes with the dawn of empire on the "plain of Shinar" (Gen. 10:10, 11:2), symbolizing the Fertile Crescent. The account of the tower of Babel in Genesis 11 is a thinly veiled parody of Mesopotamian ziggurats, which claim to reach to heaven, but which God must "come down" to see (11:4-7). Babel is another Hebrew wordplay; *balal* means "to confuse," while in Akkadian *bab-ilu* means "gate of gods," an allusion to the top of the ziggurat. The tower symbolizes the fortress architecture of domination and management of imperial conformity (11:1-3); it appears frequently as the target of prophetic denunciations (see, for example, Isa. 2:15, 33:18; Ezek. 31:10f.; Zeph. 1:16; Judg. 8:9). Its civilizational heights represent the nadir of the fall, the triumph of the wayward human impulse to reengineer the world in order to control and "improve" it.

The story outlined in such stark, archetypal strokes in Genesis 1–11 names our history, however unsettling that may be to preach. The speed of progress has been increasing exponentially by the century for ten millennia, as (1) the natural world has been increasingly demystified and subjected to ever more intense technological exploitation; (2) hierarchical social formations, economic stratification, and war have proliferated; and (3) human spiritual life and ecological competence have atrophied, resulting in growing alienation from both nature and spirit. It is impossible to argue, from today's ecological point of view, that the civilizations which have arisen over the last five thousand (or five hundred, or even fifty) years model lifeways that are as sustainable as those of the previous five hundred thousand years. Perhaps, then, the old Genesis warning tale is not so irrelevant after all.

Psalmody
PSALM 139:7-12

Paul Tillich wrote:

> To fly to the ends of the earth would not be to escape from God. Our technical civilization attempts just that, in order to be liberated from the knowledge that it lacks a center of life and meaning. The modern way to flee from God is to rush ahead . . . to conquer more and more space in every direction. . . . But God's Hand falls upon us; and it has fallen heavily and destructively upon our fleeing civilization.[16]

Psalm 139 begins and ends with David's prayer that he be searched by God (vv. 1, 23f.), and this introspection has traditionally been the focus of preaching. The middle part of the psalm, however, has interesting resonances with creation spirituality. If verses 3-6 emphasize God's omniscience from the point of view of David's conscience, verses 7-12 articulate the awesomeness of divine omnipresence. Just as the lament of verses 13-16 echoes Job's protest concerning God's care (Job 10:8-11), so does today's psalm echo God's "defense" in Job 38–41, which is the single most nature-saturated oracle in the Bible.

Note the assertion that there is no place in the cosmos in which human beings might venture where God is not already present (vv. 7-12). This assertion especially invites us to find God in creation. Again, the Bible is our ally here. The story of early Israel is all about wild landscapes: rocks and desert, rivers and springs, clouded peaks and pastured hills, caves and forests. YHWH's voice comes not to (or from!) those at the center of civilizational power, but to Moses in a burning bush (Exodus 3) and on a mountain peak (Exodus 19), and to Elijah in a desert ravine (1 Kgs. 17:2-7) and a hilltop cave (1 Kgs. 19:8-13). Heroes of the community are "born" in rivers (Moses, Exod. 2:3) and buried under oak trees (Deborah, Gen. 35:8; Saul, 1 Sam. 31:13).

These ancient traditions portray a God who not only can but who *should* be encountered through creation, a sort of "theological pan-entheism."[17] Abraham plants a tree and calls on the name of YHWH (Gen. 21:33). Torah enjoins the community to celebrate the harvest by dancing while waving branches from the local flora (Lev. 23:40). YHWH is imagined as a roaring lion (Hos. 11:10), a nursing eagle (Deut. 32:11), and an angry mother bear (Hos. 13:8). Some of the Hebrew tribes seem to have animal totems: Joseph is "like an ox" and Gad lives "like a lion" (Deut. 33:17, 20). Israel's ritual life is in tune with the seasons (for example, the harvest festivals of Leviticus 23) and the lunar cycles: "Blow the trumpet at the new moon, at the full moon, on our festal day" (Ps. 81:3). Perhaps the most archetypal expression of Israel's nature spirituality is Jacob's vision of the *axis mundi* while sleeping in the open desert, his head on a dreaming stone. Upon awakening he confesses that the land itself is God's abode: "Surely YHWH is in this place—and I did not know it! . . . How awesome is this place! It is none other than the House of Elohim, . . . the gate of heaven!" (Gen. 28:16-17).

The reach of vision in Psalm 139 goes beyond Earth to the cosmos: heaven and hell (v. 8), light and darkness (vv. 11f.). It calls to mind Paul's conviction that "not powers, nor height, nor depth, nor anything else in all creation, will be able to separate us from the love of God in Christ" (Rom. 8:38b). But we must face a bitter irony, an irony suggested already in Tillich's indictment of our technological civilization's hubris. Imagining that we have "transcended" God in our *own* global reach, we are pillaging "everywhere." Because nothing is sacred under capitalist exploitation, we are in fact profoundly separated from God's love and care precisely because we do not recognize the divine presence in creation. The legacy of our fall into civilization is a "heavy hand" on the planet indeed.

Preaching Psalm 139 on Land Sunday calls us to search hard for "light in this darkness" (v. 12) as we now reap the toxic harvest of our degradation of Earth. Today an earnest theological search for God must entail a commitment to resist empire and begin the long process of environmental restoration, even to the "furthest limits of the sea" (v. 9).

Second Reading
ROMANS 5:12-17

Our Romans passage is an interesting parenthetical reflection in the midst of Paul's great discourse on justification by faith. It concerns the etiology of sin, and its telos as well, which the apostle identifies with Adam and Christ respectively (v. 14). "The vocabulary of Christian faith suffers from misunderstanding at every turn, but no one term is as poorly understood in both society and church as the little word, 'sin,'" writes theologian Douglas John Hall.[18] While most modern critics of Christianity would concur, complaining about dour discourses that are too severe, Hall's argument is that notions of sin circulating in the North American churches are too *small*. A fatal mistake is made, he contends, whenever the church switches its focus from *sin*, a matter pertaining to the human condition, to *sins*, transgressions to be catalogued and controlled.

For Paul, sin has a history rooted in primal origins. He embraces the fall story of Genesis 1–11, acknowledging that a predatory pathology entered the world and quickly "spread to all" (v. 12). This human rupture from God and from the good creation resulted in a "reign of death" (the Greek verb is *basileuo*, the vocabulary of empire). But Paul argues archetypally that the lethal rebellion of the first human can be reversed and healed through the new human's restoration of the divine cosmology of grace and gift (Rom. 5:15-19). We find this same argument—otherwise unparalleled in the New Testament—twice more in 1 Corinthians 15:

> For since death came through a human being, the resurrection of the dead has also come through a human being; for as all die in Adam, so all will be made alive in Christ. (vv. 21-22)
>
> Thus it is written, "The first man, Adam, became a living being"; the last [Gk. *eschatos*] Adam became a life-giving spirit. (v. 45)

How are we to assess Paul's claim concerning the restorative work of Christ as the eschatological Human Being?

Modern theology, if it acknowledges this notion of restoration at all, typically folds it into a broader schema of christological redemption. But it is likely that the "just practice" (Gk. *dikaiomatos*) to which Paul refers in Romans 5:18 was Jesus' faithful resistance to the project of civilization (which, for both the Nazarene and Paul, was typified by the violent and oppressive Roman Empire), on the one hand, and his rehabilitation of the old ways of community, wilderness spirituality, and the economics of gift, on the other. The life, death, and resurrection of the eschatological Adam has, in the juridical metaphor so often employed by Paul, the power to "acquit" all those complicit in the crimes of civilization and to restore "life" to all who live under the death shadow of empire (Gk. *dikaiosin zoes*; v. 18).

Christ is thus portrayed by Paul as God's ultimate countermeasure to the fall. There had been many such efforts narrated in biblical history, beginning with the commission to Noah to preserve life from a flood meant to halt the spiral of violence (Genesis 6–9). Though only partially effective, the flood resulted in a renewed covenant, the heart of which was to reestablish respect for "blood as life" (Gen. 9:4-7). Directly on the heels of the Babel story, Abram begins the counterhistory of redemption by going "feral" from empire, leaving Mesopotamia for the margins of Palestine, where he encounters afresh the God of creation, as we saw above (Genesis 12). Moses repeats this "centrifugal" response to the centripetal forces of empire in the exodus journey, taking his people from the slave-based economy of Egypt to a wilderness rediscovery of the economy of divine grace (Exodus 16).[19] The Sinai Covenant in turn attempted to teach Israel how to live in resistance to the empires that surrounded her (thus, in Romans 5:20, Paul refers to Torah as that which exposes sin): "Remember the days of old," exhorts the Song of Moses, "the years long past" (Deut. 32:7).

And for centuries, the prophets, from Elijah to Malachi, relentlessly challenged the people to abandon the idolatry and injustice of civilization and to "turn around." "Stand at the crossroads, and look," wrote Jeremiah, "and ask for the ancient paths, where the good way lies; and walk in it" (Jer. 6:16; see Lam. 5:21). It was in *this* tradition that Jesus lived, died, and was vindicated.

Gospel
MATTHEW 12:38-40

Our passage narrates Jesus' repudiation of the local authorities' request that he legitimate his ministry with "signs." From Matthew's perspective, the authorities have already missed the dramatic evidence that proliferates in his Gospel. Jesus begins life as a political refugee fleeing the pogroms of empire (Matthew 2). He apprentices with the radical wilderness prophet John, whose critique penetrates to the roots of Israel's civilizational crisis (3:7-12); Jesus is baptized by John in the wild waters of the Jordan, far from the domesticated ritual baths of Judean cities (3:13-17). The Nazarene prepares for his ministry with a wilderness vision-quest to find out where his people went wrong (4:1-11).[20] His inaugural sermon proclaims the incompatibility of God and the mammon system (6:24), and declares that the smallest wildflower has more intrinsic value from the divine point of view than the grandest civilizational pretensions of Israel's greatest king, Solomon (6:28f.). Jesus symbolizes the "retribalization" of Israel in his naming of twelve disciples (10:1-4), and directly challenges imperial cities to repent (11:20-24). He enacts the Jubilee principle of the right of the poor to the edge of every field (12:1-8), and communicates with illiterate peasants through stories about the land: "A sower went out to sow . . ." (13:3). His seed parables envision the kingdom of God not as some otherworldly place and time, but as the reclamation of the very soil upon which Palestinian serfs toil (13:24-32).

If the authorities cannot recognize these "signs" of radical indictment and renewal, it is because they have "adulterated" themselves to empire and are looking only for spectacular confirmation of the status quo (12:39). Jesus therefore offers only the "sign of Jonah," invoking the story of the Israelite prophet commissioned by God to preach repentance to the imperial enemy (Matt. 12:39, 41). This is such an important motif for Matthew that he repeats it in 16:4, there specifically in reference to "signs of the times" (16:3).

Then comes the extraordinary comparison in verse 40 between Jonah's sojourn in the whale and the Human One's three-day journey "in the heart of the Earth" (Gk. *en te kardia tes ges*, a unique phrase in the New Testament). Obviously, for Matthew, this phrase signified Jesus' entombment after he was executed by empire and before he was raised up, which later traditions embellished with a trip to the netherworld to redeem captives there (1 Pet. 3:19). But an ecological reading might well highlight the implied horticultural metaphor of the seed that disappears deep into the Earth, only to rise again—one that Paul uses explicitly in connection with resurrection of the body (1 Cor. 15:35-49). As was the first, fallen Adam, the risen, eschatological Adam is (re)born from the "heart of the Earth [*adamah*]." Jesus, the ultimate countermeasure of God, is deeply tethered to the land in life and death, because he understood that only the old wisdom of the Earth can counter the pathologies of imperial civilization.

What will it mean for us to so "ground" our practices of justice today in a world on the brink of ecocide?

Reflections

As children of "progress," we have transformed rivers into electrical power, forests into board-feet for power and profit, and land into real estate. We have reengineered the atom, the seed, and the gene. And, as a result, says David Helton,

> Life on Earth is actually decreasing. . . . God made all those fowl of the air and fish of the sea and great whales and beasts of the fields and herbs and fruits and creeping things, and by taking His place and manipulating genes we've turned around and subdued every damned one of them. . . . We are the winners. But why aren't we saying, "This is good!"?[21]

In the last two generations—from John Hersey's *Hiroshima* to Rachel Carson's *Silent Spring* to Al Gore's *An Inconvenient Truth*—it is finally dawning upon us that we now find ourselves in what Derrick Jensen rightly calls an "endgame."[22] This is why the biblical critique of civilization as fallenness and its counterstory of redemption centered in the wilderness represent a message whose time has come again.

We must have the courage in our preaching to say plainly, as does Wendell Berry, that "we all live by robbing nature, but our standard of living demands that the robbery shall continue."[23] We are so captive to our illusions, excesses, and appetites that we can no longer *imagine* the world differently—and our little theologies of sin cannot explain why. But we are using "the addict's excuse, and we know that it will not do."[24] Berry's critique of the mercenary character of modern capitalism is trenchant, and his call to rehabilitate the "Great Economy" (his metaphor for the kingdom of God) uncompromising. "The question that must be addressed," he contends, "is not how to care for the planet but how to care for each of the planet's millions of human and natural neighborhoods, each of its millions of small pieces and parcels of land, each one of which is in some precious way different from all the others."[25] It may be, then, that the challenge for creation preaching is not so much one of cosmology as of *geography*. We need a theology of "re-place-ment."

Only love for specific land—what Hawaiians call *aloha 'aina*—can motivate us to struggle on its behalf. Place-based discourse is still marginal in mainstream political and theological discourse, but we are beginning to see a shift from anthropocentric to "biocentric" theory and "re-inhabitory politics."[26] Poet and environmental activist Gary Snyder sums up the task succinctly:

> The usual focus of attention for most Americans is the human society itself with its problems and its successes, its icons and symbols. With the exception of most Native Americans and a few non-natives who have given their hearts to the place, the land we all live on is simply taken for granted—and proper relation to it is not taken as part of "citizenship." But after two centuries of national history, people are beginning to wake up and notice that the United States is located on a landscape with a severe, spectacular, spacey, wildly demanding, and ecstatic narrative to be learned. Its natural communities are each unique, and each of us, whether we like it or not—in the city or countryside—live in one of them. When enough people get that picture, our political life will begin to change, and it will be the beginning of the next phase of American life, coming to live on "Turtle Island."[27]

Rediscovering love for place can help the church overcome the alienation resulting from our geographical and cultural displacement, and restore a sense of identity from which we can struggle for reconstruction and the life of the eschatological Adam, Christ. In the promise of Isaiah, "The surviving remnant of Judah shall again take root downward, and bear fruit upward" (Isa. 37:31).

NOTES

1. Richard Lowery, *Sabbath and Jubilee,* Understanding Biblical Themes (St. Louis: Chalice, 2000), 86.

2. Ibid.

3. See Ched Myers, "'To Serve and Preserve': The Genesis Commission to Earth Stewardship," *Sojourners* (March 2004): 28–38; and "'The Cedar Has Fallen!' The Prophetic Word vs. Imperial Clear-cutting," in *Earth and Word: Classic Sermons on Saving the Planet,* ed. David Rhoads (New York: Continuum, 2007), 211–33.

4. See Walter Brueggemann, *The Land: Place as Gift, Promise and Challenge in Biblical Faith* (Philadelphia: Fortress Press, 1977).

5. See Jacob Bronowski, *The Ascent of Man* (New York: Little, Brown, 1976).

6. See Paul Shepherd, *Coming Home to the Pleistocene* (Washington, D.C.: Island, 1988).

7. See Marshall Sahlins, *Stone Age Economics* (New York: de Gruyter, 1972).

8. See John Gowdy, ed., Limited Wants, *Limited Means: A Reader on Hunter-Gatherer Economics and the Environment* (Washington, D.C.: Island, 1998).

9. Thomas Hobbes, *Leviathan (With Selected Variants from the Latin Edition of 1668),* ed. Edwin Curley (Indianapolis: Hackett, 1994), 76.

10. Phrase used by Sahlins in *Stone Age Economics.* See also Ched Myers, "The Fall," in *The Encyclopedia of Religion and Nature,* ed. Bron Taylor (New York: Continuum, 2005), 634–36.

11. Ellen van Wolde, *Stories of the Beginning: Genesis 1–11 and Other Creation Stories,* trans. John Bowden (Harrisburg, Pa.: Morehouse, 1996), 84–85.

12. See Wendell Berry, *Home Economics: Fourteen Essays* (San Francisco: North Point, 1987).

13. See Jacques Ellul, *The Meaning of the City,* trans. D. Pardee (Grand Rapids: Eerdmans, 1970).

14. Andrew Schmookler, *The Parable of the Tribes: The Problem of Power in Social Evolution* (Berkeley: University of California Press, 1984), 79.

15. See Evan Eisenberg, *The Ecology of Eden: An Inquiry into the Dream of Paradise and a New Vision of Our Role in Nature* (New York: Vintage, 1998).

16. Paul Tillich, *The Shaking of the Foundations* (London: SCM, 1949), 40–41.

17. See Thomas Finger, "Trinity, Ecology and Panentheism," *Christian Scholars Review* 27 (Fall 1997): 74–98.

18. Douglas John Hall, "The Political Consequences of Misconceiving Sin," *The Witness* 78, no. 3 (March 1995): 8.

19. See Ched Myers, *The Biblical Vision of Sabbath Economics* (Washington, D.C.: Tell the Word, 2001), 10–17.

20. See Ched Myers, "The Wilderness Temptations and the American Journey," in *Richard Rohr: Illuminations of His Life and Work,* eds. A. Ebert and P. Brockman (New York: Crossroad, 1993), 143–57.

21. David Helton, "Hooray Humans," *BBC Wildlife* magazine (November 1991).

22. See Derrick Jensen, *Endgame, Volume I: The Problem of Civilization* (New York: Seven Stories, 2006); and John Zerzan, *Running on Emptiness: The Pathology of Civilization* (Los Angeles: Feral House, 2002).

23. Wendell Berry, "The Futility of Global Thinking," *Harper's Weekly* (September 1989): 19.

23. Ibid.

25. Berry, *Home Economics*, 18.

26. See, for example, Daniel Kemmis, *Community and the Politics of Place* (Norman: University of Oklahoma Press, 1990); and Kirkpatrick Sale, *Dwellers in the Land: The Bioregional Vision* (San Francisco: Sierra Club, 1985).

27. Gary Snyder, "Coming into the Watershed," *Wild Earth Journal* (1992), 97.

Third Sunday in Creation

Wilderness Sunday

Alice M. Sinnott

Joel 1:8-10,
17-20
Psalm 18:6-19
Romans 8:18-27
Matthew 3:13—4:2
or Mark 1:19-13

Background

Wilderness (*midbar* in Hebrew, *eremos* in Greek) features prominently in biblical texts and usually denotes desolate, abandoned, and deserted places beyond settled areas, beyond the law and social controls. In addition, it can refer to pastoral land with plenty of water and vegetation but without permanent settlements or villages. In fact, the Hebrew word originally meant "place of herding." It could even be a wooded area or have a river. For example, John the Baptist performed baptisms in a river in the wilderness. Most places beyond the immediate reach of a city or a village were regarded as wilderness. In the Bible, as in many traditional cultures, the wilderness was often perceived to be inhabited by evil spirits. Bandits and those outside the law took refuge in wilderness areas.

Biblical concepts of wilderness also suggest places that are inhospitable to human beings, as humans would have to endure thirst, hunger, deprivation of all sorts, and harsh physical conditions, and maybe have terrifying experiences because of the isolation from settled life. Paradoxically, there are also signs that the biblical tradition romanticized a nomadic past where people were free to wander and were not burdened by the rules and customs of a settled existence. In the Bible, wilderness also stands for a place of un-creation; a place of chaos where life could not flourish, a place of temptation and testing, as, for example, Jesus experienced in the wilderness in Mark's Gospel. It is a dead place where the devil prowls. Mark also tells us three times that the disciples, and then the crowds, are in the *eremos*, a "deserted place." It is remote because it is uninhabited, probably because it did not have food or water available.

Some biblical prophets and leaders were driven by the Spirit to wander in the wilderness to be tested or tempted, and such accounts invariably suggest that the wilderness was a place of trial and spiritual renewal. Those who survived in the wilderness demonstrated that they were able to overcome physical and psychological dangers, that they could survive the experience of being cut off from ready sources of food and water, and that they could even tolerate the loneliness that comes from being without the support and companionship of a tribe or a community. Among the best-known wilderness narratives are the accounts in the Pentateuch about Moses and the Israelites wandering in the wilderness. Devout Jews still celebrate the Feast of Booths/Tents, which recalls their ancestors' sojourn in the wilderness and their deliverance. Elijah and Elisha's wanderings in the wilderness also figure prominently in the narratives of the Hebrew Bible. And the prophet Isaiah described Israel's return from Babylonian exile as a journey through the wilderness (Isa. 40:3). The Gospel writers echoed this passage in their descriptions of John the Baptist (Matt. 3:3; Mark 1:3; Luke 3:4; John 1:23). Of great significance, of course, are the Evangelists' accounts about Jesus' sojourn in the wilderness for forty days.

In New Zealand, as in many lands, the perception of wilderness varies greatly, depending on the differing exposures people have to nature. Some find their "wilderness experience" on a walking track through a park or in a pocket of nature close to a city environment, such as walking in the Waitakeres in West Auckland. Others find it in the way most familiar to New Zealanders—as the experience of being in a natural environment away from crowds of people and city traffic and urban facilities. Alternatively, wilderness is often defined in a legal sense. Various legal designations of wilderness have accompanied the growth of the world's protected-areas movement. Such definitions serve to support the idea of setting aside certain areas intended to be retained largely intact in their natural state without the impact of development. In this sense, wilderness is largely a phenomenon of the twentieth century. Such laws were enacted with a view to conserving the values of wilderness areas for purposes of public education and recreation.

The wilderness concept is manifest today, for example, in New Zealand's legislation setting aside wilderness areas as national parks. In

1944, this option was first considered in New Zealand, defining a national park as "a wilderness area set apart for preservation in as near as possible a natural state, but made available for and accessible to the general public who are allowed and encouraged to visit the reserve." The New Zealand National Parks Act of 1952 included a specific provision (in section 34) permitting the setting apart "of any area of [a National] Park as a wilderness area . . . which, inter alia, shall be kept and maintained in a state of nature." In the world today, wilderness management is well established within the global protected-areas system, although approaches to management and underlying philosophy vary considerably among different countries and cultures. The importance of wilderness areas globally was recognized when the International Union for Conservation of Nature's (IUCN) World Commission on Protected Areas reviewed the categories of protected areas. In 1994, the IUCN General Assembly meeting in Buenos Aires noted the revised category: "Wilderness Areas: protected areas managed mainly for wilderness protection." The expanded definition was of a "large area of unmodified or slightly modified land and/or sea, retaining its natural character and influence, without permanent habitation, which is protected and managed so as to preserve its natural condition."

The Bible also has positive affirmations of the importance of wilderness, but not for human education and recreation. Rather, the traditions value areas outside human control or understanding *for their own sake* as wild areas beyond human reach. Adam and Eve were told not to touch the tree of the knowledge of good and evil. In the book of Job, God responds to Job by lifting up whole dimensions of creation beyond human involvement and understanding. In this sense, the cry of the Earth may be a cry to "leave me alone"—free from the encroachment of human civilization, beyond human development and cultivation, beyond the presence of humans altogether, free to grow wild. There is a tradition in many countries that seeks that kind of preservation. It may be that the future of the planet depends on a certain percentage of Earth free to develop ecosystems outside human influence.

Nevertheless, human beings may need the experience of wilderness for health and well-being. People from different cultures and backgrounds hear the call of the wilderness and respond, as is evident in the experiences that large numbers of trampers, backpackers, and climbers seek as they attempt to get away from what they perceive to be the superficialities of modern cities in search of a more authentic engagement with Earth and its gifts. Even city dwellers—who may know wilderness areas mainly from television or from works of art such as Colin McCahon's paintings of Northland and of South Otago or the North American landscapes by Asher Durand or Frederic Edwin Church—often have a deep spiritual desire to get away from it all and go in search of a wilderness experience. Those who seek to identify and to celebrate the sacredness of wilderness often stand in a long tradition of ancestors who sought out wild places. They may be seeking to recover something of their ancestral traditions, such as Celtic monks in their coracles on the open sea seeking God in uninhabited places. The contemporary understandings of wilderness in New Zealand congregations draw on a rich tapestry of traditions from the Maori, the Tangata Whenua, as well as European settlers and immigrants from the Pacific Islands, Asia, and the Middle East. Many are familiar with one or more of these traditions and other such understandings of wilderness that could serve to enhance their participation in a Wilderness Sunday celebration.

In discussing wilderness, it is important to be aware of both the geographical and the social locations of those who are to hear sermons on the subject. A small family-owned business that provides bed and breakfast for wilderness wanderers will view the wilderness theme differently from residents of a working-class, densely populated, large-city suburb, most of whom have never experienced wilderness. A youth group for whom an orientation course in the wilderness is their first-ever experience of being in a wild place will view it very differently from a youth group who regularly tramps in a national park.

It is of concern that the wilderness theme often masks a profoundly destructive social ideology. In some Bible texts, there is deep suspicion of urban settlement, while those who live in the countryside are considered to be pure. So, also, we today pit the gifts of wilderness areas of the country against the alleged corruption and destructiveness of cities and urban life generally. Frequently, the quest for a wilderness experience in New Zealand has presupposed an underlying rejection of any interest in justice for the poor or for the homeless, refugees, or other marginalized groups, all of whom must live their lives in cities and who may never visit a wilderness. On the other hand, anthropocentric viewpoints often appear in debates about what land areas may be used for housing or for national parks. In these debates, wilderness areas may be deemed unnecessary luxuries when large sums of money are at stake or when we need land for social housing or when the super-wealthy seek to build mansions in the wilderness. Our greatest dilemma is this: How can we advocate for the wilderness and celebrate its wildness without at the same time being guilty of neglecting the poor and disenfranchised, most of whom are confined to cities?

First Reading

JOEL 1:8-10, 17-20

In this text, Joel portrays Jerusalem in a state comparable to that of personal bereavement, literally like a wilderness. The scene is one of acute pathos. Instead of the wedding garments of celebration, the city must don mourning robes of sackcloth and wail a dirge. Joel summons the people of Jerusalem to such mourning, because their world has been shattered. The usual temple services have been suspended and the traditional daily rituals cannot be performed because grain, wine and oil, and animals for the sacrifices are not available. Because of the locust plague and drought, the countryside is woebegone and in desolation. Since the necessary ingredients for worship are no longer available, the law of Sinai can no longer be obeyed. Therefore, communion with God is not possible. God, who is the Lord of nature, has cut off their means of worship. They are truly in a "wilderness," facing starvation and drought.

Priests and fields alike are mourning the loss of crops of oil, wine, and grain—all perceived as generous gifts of God. The fertility hailed as a pledge of the harmony between Israel and God has disappeared: "destroyed the grain/dried up the wine/cut off the oil" (1:10). Crops that the farmers expected to harvest have withered. Therefore, the farmers are in despair, as they have nothing to eat or to sell and they have no seed for replanting. The harvest, especially the grape harvest, was usually a time of rejoicing; however, like the crops, joy, too, has dried up. The harvest songs are stilled in mouths that are dry as dust, parched with thirst, and the land itself joins in the mourning.

The prophet's poetry (vv. 17-20) depicts the catastrophe and its effect on nature. Digging in the soil finds only ungerminated seed. Cattle wander the barren fields lowing in their hunger, and sheep are scattered on the parched hillsides. Given this desperate situation, Joel composes a prayer for the priests (vv. 19-20). It is from God's hand that the judgment has fallen; therefore, the poetic lament must be directed to the God of the cosmos. There is an implicit contrast between the response of the animals and the insensitivity of the people. Each prayer has lament alternating with petition. Joel yearns for the people to take their cue from the rest of animate creation and to engage themselves in earnest prayer to God in the sanctuary. Joel's desire is that they share his heightened sensitivity to his environment and that they relate what they see around them to the God of creation and covenant. The community faces starvation because locusts have eaten everything. "Fire" suggests that any vegetation that managed to recover from the locust plague has become so parched that it might ignite from the heat of the sun. This image of fire also signifies the notion that God's judgment has dried up the land; as such, only God can reverse this catastrophe in which the fertile land has fallen back into wilderness.

Psalmody
PSALM 18:6-19

This passage can be read as a powerful poetic expression of themes already encountered in the reading from Joel, with the psalmist's urgent cry to YHWH for help in distress (v. 6). The psalmist places God's "temple" in the heavens. This is the setting for a theophany in which YHWH arrives in a violent storm, which brings to mind the Sinai theophany in the Mosaic narrative where God appears in "thick darkness." This echoing of Sinai evokes also an image of Moses entering the "thick darkness" to meet God face to face and to receive the law. The divine response to the psalmist's cry for deliverance (vv. 7-15) is reflective of God's presence and power in the creation narratives as well as in the wilderness narratives (cloud by day and fire by night). The constellation of storm images—darkness, clouds, winds, water, hailstones, and coals of fire—are creation-based expressions of deliverance provided by God (vv. 16-19).

God's presence is presaged by cosmic turmoil and is suggestive of the crossing of the Red Sea whereby Israel was "saved from the waters." Throughout the Bible, creation is pictured as a violent encounter between chaos and order, between goodness and evil, between God and the powers of darkness. Because the king was believed to embody God's determination to bring peace and fertility into the land of Israel, the creation battle against disorder and violence—the ongoing process of creation—flares up here with greater intensity because of the struggle between disobedience and national reform. Psalm 18 is a powerful affirmation of the universal reign of God in the heavens and on Earth, and it is upon this foundation that hope is built. The theophany has cosmic dimensions; at issue is nothing less than the ultimate question of who rules the world. The faith and intent of the psalmist is to keep the hope and conviction alive that God will ultimately fulfill God's steadfast loving purpose for all creation. Deliverance is spatial and personal: "[God] brought me out into a broad place; he delivered me, because he delighted in me" (v. 19), which echoes Proverbs 8:30. Contemporary commentators on this psalm are challenged to develop community rituals that glorify the God of creation. They are also challenged to encourage worshipers to leave behind fanciful notions of childhood gods or prosperity gods as assurances of God's favor.

The psalmist takes it for granted that proper cultic acknowledgment of God and righteous living go hand in hand. Importantly, however, for the psalmist, proper cultic acknowledgment of God also brings with it the rejection of idolatry. This psalm presents serious challenges. Present is the need to identify ways to foster and to shape public, communal rituals that honor and integrate worship of the God of all creation, especially in times of natural disasters such as drought, famine, loss of life, and all the accompanying tragedies of displacement and emigration. Integral to this is the need to find ways to encourage and animate the faithful to accept responsibility for providing shelter, food, and even land for the displaced and the refugees seeking to recover from the effects of disasters. Worshipers may be very accepting of a Creator God yet may balk at the notion of a Creator God who does nothing to prevent natural disasters.

Second Reading
ROMANS 8:18-27

Today, this pericope from Romans is often the centerpiece in liturgies celebrating creation. The choice to do this, I think, rests on two of Paul's claims: the glory about to be revealed outweighs the sufferings that have to be endured in the present and his use of human birth imagery to describe the future glory and the present situation of waiting. Our pericope opens with the assurance that present suffering cannot compare with the coming glory, because the whole creation is waiting for God's children to be revealed for who they really are. From here on, it is clear that Paul is talking about the entire cosmos: "For the creation waits with eager longing for the revealing of the children of God" (v. 19). Paul describes the present state of creation by drawing on Genesis 3 and other Jewish traditions that portray creation itself in bondage—in the wilderness, as it were—and therefore in need of its own exodus.

Is the answer to the problem the idea that humans should keep their hands off creation? Should humans perhaps even be removed from creation altogether so as not to spoil it any further? "Creation was subjected to futility, not of its own will but by the will of the one who subjected it, in hope" (v. 20). Paul seems to be saying that creation will have freedom because God's children will have freedom. Indeed, their glory will consist in being God's agents in restoring divine justice to the whole created world: for "creation itself will be set free from its bondage to decay and will obtain the freedom of the glory of the children of God" (v. 21). The whole creation—sun, moon, stars, sea, sky, birds, animals, plants—has been subjected to futility, not because creation rebelled as human beings rebelled but because God subjected it to corruption and decay. This is a situation equivalent to that of the Israelites in Egypt and their sojourn in the wilderness. Paul believed that all nonhuman creatures were subjected to "vanity"—here picking up the Genesis theme that God cursed the Earth. The sin of Adam and Eve meant that the Earth produced thorns and thistles. However, for Paul, creation points forward to a new world in which its beauty and power will be enhanced and its corruptibility and futility will cease.

The early Christian community in Rome addressed by Paul was experiencing something of the corruptibility and futility of their lives in the wilderness that was their lot in Rome at this time: strife in their communities and families, discrimination and fear inherent in living as a scorned minority in the Roman Empire, and an ever-present possibility of violent death. Intensely aware of this context, Paul invokes the Genesis creation narratives and the exodus wilderness accounts familiar to his Roman audience. His words of consolation are predicated on his vision of God's complete involvement in all of creation and in the lives of his audience. While the Romans were familiar with the tradition out of which he spoke, Paul had to reinterpret Hebrew traditions that addressed the place of Gentiles in relation to Jews and apply them to these new situations outside his Hebrew traditions.

Paul told his audience that the whole creation was groaning in travail, waiting for its own liberation, as their ancestors had relied on the hope of a promised future to survive in the wilderness: "We know that the whole creation has been groaning in labor pains until now; and not only the creation, but we ourselves, who have the first fruits of the Spirit, groan inwardly while we wait for adoption, the redemption of our bodies" (vv. 22-24). At the very heart of Paul's theological description of how Christians must live as an integral part of God's magnificent cosmos (vv. 22-27) is the essentially female image of the birth pangs of a mother as she is in labor to bring forth new life into the world. Paul applies this image to the created world, to the church, and to the Spirit. This is the context within which Paul explains to his Roman audience that the appropriate stance and activity for God's people while in the wilderness awaiting birth into new life is to wait and pray patiently. The dynamism of the image of groaning in labor pains suggests that the coming new world will involve the transformation of all creation.

Associated with the image of birth is that of adoption. Images of the exodus theme underlie much of this passage. Paul's concern is to stress that, while salvation is already a reality for Christians, it carries a future component that is inevitable. Hope is built into Christian experience from the start and remains one of its central characteristics. Paul stresses that one cannot expect present Christian living to be anything more than a straining forward for what is yet to come, the promised land. The church also groans in the midst of the groaning world, which is sustained and inspired by the groaning of the Spirit who helps us in our weakness. Those who cannot see the new creation for which they eagerly hope need assistance to look ahead and to pray patiently. Paul is clear that human beings are subject to decay and death and do not know how it is that God will work through them to bring about the redemption of the world. It is the Spirit's task to enable Christians to adopt a stance of humbly trusting God.

Today's world has many of the characteristics evident in the Rome that was familiar to Paul's audience. In addition, we encounter widespread destruction and exploitation of Earth's resources, the despoiling of irreplaceable habitats, the removal of indigenous peoples from their traditional lands, violence, and the fear that such violence will beget poverty, war, and numerous other tragedies. In the face of such devastation, Paul's proclamation that the whole of creation is involved in one great act of giving birth offers hope in the wilderness of exploitation.

Gospel
MARK 1:9-13

Both the Matthew and Mark readings designated for this Sunday focus on Jesus' baptism; I will focus here on Mark's account. In this passage, Mark tells us how Jesus came from Nazareth of Galilee and was baptized by John in the Jordan. Just as he "comes up out of the water"—surely an echo of his Israelite ancestors escaping through the Red Sea—"he saw the heavens torn apart and the Spirit descending like a dove on him," recalling the dove in the flood narrative (v. 10). A voice "came from heaven" saying, "'You are my Son, the Beloved; with you I am well pleased'" (v. 11). Then the "Spirit immediately drove him out into the wilderness. He was in the wilderness forty days, tempted by Satan; and he was with the wild beasts; and the angels waited on him" (vv. 12-13). In a few verses, we hear clear echoes of pivotal events in the Hebrew traditions—the journey through the Red Sea, the flood narrative, and the wilderness sojourn.

Jesus' forty days reflect the forty years spoken about in the exodus account—engagement with wild beasts, being tempted by the devil, and being ministered to by angels. Jesus had to deal with the terrors of the wilderness, coping with a lack of food and water and doing battle with the forces of chaos. Mark's portrayal of the wilderness theme that we have already outlined in Joel, Psalm 18, and Romans 8 appears here in pride of place. The vision of the Israelites journeying in the wilderness seeking a promised land lies just below the surface of Mark's Gospel, evident in the ways the vision of a new creation shapes the account at the beginning of Mark's Gospel. Here we see Jesus in his encounter with the forces of the wilderness initiating a cosmic transformation of the whole creation. Jesus' readiness and ability to engage with and survive the chaos of the wilderness sets the tone for the Markan narrative that follows. Just as the Markan Jesus is driven by the Spirit, we, too, may have to accept the idea that, as we are driven by the Spirit, we will enter a wilderness of the fear, famine, prejudice, and greed that faces us today—if we hope to be part of the transformation of people and places that are wounded, chaotic, and dangerous.

Reflections

The first two chapters of Joel refer to a plague of locusts, which has wreaked havoc on the harvests of Judah, thus exacerbating the problems of the poor. These circumstances are significant to understanding why the prophet predicts turmoil and radical change. Movement from the specific distress brought about by the plague of locusts to a more general prophecy of universal judgment characterizes the whole book of Joel. Joel 1:1—2:7 initiates this movement by combining descriptions of the plague with exhortations and prayers of deliverance.

Though Psalm 18 reads as an individual's song of thanksgiving, it also suggests a congregation at prayer. This psalm has many of the hallmarks of Israel's most ancient songs and prayers (see Exodus 15; Deuteronomy 32–33; Habakkuk 3). While the psalm evokes the glorious achievements of King David, it also reminds worshipers of the poor man David fleeing for his life in the mountains of Judah. Thus, Psalm 18 reminds the congregation never to overlook poor refugees of any age or people. This beautiful *Te Deum* is rooted in social justice and secular needs.

In the reading from Romans 8, Paul exhorts us to recognize our dignity and our great hope as God's creatures. Deep within our human essence, God has planted a seed that grows in surprising ways. God has also kneaded into all of life "yeast" that transforms us in a way similar to the transformation of dough that becomes fresh bread, the staff of life. Therefore, "the whole created world eagerly awaits the revelation" (v. 19) of what is already stirring within it, like an unborn child in the mother's body. This text explodes with magnificent possibilities, announcing that every human being across planet Earth carries within the seed of eternal life, the source of transformation into Christ Jesus.

The lesson from Mark's Gospel describes the beginning of Jesus' ministry when John baptized him, how the heavens were split open, and a voice announced lovingly and approvingly, "You are my beloved Son. On you my favor rests" (v. 11, my trans.). Yet this message of endearment was fraught with heavy responsibility. It recalled Psalm 2 and the enthronement of the Davidic king as well as Isaiah 42 and the vocation of the suffering servant. Three great and related moments in Mark's Gospel—Jesus' baptism, his transfiguration, and the prayer at Gethsemane—are each followed by struggle: Jesus' baptism followed by his confrontation with Satan in the wilderness; his transfiguration followed by the disciples' ineffectual encounter with a demon in the mute boy; and Jesus' prayer in the garden where he struggles with the will of his Father: "And he began to feel terror and anguish. And he said to them, 'My soul is sorrowful to the point of death'" (Mark 14:34, New Jerusalem Bible). In each of these episodes, a physical and mental wilderness envelops Jesus, and in the midst of each, Jesus prays. Jesus spent his forty days in the wilderness in prayer, "with the wild beasts and angels" (v. 13), caught between heaven and Earth.

RESOURCES

Adams, Edward. *Constructing the World: A Study in Paul's Cosmological Language.* Edinburgh: T & T Clark, 2000.

Bergant, Dianne, with Richard Fragomeni. *Preaching the New Lectionary Year B.* Collegeville, Minn.: Liturgical, 1999.

Braaten, Laurie J. "All Creation Groans: Romans 8:22 in Light of the Biblical Sources." *Horizons in Biblical Theology* 28 (2006): 131–59.

Dempsey, Carol J., and Mary Margaret Pazdan, eds. *Earth, Wind, and Fire: Biblical and Theological Perspectives on Creation.* Collegeville, Minn.: Liturgical, 2004.

Habel, Norman C., and Peter Trudinger. *Exploring Ecological Hermeneutics.* Atlanta: Society of Biblical Literature, 2008.

Hubbard, Moyer V. *New Creation in Paul's Letters and Thought.* SNTS Monograph Series 119. Cambridge: Cambridge University Press, 2002.

Kwakkel, Gert. *According to My Righteousness: Upright Behaviour as Grounds for Deliverance in Psalms 7, 17, 18, 26 and 44.* Leiden: Brill, 2002.

Leal, Robert Barry. *Wilderness in the Bible: Toward a Theology of Wilderness*. Studies in Biblical Literature 72. New York: Peter Lang, 2004.

Mays, James Luther. *Psalms. Interpretation: A Bible Commentary for Teaching and Preaching*. Louisville: Westminster John Knox, 1994.

Parrish, V. Steven. *A Story of the Psalms: Conversation, Canon, and Congregation*. Collegeville, Minn.: Liturgical, 2003.

Stuhlmueller, Carroll. *Psalms 1–72*. Wilmington, Del.: Michael Glazier, 1983.

Fourth Sunday in Creation

River Sunday

Barbara R. Rossing

Genesis 8:20-22;
9:12-17
Psalm 104:27-33
Revelation 22:1-5
Matthew 28:1-10

Background

We all live in a watershed, a river basin—from the Amazon River to the Nile River to the Mississippi River or even to the Cannon River in southeastern Minnesota where I grew up. River Sunday helps us draw connections between the specific rivers of our lives and the watershed of God's river of life flowing through the world.

Rivers play pivotal roles in biblical geography. God encounters people at river crossings, such as the Jabbok River where Jacob wrestled with God, or the Jordan River where the Israelites crossed over on stones. River reeds protected the infant Moses, whose name means "I drew him out of the water" (Exod. 2:3, 10). Rivers are locations for healing; for example, cleansing Namaan the Syrian from his leprosy (2 Kgs. 5:12). "There is a river whose streams make glad the city of God," the psalmist sings (Ps. 46:4). The biblical river of life, first mentioned in Genesis, flows east from Eden (Gen. 2:10). The prophet Ezekiel envisions a wondrous river flowing out from the new temple—ankle deep, knee deep, the thigh deep—bringing life to all it touches. Stagnant water becomes fresh, providing habitat for fish, birds, and people, and watering the fruit trees on each side of the river (Ezekiel 47).

In the New Testament, the river of life flows from the heart of Jesus in the Gospel of John, becoming for anyone who thirsts a spring of water gushing up into eternal life (John 7:37-38). Baptismal life centers around rivers, such as the place of prayer beside the river where Lydia and her community were baptized in Philippi (Acts 16). In Revelation, the river of the water of life flows out from the throne of God and the Lamb, right through the middle of the city of God. The invitation is addressed to everyone who thirsts: "Come, take the water of life without cost" (Rev. 22:17; my trans.).

Our task for River Sunday is to help people find and follow God's river of life in their lives. The preacher can help people see the deep connections between the biblical watershed of God's grace and the watersheds of our lives. The preacher can invite people to God's riverside to drink of the deep spiritual water of life for which we thirst, recalling the psalmist's words: "As a deer longs for flowing streams, so my soul longs for you , O God" (Ps. 42:1).

Exploring themes for River Sunday includes exploring threats of pollution and climate change that endanger rivers and watersheds. In the Appalachian Mountains, whole river valleys are being destroyed by "mountaintop-removal" coal mining. In the tar sands region of northern Alberta in Canada, toxic chemicals released into the Athabascan River from the extraction of oil are endangering the health of First Nation communities. In Asia, where 40 percent of the world's population depends on seven major rivers fed by Himalayan glaciers, glaciers are rapidly melting due to climate change. Hundreds of millions of people in Africa and Asia are experiencing droughts and changes in rainfall that disrupt normal agricultural patterns and river systems.

From the Indus River in Pakistan to the Mississippi River in Cedar Rapids, Iowa, intense rainfall has caused record-breaking flooding as the planet warms. Sadly, such increasing intensity of rainfall and catastrophic flooding are what climate models from the Intergovernmental Panel on Climate Change and U.S. Global Change Research Program predict for much of the world, including the midwestern United States. In other areas, such as the western United States and sub-Saharan Africa, droughts will dry up rivers.

The rivers of the watershed of our world's life are in danger. River Sunday can be an occasion for congregations to engage in education about climate change, fossil-fuel use, and creation care. This crisis does not have to be the sickness unto death. Our biblical texts proclaim that God wants to heal and preserve the planet and its rivers.

First Reading

GENESIS 8:20-22; 9:12-17

The story of Noah and the flood opens up wonderful possibilities for ecological preaching. The flood story culminates in what can be called the original "eco-covenant," a covenant made with every living creature. Never again will God destroy the Earth. For Jews and Christians, *Shabbat Noach*—the sabbath when the Noah cycle is read—can be a time to proclaim God's will to preserve creation in the face of perils that threaten creation today.

Our text comes from the conclusion of the flood story that began in Genesis 5:29 with the naming of Noah. The preacher can draw on the entire arc of the Noah flood story (Genesis 6–9) in setting the context, making connections also to our own ecological context through such elements of the narrative as:

- The accelerating destruction ("corruption") of the Earth caused by human violence, including violence against the creation (6:11-13);
- God's grieving heart (6:6), a heart that is first moved to destroy the Earth but then declares "never again" to any future destruction;
- The image of an "ark" that saved Noah's family together with all the creatures, an apt image for our Earth when we and all living things inhabit the planet's fragile "ark" together;
- God's command to bring two of every living creature into the ark and "keep them alive," repeated in Genesis 6:19, 20, and 7:3—a sort of divine "endangered-species act," mandating humans to take care that no species should go extinct through our negligence.

The flood story interweaves elements from both the Yahwist (J) and Priestly (P) writers, communicating profound theological and ecological insights through vivid narrative detail.

God's response to Noah's act of worship in 8:20-22 constitutes the Yahwist's conclusion to the flood story. The pleasing aroma from Noah's sacrifice rises up to God's nostrils and changes God's mind (v. 21). God's first response removes the curse that had been put on the "ground" (*adamah*) in Genesis 3:17. Verse 21 can be translated either "I will not curse the ground again" or "I will not continue to curse the ground," in either case explicitly removing the curse of Genesis 3:17. Noah's very naming had anticipated this healing mission, for Noah was named to "bring relief" from the hard labor of farming the accursed ground (Gen. 5:29). God does not completely restore the primeval state of Eden, but by removing the curse God now makes it possible for Noah and all his descendants to grow food.

In God's second response, God promises to preserve the seasons and cycles necessary for successful farming. Noah is a man of the soil, a farmer (Gen. 9:20), like the Israelite hill-country farmers for whom the Yahwist narrative was written. Theodore Hiebert points out that the promise of verse 22 lists all the major occasions of the Israelite agricultural year: "the sowing of grain in the fall (*zera'*) and its harvesting in the spring (*qasir*), the harvest of summer fruit, including primarily grapes and figs (*qayis*) and the autumn harvest of olives (*horep*)."[1] By preserving the rhythm of seasons, God promises to preserve a future for sustainable agriculture "as long as the earth shall endure" (Gen. 8:22).

Genesis 9 shifts to the Priestly writer's description of God's covenant with Noah and all creation. Christians have sometimes tended to skip over this first covenant in the Bible, focusing exclusively on the covenant with Abraham in Genesis 12 as the paradigmatic covenant. In Genesis 9, God's first covenant is a covenant with "every living creature," with "all flesh"—a fact repeated six times (twice in v. 10; also vv. 12, 15, 16, 17). God makes covenants with more than just humans. The Noah story underscores God's love for the integrity of the whole created world. All the covenantal action is from God's side. There is no reciprocity on the part of humans or creation. The heart of the covenant promise is God's repeated pledge of "never again" (found also in the Yahwist account, Gen. 8:21). Never again will there be a flood to destroy the Earth.

God sets a rainbow in the heavens as the sign of the promise. It is striking that God is the one who will see the rainbow and "remember" the covenant never again to destroy the Earth (9:16). God's remembering echoes Genesis 8:1 when God "remembered" Noah and his family and all the animals in the ark, causing the waters to recede. Throughout the story, God remembers the whole creation, including humans.

God's covenant with Noah and all creatures is an "everlasting covenant" (*berit olam*, 9:16). The flood story and God's covenant with creation mark a decisive change in God's dealing with the world, a change toward graciousness. God "recharacterizes" the divine relation to the world in promising never again to destroy, notes Terence Fretheim.[2] It is not humans but God whose mind is changed by the flood.

While the everlasting covenant will never be broken by God, Israel's prophets warned that humans are capable of breaking what God intended as an everlasting covenant from their side. Isaiah counsels that human injustice and transgression against God's "everlasting covenant" could bring about the very undoing of creation (Isa. 24:4-5). Today, when humans are altering the climatic patterns of seasonal rainfall, the cold, and the heat (Gen. 8:22) that God promised never to destroy, we must consider prophetic warnings about the consequences of our breaking of God's everlasting covenant.

The covenant of Genesis 9 is a covenant also for "all future generations" (v. 12). This intergenerational dimension of the Noah covenant is perhaps the most important aspect of the Noah story in our time of climate change. Jonathan Sacks, the chief rabbi of Great Britain, makes this point: "We have to honour our covenant with future generations so that they will be able to live. And that is the call of God in our times."[3]

Psalmody
PSALM 104:27-33

Psalm 104 celebrates the richness of God's creation by cataloging the biodiversity of different habitats. The psalmist praises God in the second person ("you") for assigning specific ecological niches to different creatures and for providing food for each. The ordering of creation also includes setting boundaries. Verse 9, a direct reference to the flood and the covenant of Genesis 9, decrees a boundary for the waters so that they will never again cover the Earth. Verses 6-13, while not assigned for River Sunday, marvel at the rivers that flow in valleys that God appointed for them, giving drink and home to a whole array of animals and birds.

Earth's habitats and natural cycles are celebrated independently of their utility to humans. The sky, sea, and land are home to an exuberance of creatures, amazing in their diversity. In the verse preceding our text, God is even described as playful in creating Leviathan for the sheer sport of it. Food is generously provided for humans, as well as for all creatures. All look to God to give food in due season. God feeds us by hand (v. 28), like a parent or a farmer tending a young animal.

Verses 27-33 are sometimes read at Pentecost, with the emphasis on God's creating Spirit. The psalmist says that we are all dependent on God's breath to give us life, recalling Genesis 1:1 when God's Spirit moved over the waters. In Psalm 104:30, the emphasis is not on the first creation so much as the ongoing sustenance and renewal of creation, utterly dependent on God's Spirit, God's breath. God's Spirit is pictured as the world's life-support system, renewing the face of the ground each springtime. In portraying God's breath as atmosphere, the psalmist gives an ecological metaphor that can help us address the crisis of our atmosphere today—suffering from increasing carbon dioxide concentrations. This psalm's notion of creation as an ongoing process is congruent with modern science.

Moreover, God finds great "joy" in the ongoing unfolding of creation. While in the Hebrew Bible people and creatures are often exhorted to rejoice, Psalm 104:31 is the only occurrence of the verb *smh* to express God's own joy. The psalmist prays for God to continue to "rejoice" in the works of creation.

Second Lesson
REVELATION 22:1-5

The New Jerusalem of Revelation 21–22 offers one of the most wonderful and hope-filled visions of our future in all of Scripture. The vision comes at the end of the book's apocalyptic journey—a journey into the heart of the universe and the heart of Rome's imperial power, a journey of radical hope and transformation. The entire book of Revelation leads up to this wondrous vision of renewal and joy.

Written at a time when Rome was at the height of its power, Revelation invokes apocalyptic imagery and patterns from the Old Testament as a way of critiquing Roman imperial injustice. It offers an alternative vision for our future in God's city of well-being. Revelation seeks to make God's vision of beauty so persuasive and real that the audience will "come out" of the evil empire (Rev. 18:4) in order to enter into the promised land of blessing and healing.

Creation plays a central role throughout Revelation's story. The image of Jesus as a Lamb, the central image of Christ in this book, connects Jesus to creation. When the Lamb is introduced, a whole chorus of animals, sea creatures, and creatures under the earth burst into songs of praise (Rev. 5:13). Creation participates in the conflicts and tribulation that unfold in the middle chapters, leading up to God's judgment against evil destroyers who destroy creation (Rev. 11:18). God is a God who comes down to Earth, dwelling with creation and renewing it.

Revelation 22 follows the second narration of the descent of God's holy city (Rev. 21:9-27), an architectural tour modeled on the angel's tour of the new temple in Ezekiel 40–48. Revelation makes important changes that open up Ezekiel's priestly vision to everyone. One striking modification is that the New Jerusalem has "no temple" (21:22). God's presence now extends to the entire city's landscape, with all of God's people serving and reigning with Christ as priests (Rev. 1:6, 5:10, 20:6, 22:3, 5). Whereas Ezekiel's temple gate was shut so that "no one shall enter by it" (Ezek. 44:1-2), the gates into New Jerusalem are perpetually open—they are "never shut by day and there will be no night there" (Rev. 21:25). Even foreigners are invited to enter into this radiant city, whose lamp is the Lamb, Jesus.

The image of the "throne," which recurs twice in this passage, is a central image for Revelation. John's apocalyptic journey began with a tour of the heavenly throne room in Revelation 4–5. But where is the "throne of God and the Lamb" located in Revelation 22? The text suggests that God's throne will move down from heaven, where it was in chapter 4, and will be located in the middle of the city that descends from heaven to Earth (see 21:2). Thus, the New Jerusalem can be read as a wonderfully Earth-centered vision for our future, a vision of hope for the world. Contrary to the escapism or "heavenism" that dominates some fundamentalist interpretations today, Revelation suggests that our future dwelling with God will be on a radiant Earth.

Green space and God's river of life fill out the final description of the city. Revelation 22:1-5 recreates the garden of Eden in the center of a thriving urban landscape, drawing on Ezekiel's vision of a wondrous tree-lined river flowing out from the temple:

> Water was flowing from below the threshold of the temple toward the east.
> . . . On the banks, on both sides of the river, there will grow all kinds of trees for food. Their leaves will not wither nor their fruit fail, but they will bear fresh fruit every month, because the water for them flows from the sanctuary. Their fruit will be for food, and their leaves for healing. (Ezek. 47:1, 12)

In Revelation, the river of life flows not from the temple but from the throne of God and the Lamb, through the center of the processional street of the city. Ezekiel's fruit trees on both banks become the wondrous "tree of life" in Revelation 22:2, invoking Eden and paradise traditions. The fruit of the ever-bearing tree of life satisfies the hunger of everyone who is faithful (Rev. 2:7), overcoming the prohibition of Genesis 3:22.

The tree's leaves, as well as its fruit, offer blessing and healing. Revelation universalizes Ezekiel's already lavish vision by adding the "healing of the nations," to the tree's medicinal leaves (22:2; cf. Ezek. 47:12), the tree of life with its medicinal leaves offers a vision of an alternative political economy in which the essentials of health and life are available for all God's children, even for those who cannot afford them.

The tour of the city concludes with reference to God's servants, who offer service and worship (*latreusousin*) before the throne (v. 3). God's servants shall reign forever and ever. At a time when the Roman Empire claimed to reign forever (*Roma Aeterna*), Revelation boldly proclaimed that it is God who reigns forever—not the Roman Empire—and that God's servants will also reign with God. Note, however, that there is no object of the verb *reign*. God's servants do not reign over anyone else. The text invites us to explore ways to understand our reign not as domination over but as sharing in God's healing of the world.

Throughout the ages, Revelation's river of life, flowing through the New Jerusalem, the city with the gleaming golden street and pearly gates, where death and tears are no more, has given form and voice to the hopes and dreams of God's people. Martin Luther King Jr. drew from this river in his "I have a dream" speech. Other visionaries and dreamers have taken us again and again to this wondrous riverside, in songs, in stories, in sacraments, to help us see and experience God's holy city with its vision for life and healing, the waters of reconciliation and justice—right in the middle of our world.

These glimpses of a renewed Earth can inspire and motivate us. Through each of our cities, by whatever name, there is a river flowing from the heart of God and the Lamb, a life-giving river in which each of us was baptized and by which each of us is renewed.

Gospel
MATTHEW 28:1-10

The promise of "I am with you always" (Matt. 28:20) roots the Gospel of Matthew firmly on Earth. Unlike Luke, Matthew does not portray Jesus as ascending up to heaven at the end of the story. Rather, Matthew proclaims the resurrected Jesus as here with us for all time, until the close of the age. This Earth-bound focus of Matthew can shape our ecological preaching.

Matthew's empty-tomb story underscores the cosmic significance of Jesus' life and death. Earth itself participates in the drama of his crucifixion and resurrection. The Son of Humanity was lain "in the heart of the Earth" for three days and three nights (*en te kardia tes ges*, Matt. 12:40). Now, at his resurrection, comes what Anglican bishop James Jones calls "a seismic response from the earth's heart." This earthquake echoes the earthquake at Jesus' crucifixion two days earlier, which split rocks and opened tombs (Matt. 27:51-52). Crucifixion and resurrection shake the foundations of heaven and Earth, fulfilling Old Testament prophecies such as Ezekiel 37:12-13 that "I will open your graves and lead you out of your graves." Bishop Jones counsels preachers to give equal importance to the earthquakes of Matthew's Gospel (8:23-27, 24:7-8, 27:51-54, 28:2) as we do to the tearing of the temple curtain. "I have overlooked the fact that in the Passion narrative the earth speaks as powerfully as the curtain. . . . The truth is that the earth did not stay silent as it witnessed the Son of Man's death and resurrection."[5] The earthquakes at Jesus' death and resurrection embody nothing less than the profound participation of the Earth in the mission of Jesus.

The Roman imperial regime's political grip is also shaken, as symbolized by the terrified Roman guards who are like dead men. Resurrection is a profoundly political event in Matthew, proclaiming that the Roman imperial rule of death did not have the last word.

Matthew strengthens Mark's focus on the faithfulness of the women as model disciples. As in Mark's Gospel, all the male disciples fled before Jesus' crucifixion. By contrast, the "many women" who had followed Jesus from Galilee and "ministered" to him stood by him through his crucifixion, looking on from afar (Matt. 27:55-56). Mary Magdalene and the other Mary also witnessed Joseph of Arimathea's burial of Jesus' body and the sealing of the rock-hewn tomb with a large stone (Matt. 27:61). These two women keep vigil opposite the tomb, unwavering in their faithfulness to Jesus even in his death.

The two Marys go again to Jesus' tomb two days later, in continuity with their previous faithfulness. They go to "see," presumably in anticipation of his resurrection. A mighty angel rolls back the stone and invites the women to see the empty tomb where Jesus had lain. Jesus has risen, he is not here!

The angel's promise that Jesus has "gone ahead" into Galilee offers rich possibilities for Earth-centered preaching. The Greek verb for "going ahead" (*proagei*) conveys the sense of "leading," the same word Matthew uses to describe the star that would "go ahead" of the Magi and lead them to the infant Jesus (Matt 2:9). Jesus used the word before his death in promising his disciples that he would "go ahead" of them to Galilee (Matt. 26:32). "Jesus is going ahead—not going away," notes Elisabeth Schüssler Fiorenza, underscoring the horizontal dimension of the angel's words.[6] The "empty tomb," she adds, "does not signify absence but presence: it announces the Resurrected One's presence on the road ahead, in a particular space of struggle and recognition." Jesus goes ahead of us to lead us into the world—into a transformative way of life that testifies to the power of resurrection on Earth.

The disciples are commanded to go to Galilee, because Galilee is the location of the mountain on which Jesus had earlier given them his teachings, suggests Marianne Sawicki. "In effect, the Christian who wants to see the Risen Lord is being directed to the Beatitudes and the Sermon on the Mount—or, rather, to *obedience* to these teachings."[7] The commissioning of the eleven on the mountain in Galilee in Matthew 28:16-20 confirms obedience to Jesus' teachings in the Sermon on the Mount as the goal.

If Matthew's emphasis (like Mark's) is on Jesus' "going ahead" of the disciples in a horizontal sense—rather than going up into heaven—then Matthew is teaching us to look for experiences of resurrection presence not only in Galilee but also in Galveston, Galesburg, and Grand Forks—on all the roads of our lives on Earth. Resurrection means that Jesus opens up a future for us here. The stone has been rolled away. Like the women, we can run to meet that liberating future for Earth—a vision of the kingdom of God "on earth as in heaven" (Matt. 6:10).

Reflection

Watershed discipleship can revitalize ministry today, as congregations explore how the biblical watershed of God's river of life relates to actual rivers and watersheds. Preachers and parishes can learn to "read" their bioregion just as they learn to read and interpret the Bible. Celebration of River Sunday might include a "Healing Watershed" component that immerses parishioners in an awareness of a local watershed, learning about a river's geography and beauty as well as about its vulnerabilities and perils. At the Lutheran School of Theology at Chicago, where I teach, we offer a "Toxic Tour of the Calumet Watershed" where students see firsthand the toxicity of landscapes polluted by heavy industry, and also visit ecological restoration efforts. River Sunday can be an occasion for a canoe trip on a local river, for a gathering at a riverside, or for an outdoor baptism or renewal of baptism. A "river" or fountain of living water can even be brought into the church's sanctuary. A Lutheran congregation in Woodstock, Georgia, held a year-long emphasis on water that included activities such as a men's fly-fishing and spiritual retreat, culminating in Water Sunday depicting Revelation's river of life as a fountain flowing through the sanctuary.

The important point to underscore is that the Bible's waters are not just metaphorical waters, theological waters. They can also have something to say about the real rivers of our lives. Roman Catholic bishops in the Pacific Northwest issued a pastoral letter on the Columbia River watershed, seeking an ecological approach that considers the needs of all residents, including salmon, who share in the "living waters in the sacramental commons of the Columbia Watershed."[8] Revelation's vision of the holy city, with the river flowing through its main street, can become for us a vision of ecological renewal, of access to living waters for all, connecting the rivers and waters of our world to the future of God's river of life.[9]

RESOURCES

Bauckham, Richard. *The Bible and Ecology: Rediscovering the Community of Creation.* Waco: Baylor University Press, 2010.

Brown, William. *The Seven Pillars of Creation: The Bible, Science, and the Ecology of Wonder.* New York: Oxford University Press, 2010.

Davis, Ellen. *Scripture, Culture, and Agriculture: Reading the Bible Through Agrarian Eyes.* New York: Oxford University Press, 2009.

Hiebert, Theodore. *The Yahwist's Landscape: Nature and Religion in Early Israel.* New York: Oxford University Press, 1996. Paperback edition: Minneapolis: Fortress Press, 2008.

Limburg, James. "Down-To-Earth Theology: Psalm 104 and the Environment." *Currents in Theology and Mission* (1994): 340–46.

Rossing, Barbara. "God Laments With Us: Climate Change, Apocalypse and the Urgent Kairos Moment." *Ecumenical Review* 62 (July 2010): 119–30.

NOTES

1. Theodore Hiebert, *The Yahwist's Landscape: Nature and Religion in Early Israel* (New York: Oxford University Press, 1996 [paperback ed.: Minneapolis: Fortress Press, 2008]), 45.

2. Terence Fretheim, *God and the World in the Old Testament: A Relational Theology of Creation* (Nashville: Abingdon, 2005), 82.

3. Jonathan Sacks, "The Relationship Between the People and God," Lambeth Conference, July 2008, http://www.aco.org/vault/Sacks_The_Relationship_between_280708.pdf, accessed February 2, 2011.

4. William Brown, *The Seven Pillars of Creation: The Bible, Science, and the Ecology of Wonder* (New York: Oxford University Press, 2010), 147.

5. James Jones, "Jesus: Savior of the Earth," in *The Green Bible* (San Francisco: Harper Collins, 2008), I–69.

6. Elisabeth Schüssler Fiorenza, *Jesus: Miriam's Child, Sophia's Prophet* (New York: Continuum, 1995), 126.

7. Marianne Sawicki, "Recognizing the Risen Lord," *Theology Today* 44 (1988): 446, http://theologytoday.ptsem.edu/jan1988/v44-4-article2.htm, accessed February 2, 2011.

8. My paraphrase. For the original full text, see "The Columbia River Watershed: Realities and Possibilities," 1999, http://www.thewscc.org/columbia-river, accessed February 2, 2011.

9. See Barbara R. Rossing, "River of Life in God's New Jerusalem: An Ecological Vision for Earth's Future," *Currents in Theology and Mission* 25 (1998): 487–99.

YEAR B

THE WORD SERIES

First Sunday in Creation

Earth Sunday

Gerald West

Genesis 1:1-25
Psalm 33:1-9
Romans 1:18-23
John 1:1-14

Background

Biblical texts have no fixed meaning. While a certain meaning may become entrenched, there are always other contending meanings. This is true not only of our own appropriations of Scripture, but also of the very production of Scripture itself. The Genesis text that opens the Bible and that begins our worship and reflections on this Earth Sunday is an excellent example. Produced, probably, in a context of exile and colonization, when the elites of Judah were attempting to assert their own identity and theology in the midst of Babylonian and then Persian hegemony, Genesis 1:1-25 addresses this site of production, as well as many other sites of reception over the centuries.

This may seem an odd way to begin this liturgical reflection, but we do well to pause and remember that the same urge to dominate and domesticate Earth that we revisit and resist in this Season of Creation series has been present in the reading of Scripture. We desire a definitive and declarative "meaning" of Scripture. The impulse to dominate and domesticate is driven in part by our deep sense that Scripture matters, and so we yearn to hear its voice distinctly. But, in part, the desire is also to control, to hear the voice we expect Scripture should speak with.

We can do no other than bring our interests and questions to the text, and as people of faith we justifiably expect our sacred texts to speak to these interests and questions. And they do. But as they do, we should never forget for a moment that they, the biblical texts, are only able to speak because our ideo-theological orientations have been brought to bear on them. To put it crudely: without a reader, the text is silent. The particular ideo-theological orientation we bring to an encounter with the Bible in this Season of Creation is an ecojustice orientation. But as people of faith who locate ourselves in forms of continuity with Scripture, we also recognize and respect the details of Scripture. We cannot or should not conjure only what we would like to hear from Scripture. We should be able to hear the voice that speaks over against our preferred reading. After all, Scripture speaks with more than one voice, particularly when we pay attention to the details.

This is especially the case with the book of Genesis, as Mark Brett so eloquently argues. He discerns an "intentional hybridity" in the fabric of the Genesis text, a text where there is "a blending of two or more voices, without compositional boundaries being evident, such that the voices combine into an unstable symphony—sometimes speaking univocally but more often juxtaposing alternative points of view such that the authority of the dominant voice is put into question."[1] "In the case of Genesis," he continues, "the overriding ideologies have been juxtaposed with so many traces of otherness that the dominant voices can be deconstructed by audiences who have ears to hear."[2]

First Reading
GENESIS 1:1-25

Genesis 1:1-25 is usually considered, at least by biblical scholars, as part of the larger unit of Genesis 1:1—2:4a. It is only with the advent of ecological interests and questions that Genesis 1:1-25 has been considered as a literary unit. Norman C. Habel, for example, reads these verses as "a consistent story about Earth that affirms the intrinsic value of Earth."[3] Indeed, continues Habel, "when Genesis 1 is read as a story of Earth, the account of God creating humans [in Genesis 1:26-29/31] does not represent a climax to the narrative, but a sharp conflict of plot and perspective within the narrative."[4] Reading Genesis 1:1-25 with the Earth as a central character of the story is appropriate on Earth Sunday.

The Earth is introduced immediately in verse 1. It is possible to read verse 1 as indicating that God existed before the heavens and the Earth, the creation of which would then have been God's first creative act.

By contrast, an Earth-centered reading, which also fits with the Hebrew grammar of the text, would take verse 1 as a summary of the entire process of creation—in which case the Earth is co-eternal with God.[5] This is no forcing of the grammar; it is a valid and plausible interpretation of the Hebrew. In this reading of the text, the origins of the Earth are not the text's concern. The text is concerned to foreground the Earth alongside God.

The second distinctive feature of the Earth, found in verse 2, is that it is unformed and that not even God has fashioned it. The Earth has its own integrity "before" (in both a temporal and a spatial sense) God. The Earth is the subject of verse 2. The adjectives used here need not be interpreted or translated in negative terms. Though this verse may reflect an engagement with the chaos imagery associated with creation in the *Enuma Elish* and other ancient Near Eastern creation narratives, there is nothing in verse 2 that requires this reading. The Earth is simply unformed. The darkness that covers the Earth in the beginning is further support of an Earth with its own integrity and identity. But the second part of verse 2 hints at change, for God hovers over the waters, which represent the dominant feature of the unformed Earth.

Verses 3-5 introduce the first change God brings about, which is not to the Earth, but to the darkness. Again, it is not necessary to interpret "darkness" in a negative way, for verse 5 makes it clear that both light and darkness have a designation and an identity. The Earth has always been there, but we, the readers, do not see it until there is light; and so God says, "Let there be light." We are now able to witness and to bear testimony to the nature of this Earth. So ends the first day, with an unformed Earth— with its original identity and integrity now visible.

Though clearly the dominant force, God enters into a partnership in verses 6-10 with the Earth, fashioning what is already there, creating an infrastructure for life. The results of this initial partnership, tentative perhaps, are declared to be good. Recognizing that the Earth is responsive to a partnership-for-life with God, the Earth is now, on the third day, given a prominent role in the production of life (vv. 11-13). This collaborative work is also considered to be good. The most fundamental form of life has been formed with its own reproductive power (v. 12). And it, too, is good, in its own terms, before it has a purpose beyond its own fecundity. In terms of the inverted hierarchy of this ecojustice reading, the highest form of life is plant life (and so vegetarians, too, should eat with reverence).

At this point, there is a kind of pause or digression, it would seem, in the process of forming the Earth. Between the Earth producing on the third day and the waters (a constituent element of the Earth) producing on the fifth day, day four (vv. 14-19) is given over to making an infrastructure for the day and the night, the light and the darkness, which had been divided on the first day. In verse 17, there is an explicit linking of "the dome of the sky" and "the earth," such that the infrastructure of the sun, the moon, and the stars is also a sign of the relationship between and the unity of the sky and the earth. The sky is a part of the Earth. I have used the lower-case and the upper-case forms of "E/earth" here to indicate that I see a part-whole relationship between "earth" with a lowercase e and "Earth" with an uppercase E. The former could be translated "land," leaving the latter to designate the composite whole. So, day four serves as a reminder of the integrity and unity of the Earth, notwithstanding the forming that is taking place. But perhaps they are also a sign of something else. The repetition of the verbal form *mashal* (to rule/govern/be responsible for), used three times in this section, is also a sign of the kind of relationship between the constitutent elements of the Earth. They each have a role, but it is not a hierarchical role that has to do in any sense with unequal power. This may, indeed, be the primary point of day four's work and an indication of what the similar verbs in verse 28 might mean. It is this kind of "relational" responsibility that is good.

Verses 20-23 again call on the agency of the Earth, this time from the waters of the Earth. The respective waters bring forth life related to their reality, whether the waters above (the sky dome) or the waters below (the seas). Again, the unity of the Earth is emphasized, as is the cooperation of its constituent parts. Similarly, verses 24-25 call on the agency of the "land" component of the Earth to co-create with God. The agency lies first with the land of the Earth (v. 24, as is the case in v. 20 with the waters of the Earth), but then God joins (in v. 25, just as God had done in v. 21), signaling once again the collaborative act of creation. Such collaboration and its fruits are good.

Much is made of the difference between the verbs used for the creative process, whether *bara* (used in vv. 1 and 21, three times in 27, and 2:4) or *asah* (in vv. 7, 16, 25, 31, twice in 2:2, 2:3, and 2:4), and it may be that *bara* does designate different moments in creation or different kinds of creation, in which God is the primary partner. Genesis 1:1-25 is clearly as much about God as it is about the Earth. The point this reading makes, on this Earth Sunday, is that the Earth is a partner, a subject, and not just the object of God's activity. The Earth is an agent. Indeed, in verses 11-12, God watches, without intervening, as the Earth alone brings forth the fundamental layer of life.

The story so far, says Norman C. Habel, "emphasizes the intrinsic value of Earth as the center of the cosmos and the source of life. All components of the cosmos are related to Earth as an integrated interconnected whole, free from hierarchies of power in relation to Earth."[6]

But, according to Habel, the story then takes a dramatic turn: "With the appearance of human beings onto the scene [in verse 26], however, the power relations shift radically."[7] Brett, too, marks this shift: "The plants and animals are created 'according to their kinds' (Gen. 1.11, 12, 21, 24, 25), without any overt indication of hierarchy, but a distinction certainly arises with the creation of the species which is made in the image of *Elohim*."[8] I, however, would want to emphasize the continuities and similarities between verses 1-25 and what follows; I would want to wrestle with the verbs in verse 28 until they bring forth life and not death.[9] But perhaps I must bow to the detail of Scripture in what follows, hearing in what follows the seeds of human autonomy, arrogance, domination, and destruction in the very words of sacred Scripture. But not today, not on Earth Sunday!

Psalmody
PSALM 33

The psalm for today, Psalm 33,[10] takes us deeper into the relationship between God and the Earth, exploring dimensions of their correspondence not probed in Genesis 1. After the opening call to praise (vv. 1-3), verses 4-7 probe both the nature of God and that of the Earth. God is to be praised "for" (the logical connector between vv. 1-3 and vv. 4-7) the kind of God that God is and the kind of Earth that God has created. In verse 4, the "word" and "work" of God are linked in a parallel structure:

> For the word of the LORD is upright,
> and all his work is done in faithfulness.

As in Genesis 1, what is said and what is done correspond. But the emphasis is different. Here we encounter an ethically engaged God. It is not primarily what God says and does that is important (as in Genesis 1); rather, the focus is firmly on the ethical nature of God, expressed in the ethical character of God's word ("upright") and work ("faithfulness"). The first part of verse 5 reinforces this ethical emphasis: "God loves righteousness and justice." And then, without a pause, the focus shifts from

God to the Earth, for the parallelism of verse 5 binds its first and second sentence: "the earth is full of the steadfast love of the LORD." The Earth is the embodiment of God's ethical identity.

Verses 6-7 then "rewind" or "zoom in," explaining more fully how the Earth came to be the embodiment of God's ethical character. It is not just the power of God's word that makes the Earth what it is, it is the ethical nature of this word and its corresponding deed, as expressed clearly in verses 4 and 5a. So, the "making" (as in Genesis 1, *asah*) of the heavens and all their host (v. 6) and the dividing of the waters (v. 7, as in Genesis 1) are ethically charged acts, imparting not only a physical identity but also an ethical identity to the Earth. The personal imagery in these verses (more marked than in Genesis 1), in which God has a mouth and implied eyes and hands, reveals an intimacy between God and the Earth.[11] No wonder, then, that "the earth is full of the steadfast love of the LORD," given God's intimate and personal connection with Earth. And as in Genesis 1, there are aspects of this "account" in which God brings into being (v. 6) and in which elements of the Earth already exist alongside God (v. 7).

The shift in verse 8 is similar in some sense to the shift from Genesis 1:25 to 1:26, for we move in verse 8 from an independent and ethically charged Earth to its human inhabitants. Unlike Genesis 1:26, however, where humans have a special place in the hierarchy of creation (perhaps), here in the psalm, humans, "the inhabitants of the world," are to "fear the LORD," which in the literary context of the psalm so far includes the Earth—which shares the ethical character of the Lord. Indeed, the parallelism of verse 8 and the third-person masculine plural jussive form of the verb *yare* (fear) make it clear that the reference in verse 8a does not refer to the Earth (which is feminine) fearing the Lord, but to "all [the inhabitants of] the earth" fearing the Lord. In this context, "all the earth" is a metaphor for humanity. There is no grammatical opposition here between the Earth and the Lord. The Earth and the Lord stand together over against humanity.

The reason that humanity must "fear" and "stand in awe" of God is because of the ethical nature of God and of the Earth. Verse 9 emphasizes the brute fact of the correspondence between God and the Earth. Verses 10 and 11 make the point that humanity is expected to live according to the ethical identity of its home and its God. That humanity does not do so is already apparent in these verses, for the verses contrast the "counsel" and "plans" of humanity with the "counsel" and "thoughts" of God.

Verse 12 is a reminder that humanity has a choice; we can choose to live in ethical harmony—in uprightness, faithfulness, righteousness, and justice—with the Earth and God. Verses 13-15 are a reminder that God (and the Earth) are watching and judging how humanity chooses to live on this ethically imbued Earth.

Verses 16-17 deliver a preliminary judgment. Humanity has chosen an ethically destructive path, choosing hierarchy and military power as its way.[12] But such ways will only lead to death and famine, as verse 19 declares. The reference to famine here makes it clear that God's judgment is the Earth's judgment; they are the same judgment. An ethic of hierarchy and might-is-right will receive its judgment here on Earth, as it is in heaven.

Nevertheless, verses 18-19 and the liturgical response—our response— in verses 20-21 make it clear that we continue to have a choice about how we live on Earth and under heaven. The "steadfast love" (*chesed*) of God,[13] which is part of the very fabric of the Earth (v. 5), is our hope (vv. 18, 22). By choosing justice, righteousness, uprightness, and faithfulness toward each other and toward the Earth, we participate in the *chesed* of God.

Second Reading
ROMANS 1:18-23

This reading from Romans could almost be, and perhaps is, a comment on Psalm 33. In both, there is a similar recognition that God and the created order, the Earth, share an ethical identity (vv. 19-20). There is a similar recognition of a relationship between godliness and righteousness/ justice (v. 18). And there is a similar recognition that God and "the things God has made" (v. 20) share a particular kind of ethical orientation, an orientation toward righteousness/justice (v. 18).

But this text has its own logic, which begins in verses 16-17. Verses 16-17 introduce the focus of Paul, namely, "the gospel," its purpose and shape. The gospel has a purpose, which "is the power of God for salvation to everyone who has faith." And the gospel has an ethical shape, "for in it the righteousness of God is revealed." The gospel is God's power for salvation and a revelation of God's righteousness/justice.

It is important for our reading this Earth Sunday to see that our text is logically connected to the verses that precede verses 16-17. The conjunction "for" links the verses, as does the verb "reveal" (*apokalupto*), in the third-person singular, present passive in both verse 17 and 18. But what is the logic of this link? Up to this point in the letter, "the gospel" is the vehicle of revelation. God is the originator of the gospel (v. 1); the prophets and the Scriptures convey God's promise of the gospel (vv. 2-3); Jesus is the gospel (v. 4); and Paul is an apostle and servant of the gospel (vv. 5 and 9). Verses 16-17 then summarize the purpose of the gospel, which is "the power of God for salvation to everyone who has faith," and the shape of the gospel, which is "the righteousness of God." But our reading begins (v. 18) not with the righteousness of God but with the wrath of God, and not with what the gospel reveals but with what heaven reveals: "For the wrath of God is revealed from heaven."

It is almost as if we leave the realm of the gospel and enter another realm of another kind of revelation. God is clearly the implied agent of both, but the focus in Romans 1:18-23 is fixed on this other realm of revelation. It is the realm of creation (*kosmos*) (verse 20). The good news about this realm is that it has been a faithful representation of and witness to the power and ethical nature of God: "For what can be known about God is plain to them, because God has shown it to them. Ever since the creation of the world, his eternal power and divine nature, invisible though they are, have been understood and seen through the things he has made" (vv. 19-20a). In contrast to Psalm 33, the human problem here is not hierarchical power and military might, but a failure to recognize fully that the Earth is a faithful representation of God.

There is some subtlety here, for verse 21 seems to indicate that humanity has understood who God is from creation, but not the full extent of what knowing both God's power and God's ethical character requires. To "know God" (v. 21) implies or requires an entering into a right/just relationship with the created world and God. The failure to do so is characterized as "ungodliness and injustice" (v. 18); and verses 21-23 seem then to catalog the steps toward this condition. The first step (v. 21a) toward ungodliness and wickedness is knowing the ethical nature of God in/and creation but refusing to embrace the relational dimension required by both, signaled here by the failure of people to honor or to give thanks to God (and the Earth). Although the former (ungodliness) is stated, the latter (injustice) may also be implied in it and/or inferred from it, for the resulting "injustice" extends to every dimension of our humanity, including our relationship with God, with other humans, with ourselves, and with the rest of creation (see, for example, Genesis 4:13-14).

While the first step toward ungodliness and injustice is the desire for autonomy, the second step (vv. 21b-22) is the development of ideo-theological systems that entrench this desire for autonomy, systems that consider relationality as foolishness and autonomy as wisdom—the precise opposite of what the creation of the world (the Earth) demonstrates.

The desire for autonomy and the injustice that results has always led humanity both to suppress the truth about God (and the things God has made) and to construct ideo-theological systems that justify injustice. The result (v. 23) of these steps is idolatry, idolatry in the form of a system of belief that denies the truth about God and creation.

While Paul characterizes the kinds of consequences of idolatrous ideo-theological systems in the verses that follow, he says almost nothing about what exactly "the creation of the world"—both as a process and as a product (for both are included in the Greek phrase in v. 20)—demonstrates about justice and godliness. The shape of the argument is clear, but not its content. The reason for this is that Paul believes that "the things God has made" (v. 21), even though they continue to bear witness to godliness and justice, have become increasingly distorted by the decay precipitated by humanity's persistent attempts at autonomy. The same argument used in Romans 1:24-32, namely that "God gave them [humanity] up" (vv. 24, 26, 28), is used of a "groaning" creation in Romans 8:18-27. This text will be dealt with in depth on Wilderness Sunday, but it is important to reflect on it briefly here.

In our text for today, it is not God who instigates human autonomy; God simply allows the consequences of this ideo-theological orientation to play themselves out. In my view, this is how we are to understand Romans 1:18: the *kosmos* itself is wracked by the wrath of God, not because God is angry with it, but because its ethical nature reacts against human autonomy. As I said earlier, in this verse we enter a realm other than the gospel. In this realm, "the creation of the world" demonstrates its own and God's ethical order. When that ethical order is rejected, according to Paul's "narrative,"[14] decay (*phthora*) sets in (8:21). And just as God "gives over" humanity to the consequences of their unjust ideo-theological systems, so "creation was subjected to futility, not of its own will but by the will of the one who subjected it, in hope that the creation itself will be set free from its bondage to decay and will obtain the freedom of the glory of the children of God" (8:20-21).

"Creation" (*ktisis*) in Romans 8:18-27,[15] which is inclusive of nonhuman creation, has a dignity and an integrity of its own, with God's ethical character visibly woven into its very fabric. But the human desire for autonomy, originating with Adam[16] but including almost certainly the unfolding story of humanity in Genesis 1–11 and beyond,[17] has brought about decay in the fabric of the created reality. The logic of Paul's argument spanning these two texts seems to suggest that humanity of its own accord chose to live by its own "futile" systems (1:21), thereby bringing decay to the human relationship with God and the Earth. God chose not to intervene, thereby subjecting creation to "futility" (8:20; the Greek word is the same as in 1:21); in other words, allowing the Earth to decay along with humanity, recognizing that the Earth, even in its decay, represented God's power and justice (1:19) and that the Earth, as it decayed, added its groaning voice (8:22) to the voices of those who have heeded the good news of God's power and justice in Christ and of the Spirit (8:23) in calling humanity to turn away from autonomy to relationality.

So while creation has been given over to the humanity-induced decay, it is not a condition that will last forever and it is not without hope. Indeed, Paul's argument (8:18-27) is that the delay in God's distinctive intervention in Christ is precisely to demonstrate to humanity where its relational hubris leads. Once humanity recognizes that it can no longer operate independently of God and the Earth and becomes once again "children of God" through Christ (8:14), its redemption will lead the way to a restoration of the groaning creation (8:19).[18] The damage that humanity has done to creation must be "righted" by humanity's salvation.

The decay brought about by humanity's refusal to live within the ethical relationalities of God, inscribed by God in creation, is more than physical; it is also ethical.[19] As Romans 1:18 indicates, ungodliness and injustice are relational terms. In ecojustice terms, however, we must accept that our reading cannot ignore the theocentric dimension of these texts.[20] While God is clearly the primary agent, however, we do see glimpses of a cosmos that has its own integrity, which, when disrupted by humanity's hubris and injustice, has consequences for every component of creation. Furthermore, the creation "is not merely the stage on which the drama of human salvation takes place. There is a strong sense of creation's 'purpose,' its own eschatology, since its destiny is its participation in the glory and liberation of the children of God."[21]

We cannot ignore the anthropocentric dimension of these texts, as the quotation above indicates. But we can perhaps chasten and humble this anthropocentrism, since Romans 8 "depicts creation, humanity, and the Spirit as conjoined in a chorus of hopeful groaning."[22] Furthermore, a Christian "ecological anthropocentrism" might draw from Romans 1 and 8 a specific challenge for Christians, "because they are the ones in whom the promise of renewal and transformation is already coming to fruition,"[23] or should be.

> Insofar as hope for the future thus informs present action, so too hope for creation might [should] inform patterns of human living, such that the

'not yet' of creation's (and humanity's) liberation becomes evident in the 'already' of environmentally responsible living, not only for the sake of fellow human beings, who will suffer the effects of climate change, and so on, but also for the sake of the creation itself, and all the creatures which know suffering and decay.[24]

Gospel
JOHN 1:1-14

The Gospel reading on this Earth Sunday is from the New Testament's equivalent of Genesis 1. Like the Genesis text, John 1:1-14 takes us back to the beginning. Except now there is nothing with God in the beginning—no Earth, only the Word. So in some sense we might say that John 1 rereads Genesis 1, rewriting it to make his own theological point. Indeed, some scholars have argued that John is not only rewriting Genesis 1; he is also rewriting Paul, Mark, Matthew, and Luke. They all begin their accounts of Jesus within human history. But not John. John's opening words move readers outside of time and space. The point John is making is the preeminence of Jesus, over against all else: "In the beginning was the Word, and the Word was with God, and the Word was God. The Word was in the beginning with God" (vv. 1-2).

Such a beginning is not auspicious for our Earth Sunday. Even though the creation is mentioned quite early on in the text, in verse 3, "the creation of everything (*panta*) in the physical world is covered in summary fashion in one verse"—with the emphasis, as Norman C. Habel argues, being "on what Word brings to creation rather than on creation itself."[25] Even when life (*zoe*) is mentioned in verse 4, it is not the "life" of Genesis 1 but the "spiritual" light of the Word. If we were to continue in this line of interpretation, trying to understand how John 1 rereads/rewrites Genesis 1, as Habel does, we would not find much "to earth" this text. John seems to "spiritualize" almost every echo of Genesis 1. And in what is perhaps an echo of Romans 1, John goes further than Paul in seeing an almost total separation between "the world" (v. 10) and God.

The only glimmer of an Earth-consciousness that Habel can find is the powerful image of the Word that "became flesh and lived among us" (v. 14). For surely, as Habel says, "[f]lesh is the stuff of the living creatures of the physical world."[26] But even here, he admits, there is no explicit mention and little sense of the stuff of the Earth independent of humanity. What is more, verse 13 makes it very clear that the terrain of the "blood" and "flesh" is not adequate for the Word's purposes. The Word becomes flesh only briefly, "pitching its tent among us" (v. 14) in order, the argument seems to go, for us to recognize the limits of the flesh and the glory of the Word (v. 13). John's rereading of Genesis (and Romans) therefore poses a series of questions to us on this Earth Sunday: "Is Earth valued or devalued? Does Earth remain but a temporary residence of the very *logos* that once created it? Does the *logos* discover that flesh is good? And, if so, what does this mean?" Furthermore, "Does the text of John 1 then begin with an incomplete, defective, darkness-dominated Earth below? Is that Earth, too, to be redeemed, revalued, restored to its primal state as 'good'?"[27]

Taking up the challenge of these questions, Elizabeth Wainwright responds to Habel by reading John 1 not against Genesis 1 but against three Wisdom texts: Proverbs 8:22-31; Sirach 24:1-12; and Wisdom 7:22—8:1.[28] Using these as intertexts of John 1, Wainwright reads John 1 as a song that may have "originated as a song of praise to Sophia/Wisdom or even Jesus/Sophia."[29] Attentive to the androcentric and dualistic ideo-theological orientations of Wisdom texts, her own reading privileges "the resistant voice of Earth that can be heard when John 1 is read intertextually" with these Wisdom texts.[30] Viewed through these intertexts, the subject of John 1—namely, Word/Sophia/Wisdom/Jesus—becomes far more deeply related to the stuff of creation.

Similarly, Vicky Balabanski also takes up the challenge of Habel's questions, but her reading probes the intratextual dimensions of John's understanding of "the world," the *kosmos*.[31] Discerning four different ways in which John uses the concept of *kosmos*, only one of which is thoroughly dualistic, she reads John 3:17 (in which there are three references to *kosmos*) in a nondualistic way "that acknowledges our mutuality with Earth."[32]

My own reading of John accepts, with these three scholars, that the dominant voice in John offers little to our Earth-centered concern on this Earth Sunday. Fortunately, however, there is more than one voice in the Gospel of John, even if the other voices are only fragmentary. In what follows, I will attempt a preliminary liberationist reading of one fragmentary trajectory. Ecojustice is only one dimension of a multifaceted liberationist ideo-theological reading; yet by adopting a liberationist reading, I hope to show how it may offer resources to read John 1 (and the whole of John) in a way that is more inclusive of the Earth.

The first fragment in this line of fragments I find in the text for today: "And the Word became flesh and lived among us" (v. 14). Even in John, the flesh here is real flesh, even if it is just for a moment in time. Indeed, I would hold on to the image of temporariness in the verb "to dwell" (*skenoo*). The image of a tent has been associated with the tent that was the tabernacle, and the reference to "glory" later in the verse has reinforced this association. Unfortunately, however, this association has led readers in the direction of power (Exod. 40:34-35) rather than to the vulnerability of tent living, whether it be the tents of nomads or the tents of refugee camps on the margins.

The reference to the margins, their vulnerability, and their close reliance on the Earth is a fragmentary trajectory that begins here. This trajectory is confirmed in "the voice of one crying out in the wilderness" (John 1:23). It also confirmed in this chapter by the designation of the Word as "Jesus son of Joseph from Nazareth," for indeed, "can anything good come out of [the marginal/marginalized] Nazareth?" (1:45-46). This fragmentary line continues with Jesus' ethical identification of Nathanael as "an Israelite in whom there is no deceit" (1:47), who is located "under the fig tree" (1:48)—a place of sustenance for those on the margins, driven there because of their refusal to embrace a life of deceit. The Earth nurtures those like John the Baptist and Nathanael who reside, like Jesus, on the margins.

The trajectory becomes especially clear in the story of the wedding in Cana, for in this story the agenda of Jesus is revealed first of all to the servants. This is explicitly stated in John 2:9. Servants, those marginalized by the dominant economic system, are the first to recognize the first sign. That the tributary mode of production of this time is the target of critique in this fragmentary trajectory is equally clear as Jesus moves from Cana to Jerusalem (2:13-16), where he takes sides with the servants, victims of the Temple-state system. Since the time of monarchy (see 1 Samuel 8), the leadership of "Israel," whom John refers to in his time as "the Jews," have used a tributary mode of production to drive peasant farmers into debt in order to foreclose their land and then exploit their labor. While a critique of this economic and ecological system is, in my view, the dominant trajectory in Mark's Gospel, it is only a fragment in John—but it is there!

There are even hints of this fragment in John 3, where Jesus engages in the reeducation of "a Pharisee named Nicodemus, a leader of the Jews" (John 3:1). The subversive nature of this encounter is clear, for Nicodemus came "by night." And although the dominant "spiritual" trajectory is foremost in this narrative, there is a glimpse of the fragmentary line I am following, for one might interpret the saying of Jesus in 3:17 as follows: "God did not send the Son in/to the margins of the world to destroy the world, which had been corrupted by the deceit of the tributary mode of production, but in order that the entire socioeconomic system might be redeemed through him." The talk of "judgment" coming "into the world" in order to expose those who "loved darkness rather than light because their deeds were evil" (3:19) makes sense in this marginal reading.

The shift to the countryside (3:22), the site of the devastation wrought by the tributary mode of production, which was centered in the cities, especially Jerusalem, and then the movement to Samaria, another marginal area to which Jesus "had to go" (4:4), and finally the recruitment of the socially excluded Samaritan woman—all testify to the presence of this fragmentary voice. And the recurring images of water and food further connect the socioeconomic concern of this trajectory to the Earth.

Not only does the healing of the royal official's son in Capernaum (4:46) demonstrate a commitment to the here-and-now, but once again it is explicitly mentioned that servants are the ones who first recognize the agenda of Jesus (4:51-52). As this is the second time I have used the notion of the "agenda of Jesus," it may be useful to explain briefly how my hermeneutical approach operates in this case. I am not arguing that John's agenda is primarily concerned about this minority report, this minority voice that I am pursuing. What I am arguing is that the reality of Jesus' agenda cannot ever be entirely co-opted by another agenda, not even by John's very insistent agenda. In poststructuralist terms, for those interested in such things, structures of presence always imply absent elements, whose exclusion enables their *own* "presence" to be proclaimed. In building his theological argument, John has to include those elements he excludes!

The next chapter in John is a good example of the tension between Jesus' agenda and the agenda of John. This is one of the high points of John's teaching about the relationship between Jesus, the Son, and the Father. But it begins with Jesus noticing, in the midst of a busy festival, those who because of their marginal status are excluded, the "many invalids—blind, lame, and paralyzed" (5:1-9). The minority voice draws attention to Jesus "seeing" what no one else sees; to Jesus communicating with someone from the margins (as with the Samaritan woman); to Jesus healing someone; and then to Jesus "finding" him later in order to build relationship and community (5:14). John uses this minority voice, but he builds on it and around it his own concern with the superiority of Jesus over against the Temple and the religious tradition, because of Jesus' special relationship with the Father. We can hear both voices, that of Jesus as well as that of John—to those who have ears to hear.

139

This is not the occasion to develop this trajectory more fully, but I hope I have shown enough of it to give an indication that the lives of those who are most closely tied to this world, this *kosmos*, are the subjects of this minority, marginal voice in John. There is an almost obsessive concern of the servant Jesus with all those who have become in some way a part of the new community Jesus is establishing (but which John does not always emphasize)—including those we have already met and including the "large crowd" he feeds (John 6:5); the "boy" who shares his food (6:9); the "woman who had been caught in adultery" (8:3); the man born blind (9:1); his friends Lazarus, Mary, and Martha (11:1); "some Greeks" (12:20); and even Judas, whom Jesus includes when he washes his disciples' feet and shares his final meal (13:1-30). He becomes "troubled in spirit" (13:21) when he considers that this fragile community, and the Earth on which it depends, will be betrayed. Hence, the many post-crucifixion appearances (20:14, 19, 26, 21:1), assuring the betrayed community that he is with them and that together, by sharing their resources (21:6, 9-13, 15-17), they will be cared for and fed for the work that lies ahead of them.

A liberationist reading includes an ecojustice reading, because without justice for the Earth, there will be no justice for the poor and marginalized. While justice for the Earth lies on the margins of John's Gospel, there are glimmers of it within the fragments I have woven together into a liberatory voice, which, though marginalized in John's Gospel, is nevertheless discernable to those who have ears to hear.

Which brings us back to our first reading for this Earth Sunday, Genesis 1:1-25. In my view we should not emphasize the contrast between the creation of humanity (Gen. 1:26-29) and what precedes it. Humanity is integral to the Earth. Just as we cannot, given my liberationist ideo-theological orientation, have ecological justice without a place for humanity, so we cannot have socioeconomic justice without a place for the Earth.

Reflections

In preaching on these texts I would highlight two related things. First, I would emphasize that we bring "new" contextual realities and questions to the Scriptures. We must be open to hear Scriptures speak with a "new" voice. Indeed, what makes these texts "Scripture" is that they have the capacity to speak a word into any context. Second, I would emphasize that Scripture does not speak with one voice. Scripture is always, in my view, a site of dialogue or even contestation, as different voices struggle together to hear the voice of God. We should not be worried, therefore, that we sometimes have to "wrestle" with Scripture in order to receive its blessing (Gen. 32:26).

NOTES

1. Mark G. Brett, "Earthing the Human in Genesis 1–3," in *The Earth Story in Genesis*, ed. Norman C. Habel and Shirley Wurst, The Earth Bible, vol. 4 (Cleveland: Pilgrim, 2000), 85.

2. Ibid.

3. Norman C. Habel, "Geophany: The Earth Story in Genesis 1," in *The Earth Story in Genesis*, ed. Habel and Wurst, 35.

4. Ibid.

5. Mark G. Brett, *Genesis: Procreation and the Politics of Identity* (New York: Routledge, 2000), 74.

6. Habel, "Geophany," 45.

7. Ibid.

8. Brett, "Earthing the Human in Genesis 1–3," 76.

9. See, for example, David W. Cotter, *Genesis, Berit Olam Studies in Hebrew Narrative & Poetry* (Collegeville, Minn.: Liturgical, 2003), 18; and Gunther Wittenberg, "In Search of the Right Metaphor: A Response to Peet van Dyck's 'Challenges in the Search for an Ecotheology': *Part One: Metaphor and Dominion, Old Testament Essays* 32, no. 2 (2010): 215–34.

10. For an ecological perspective on the Psalms, although not this psalm, see Norman C. Habel, ed., *The Earth Story in the Psalms and the Prophets*, The Earth Bible, vol. 4 (Cleveland: Pilgrim, 2001).

11. As Norman C. Habel notes in his discussion of Genesis 1, here, too, in Psalm 33:6, "the word and the breath are alternative images to express the presence of God as a creating power; they are two modes of God as Creator." Habel, "Geophany," 40.

12. On how this psalm and other psalms speak to the issue of military power in the context of justice, see David Pleins, *The Psalms: Songs of Tragedy, Hope, and Justice* (Maryknoll, N.Y.: Orbis, 1993), 78–80.

13. For more on the role of *chesed* in this psalm, see Konrad Schaefer, *Psalms, Berit Olam Studies in Hebrew Narrative & Poetry* (Collegeville, Minn.: Liturgical, 2001), 81–84.

14. Cherryl Hunt, David G. Horrell, and Christopher Southgate, "An Environmental Mantra? Ecological Interest in Romans 8:19-23 and a Modest Proposal for Its Narrative Interpretation," *Journal of Theological Studies*, NS 59, no. 2 (2008): 546–79.

15. The verbal form of *ktisis* is used with *kosmos* in Romans 1:20. For a discussion of the various ways in which *ktisis* has been understood by generations of readers, see Harry Alan Hahne, *The Corruption and Redemption of Creation: Nature in Romans 8.19-22 and Jewish Apocalyptic Literature* (London: T & T Clark, 2006), 177–81.

16. For a more detailed analysis of the relationship between Romans 5:12-21 and Romans 8:18-22, see Brendan Byrne, "Creation Groaning: An Earth Bible Reading of Romans 8:18-22," in *Readings from the Perspective of Earth*, ed. Norman C. Habel, The Earth Bible, vol. 1 (Cleveland: Pilgrim, 2000), 193–203.

17. Hunt, Horrell, and Southgate, "An Environmental Mantra?" 561.

18. Byrne, "Creation Groaning," 215–16.

19. See also Hunt, Horrell, and Southgate, "An Environmental Mantra?" 569.

20. Ibid., 572.

21. Ibid., 574.

22. Ibid., 575.

23. Ibid.

24. Ibid., 575–76.

25. Norman C. Habel, "An Ecojustice Challenge: Is Earth Valued in John 1?" in *The Earth Story in the New Testament*, ed. Norman C. Habel and Vicky Balabanski, The Earth Bible, vol. 5 (Cleveland: Pilgrim, 2002), 78.

26. Ibid., 81.

27. Ibid., 82.

28. Elizabeth Wainwright, "Which Intertext? A Response To 'An Ecojustice Challenge: Is Earth Valued in John 1?'" in *The Earth Story in the New Testament*, eds. Habel and Balabanski, 83. For a reading of Romans 8:18-30 in the light of Wisdom 1–2, see Marie Turner, "God's Design: The Death of Creation? An Ecojustice Reading of Romans 8:18-30," in *The Earth Story in Wisdom Traditions*, ed. Norman C. Habel and Shirley Wurst, The Earth Bible, vol. 3 (Cleveland: Pilgrim, 2001), 168–78.

29. Wainwright, "Which Intertext?" 83.

30. Ibid., 84.

31. Vicky Balabanski, "John 1—The Earth Bible Challenge: An Intra-Textual Approach to Reading John 1," in *The Earth Story in the New Testament*, eds. Habel and Balabanski, 89–94.

32. Ibid., 94.

Second Sunday in Creation

Humanity Sunday

Norman C. Habel

Genesis 1:26-28
Psalm 8
Philippians 2:1-8
Mark 10:41-45

Background

The various Sundays in the Season of Creation have titles that highlight a domain of creation—Mountain Sunday, River Sunday, Earth Sunday, and so on. By including Humanity Sunday, the intention is to emphasize that human beings are part of creation and belong to the concrete domains of creation. Earth is not simply a stopping place for human souls en route to heaven. We are not merely "pilgrims on this barren land," as one of our hymns proclaims. Earth is home for humans.

As humans, we have also come to realize that we are not separate or disconnected from the various forces and domain of nature. We are totally dependent on the various ecosystems of Earth for survival, ecosystems that have existed for millennia. The movement of oxygen in the atmosphere is necessary for us to breathe. The movement of moisture in the clouds and the seas is essential for us to enjoy a drink. The movement of worms in the soil is vital for us to receive our daily bread.

We are children of Earth, made of earth, air, and water. Earth penetrates our being and replaces each cell in our body every seven years. We eat Earth, are made from Earth, and excrete Earth. We are Earth beings. On Humanity Sunday, we celebrate our connection with creation, our dependency on Earth, and our intimate relationship with a Creator who continues to meet us "in, with, and under" this creation.

As we explore the texts for this Sunday, we will be reading passages that are well known to our listeners, the subject of numerous sermons, and, in fact, the primary source for several Christian doctrines. Theologians and preachers have defended their interpretations of these texts for centuries. To read these texts afresh in the context of the Season of Creation therefore demands that we come with an open mind to traditional interpretations with which we are very familiar. We approach these texts as Earth children, sympathetic with the perspective of Earth.

It is also important that we read the texts for this Sunday as a whole, recognizing that there is a major transition from the perspective of the Old Testament texts to that of the New Testament texts. As readers who are in Christ, we may not get the full significance of an Old Testament text if we do not discover the way this tradition is interpreted by the Christ event, the gospel!

As we explore these readings in the context of the Season of Creation we will not only recognize some of the major ways in which these texts have been interpreted in the past, but we will also highlight some of the insights that emerge when we read from the perspective of Earth. As children of Earth we are invited to read from the perspective of Earth and creation, rather than simply from the perspective of humans.

Reading these particular texts in context, the key question before us is: Are human beings created to rule or to serve creation?

First Reading
GENESIS 1:26-28

The *imago Dei* of this passage has been widely discussed and hotly debated since the time of the Church Fathers. The numerous interpretations of this passage leave the Bible student dizzy in the head. And this is not the time to survey the massive array of understandings of the *imago Dei* text and the accompanying verses. Suffice it to say that at least two factors have been significant in most readings of this *imago Dei* passage. The first is the influence of *dualism*, and the second is inherent *anthropocentrism*.

Dualism can be traced back to the influence of Greek thought on Western interpretations of reality. A dualistic approach leads to a sharp division between humanity and nature, mind and matter, soul and body. A long tradition that goes back to figures like Philo, who was influenced by dualistic Greek thought, promotes the idea that the image refers to a non-physical dimension of humans—the mind, reason, consciousness, or a spiritual core. The usual meaning of the Hebrew word for image (*tselem*), however, is something concrete and visible—for example, a statue of a deity (2 Kgs. 11:18; Dan. 3:1) or a picture on a wall (Ezek. 23:14). If we dare to see our physical selves as living expressions of "the image of God," we face a whole new set of questions about our relationship to God and God's very concrete creation!

Past readings have also been understandably anthropocentric. According to the text, humans are to function as creatures in God's image by multiplying on Earth, by "ruling" over other creatures, and by "subduing" Earth itself. Until recently, these specific roles of humanity have been taken to mean that humans are expected to dominate—to tame creatures, to harness nature, and to rule in God's place on Earth. One of the sources cited to support this reading was the practice of ancient kings who frequently erected their image in a certain domain to announce that the region in question was under their rule. The image represented the king. Human beings, in this text, are therefore understood to be kings whom God has placed on Earth to exercise power—the divine right of humans to conquer or to control nature as any king of the ancient world might do.

In the historical process of European colonization, this text provided an impetus for "conquering" the wilds, clearing the landscape, and ruling as God's people. To some extent, the climate crisis our planet now faces is due to the claim of Western Christians that they had the right to exploit nature.

Some more recent readings of this text have sought to temper the terms *rule* and *subdue* and render them as "exercise stewardship." Unfortunately, this approach tends to retain the anthropocentric way of viewing humans as the designated rulers of Earth, even if they are rulers for the king rather than kings themselves.

We are left with the question we posed above: Are we as Christians to rule or serve creation?

In this regard, there are several ways in which we can read this text from the perspective of Earth. The first is to read the text in light of the second story of creation told in Genesis 2. If we do so, there are two possible outcomes: either we try to harmonize Genesis 1:26-28 and Genesis 2:15 so that they say much the same thing or we face the reality that these two texts present us with the tough choice: to rule or to serve. I believe the latter position is more faithful to these two texts.

The Genesis 2 account begins by announcing that the ground (*adamah*) was not yet green, because there was no person or power to "serve" or nurture her. While the verb *abad* in verse 5 is sometimes rendered "to till," the normal meaning of the term is "to serve." This primal absence of someone to "serve" Earth moved God, the gardener, to take some of the soil from the ground and, like a potter, to mold the soil into a figure called an *adam*, a human being. So in Genesis 2, humans were created from Earth for the purpose of "serving" Earth. Earth was not created for humans.

In the Genesis 2 account, then, God works with Earth to green the landscape with a forest of beautiful and bountiful trees. From that forest, rivers flowed in all directions. The first scene of this account concludes when God gives the first human the task of completing what was missing at the very beginning of the story. The human has the task of greening the ground—in the specific words of the text: "Then the LORD God took the man and put him in the garden of Eden to *serve and preserve* it" (Gen. 2:15).

The role of humans in Genesis 2 is to "serve and preserve" this Earth. "Serving" is what people did when they devoted their attention to a person or to a task. Members of the court served the king. Laborers served in the fields. Priests and worshipers served their God in the temple. Here humans are to "serve" Earth, that is, dedicate themselves to Earth by attending to her needs.

When we compare the verbs used in Genesis 1:28 and Genesis 2:15, we can see just how different they are.

Genesis 1:26-28	Genesis 2:15
"rule" (*rada*)	"serve" (*abad*)
"subdue" (*kabash*)	"preserve" (*shamar*)

What we have here are two chapters, side by side, that have verbs in pivotal passages which are diametric opposites. One contradicts the other. "Rule" is the opposite of "serve" and "subdue" is the opposite of "preserve." We therefore need to decide which text has priority and why.

Some scholars cite Psalm 72 as an example in which the king's rule is expected to reflect God's justice. A closer reading of this text, however, reveals an explicit reference in verses 8-11 to the king "ruling" (*rada*). The psalmist prays that the dominion or "rule" of the king will be from sea to sea and that, as a result, kings will fall down at his feet and all nations will "serve" him. When a king "rules," enemies "serve."

If we now take another step and empathize with Earth in Genesis 2, we readily appreciate the kinship reflected in this passage between Earth and humans as well as between humans and other living creatures. All creatures are Earth that has become animated. Earth nurtures humans and humans are expected to nurture Earth.

We can also hear the voice of Earth crying behind the divine mandate to dominate in Genesis 1:26-28. Earth says:

> "Why should I be dominated, subdued, and crushed? Why should I be treated as a 'slave' of humans? The verb *kabash* is even used of raping women (Esth. 7:8; Neh. 5:5). Why should I be so treated?
>
> "After all, I was a co-creator with God. I brought forth vegetation and made Earth green. I brought forth from within me all the animals and creeping creatures. Why then should I be humiliated and reduced to being the slave of humans?"

The question remains: Am I, Earth, destined to "serve" humans?

Psalmody
PSALM 8

Psalm 8 has long been a favorite song for church choirs and gospel singers. The opening verses recognize the majestic presence of God in the skies, and hail the heavens themselves as the amazing work of God the Creator. In this glorious cosmos, God's name deserves to be praised with expressions of splendor—even from the mouths of babes.

What excites our human egos, however, is that this majestic God of the heavens has chosen to invest a comparable glory in one of Earth's creatures, namely, human beings. God is portrayed as a celestial king who "visits," "remembers," "crowns," and "transfers dominion" to human beings on Earth. Surely this psalm is a poetic rendition of the *imago Dei* mandate of Genesis 1:26-28! The right of humans to rule as kings over the creatures of Earth is not simply part of the created order, as Genesis 1 might suggest. Instead, this crowning of humans is depicted as a special act of God, namely, the coronation of human beings as God's rulers on Earth.

Here again, the royal language elevates humans to the status of lordship over the natural world. Their dominion extends not only to all living things on the land, in the sea, and in the air, but also to all the work of God's hands. Nothing is excluded. Humans reign supreme over all of creation! By so doing, the natural world is devalued: nature is placed "under the feet" of humans and thereby assumes the position of a slave or a defeated foe. What could be more degrading!

One writer who dares to challenge this glorious—and, dare we say, unrealistic—view of humanity as expressed in Psalm 8 is the author of the book of Job. In Job 7, he declares that humans are in fact the real slaves on Earth, with sad and empty lives, as exemplified by Job (vv. 1-2). They are like "slaves" who long for the shade of evening, like "hirelings" who hope for some wages (v. 2). They are forced to labor on Earth!

Using the very language of Psalm 8, the author of Job insists that God does indeed "visit" humans every morning. Why? To harass and hound them (vv. 17-19)! Job's experience of human existence is precisely the opposite of that depicted in Psalm 8. Elsewhere, Job also accuses God of using his wisdom to "overthrow Earth" (12:13-15). Job, it seems, identifies with Earth. This alternative orientation of Job, however, has generally been ignored in Christian worship. Celebrating the mandate to dominate has been the prevailing mind-set in work and worship.

What if we now follow the cue of Job and identify with Earth and the creatures of Earth in Psalm 8?! All that God has created is here said to be put "under the feet" of human beings. By making slaves of all creation, nature is devalued, humiliated, and relegated to ignominy.

The voice of Earth can no longer be silenced:

> "I am not the pawn, the plaything, or the slave of humans. Those who portray me in this way have misread the mind of the Creator. Return to the story of Genesis 1. What happens on Day Three? God does not simply say: Let there be Earth! No, God summons the waters to part, to burst. Then God calls me to emerge from the waters, to appear like a child being born. Then God names me 'Earth' and invites me to green the landscape. I am God's partner in creating life on Earth. And when I am born, God looks at me and declares, 'Very good!!' God reacts with delight and uses the same words Moses' mother used when her son was born."

So we interpreters are faced with two traditions: one that glories in the role of humans as kings who are given the right to conquer Earth, and one in which God rejoices with Earth as a partner in the creation process. Or, as another psalmist sings: "May YHWH rejoice with his works" (Ps. 104:31).

Second Reading
PHILIPPIANS 2:1-8

Once again, we are faced with a text that has played a major role in Christian theology. Here the mystery of Christ's humiliation and incarnation are often summarized by the term *kenosis*, or "emptying." Precisely what Paul meant by this cryptic phrase has long been debated. A frequent interpretation is that Christ, as the very Son of God, who was in reality God, emptied himself of the divine glory, power, and majesty associated with his divinity, humbled himself, and became a human being like other humans beings, even to the point of dying on a cross.

One of the many traditions associated with this text is the dualistic concept that the *logos* became the human soul of Christ, which means that Christ was not fully human—body and soul. The text, however, makes it clear that Christ Jesus, who has the essential attributes (*morphe*) of God, becomes a genuine human being capable of suffering and dying.

As the risen Christ, however, the name of this humbled human is exalted and becomes the object of praise and veneration by all in heaven and on Earth. The self-humbling of Christ is the supreme example of how his disciples should live, "in humility each regarding others as better than themselves" and "doing nothing from selfish ambition or conceit" (v. 3).

Taking into account the previous readings and the wider context of creation, new insights may be discovered in this text. The first of these insights concerns Psalm 8. Most scholars recognize that Philippians 2:6-11 was originally an early Christian psalm or hymn. As such, the text reflects a deep expression of faith celebrated in early Christian worship. Early Christians not only revered the name of the Risen Christ, they also worshiped with Christ as the emptied and humbled Son of God.

Having reread Psalm 8 with empathy for Earth and the creatures of Earth, we may recognize how this Philippians hymn reverses the imagery of Psalm 8 and to some extent reflects the orientation of Earth. This human called Jesus Christ not only divests himself of the royal majesty, power, and rule of God, but in so doing becomes a true human being, a humble servant. And that image of a genuine human being is the radical opposite of the image in Psalm 8. In Christ, the image of humans as royal overlords in creation is countered. Christ is himself the true *imago Dei*; as such, he exposes the deficiency of the claim that the *imago Dei* involves dominion and royal lordship as an integral part of being human.

Another insight we may discern involves the term slave or servant. Christ not only becomes a human being, he also becomes a slave! Some disciples may have wanted to hail Jesus as a king, like the Messiah promised of old. Jesus, however, is no typical human king, but a servant like the first human in the garden of Eden. And Paul enjoins his people to have the same mind as Jesus, the mind of a servant. From the point of view of Earth, this servant mind-set may well imply that humans also ought to serve Earth and not, as Paul says, to focus "on your own interests."

The full implications of the incarnation celebrated in this hymn may only be fully appreciated when we recognize what we noted above about our nature as Earth beings. A human being is made of Earth—soil, atmosphere, water, and more. By becoming flesh, as John reminds us (John 1:14), the *logos* or Word "becomes" an integral part of Earth. Jesus Christ may well be the Son of God, but the idea of "being found in a human form" means that he is also a child of Earth, an Earth being. As such, Christ is also a servant of Earth.

Gospel
MARK 10:41-45

Many of us recall preachers berating James and John, the sons of Zebedee—and their ilk—for daring to ask Jesus for the right to sit with him in glory! Presumptuous, indeed! They anticipated a day when they would share the glory—one on the right and one on the left hand of Christ. Naturally, the other disciples were rather upset. They were also probably ambitious and wanted some of the glory.

Jesus intervened with a famous speech that put the disciples in their place. In the past, the emphasis has generally been on the need to rethink our relationship to Christ. And rightly so! We are to follow the example of Christ and learn to serve rather than sit in glory. We are to follow the way of the cross rather than anticipate the day of glory!

The example of Christ, moreover, is an expression of the very essence of the gospel. His coming to "serve" is explicitly linked to his role as redeemer. He is ready to live and die, giving his life as a ransom for "many"—meaning all! His life is one of absolute sacrifice and service for others.

There has been some contemporary debate about the precise meaning of "ransom." Traditionally, this term has been viewed as a particular expression of the atonement, namely, that Jesus Christ, through his voluntary sacrifice of himself on the cross once and for all on behalf of and instead of sinful humanity, made satisfaction for the sins of the world and restored communion between God and humanity.

If we now read these words of Jesus in the context of our earlier readings, the implications of Jesus coming to "serve" are even more forceful. Jesus speaks of himself as "the Son of Man"! The background to this title is the vision of Daniel 7. In that vision, the Son of Man or Son of Adam is given dominion, glory, and kingship so that all peoples "serve" him.

However, Jesus reverses the royal concepts associated with the title Son of Man. As the Son of Man, Jesus has chosen to "serve" and not to "rule" like the royal figure in Daniel. As the Son of Man—that is, as representative of "humanity"—he does not claim the royal rights of the first humans in Genesis 1:26-28. Rather, he assumes the status of servant as reflected in Genesis 2:15. Jesus interprets what it means to be a genuine human being—to serve rather than to rule.

The contrast between ruler and servant is also made explicit when Jesus condemns the rulers among the Gentiles who "lord" it over their people and whose so-called great ones are tyrants. By contrast, the way of Christ and those who follow him is the way of serving—being ready to become "slave of all." Here Jesus endorses the mission of the first humans in Genesis 2:15 and repudiates the mandate to dominate in Genesis 1:26-28.

When Christ comes to serve and to give his life for many, does that include more than humans? If so, then the implication of Jesus' words is that as human beings we, too, are called to be servants of Earth. Christ renews our commission to nurture nature.

Another occasion when Jesus reflects the same point of view is on the mount of transfiguration. When surrounded by glory on the mountain, Jesus rejects the suggestion of Peter that tabernacles be erected there for posterity. Rather, Jesus goes quietly down the mountain to be with those in need, reminding his disciples that he has come to experience suffering rather than glory (Mark 9:2-13).

One more implication deserves consideration. If, as we see from unambiguous New Testament texts, Jesus is indeed the true expression of the image of God (for example, Col. 1:15), then his portrayal of himself as "one who serves" rather than as "one who rules" makes it clear that the concept of the *imago Dei* in Genesis 1:26-28 has been overridden and the *imago Dei* in Genesis 2 has been affirmed. Those who reflect the way of Christ as the full revelation of the image of God will not rule creatures and subdue creation. Instead, they will serve and preserve the planet.

Reflections

To rule or to serve? The gospel messages we have uncovered in the New Testament readings for Humanity Sunday make it clear that we are called to serve creation rather than rule and subdue it. We have a commitment to nurture this planet rather than exploit it. That commitment flows from the very gospel message spoken by Christ himself, the true image of God.

RESOURCES

Carley, Keith. "An Apology for Domination," in *Readings from the Perspective of Earth*, ed. Norman C. Habel, The Earth Bible, vol. 1:111–24. Cleveland: Pilgrim, 2001.

Garr, W. Randall. *In His Own Image and Likeness: Humanity, Divinity, and Monotheism.* Leiden: Brill, 2003.

Habel, Norman C. "Playing God or Playing Earth? An Ecological Reading of Genesis 1:26-28," in *"And God Saw That It Was Good": Essays on Creation and God in Honor of Terrence E. Fretheim*, 33–41. Word and World Supplement Series 5. St. Paul: Luther Seminary, 2006.

———. *An Inconvenient Text: Is a Green Reading of the Bible Possible?* Adelaide: ATF, 2009.

Limburg, James. "Who Cares for the Earth? Psalm Eight and the Environment," in *All Things New*, ed. A. J. Hultgren, et al., 43–52. Word and World Supplement Series 1. St. Paul: Luther Seminary, 1991.

Palmer, Clare. "Stewardship: A Case Study in Environmental Ethics," in *The Earth Beneath: A Critical Guide to Green Theology*, ed. Ian Ball, et al., 67–86. London: SPCK, 1992.

Santmire, H. Paul. *Nature Reborn: The Ecological and Cosmic Promise of Christian Theology.* Theology and the Sciences. Minneapolis: Fortress Press, 2000.

Suzuki, David, and Kathy Vanderlinden. *You Are the Earth.* Sydney: NSW, 1999.

Season of Creation (2011). http://www.seasonofcreation.com (accessed March 2011). Dramatized readings of Genesis 1:26-28; Genesis 2:7-8, 15, 19; and Mark 10:42-45 are included on the Web site in one version of the liturgy for Humanity Sunday.

Third Sunday in Creation

Sky Sunday

Susan Miller

Jeremiah 4:23-28
Psalm 19:1-6
Philippians 2:14-18
Mark 15:33-39

Background

This Season of Creation commentary that celebrates Sky Sunday seeks to develop an ecological reading of several passages featuring the sky, along with the sun, moon, and stars. These accounts point to the beauty of the expanse of skies and celebrate both light and darkness. In the Bible, the term *heavens* is used both for the physical location of the skies and for the dwelling place of God. The heavens and the Earth frequently appear together as a phrase describing the created world. At the beginning of Genesis, God creates the heavens and the Earth. God's first act of creation is the separation of light from darkness, and the alternation of evening and morning forms the first day. God creates the sun to rule the day and the moon to rule the night, and they are placed in the dome of the sky to give light to the Earth. God dwells in the heavens, whereas human beings live on Earth. In Genesis 2, God forms Adam from the dust of the ground and breathes into him the breath of life. Human beings are formed from the clay of the Earth and are thus aligned with the Earth. The skies are associated with the divine, spiritual realm, and the Earth is linked with the material realm.

The association of God with the skies may be seen in the book of Exodus when Moses climbs Mount Sinai to receive the law from God.

On the third day, God appears, accompanied by thunder and lightning, and a thick cloud covers the earth. Mount Sinai is wrapped in smoke and the mountain shakes violently. The transcendence of God is indicated by the cloud of darkness, and no one is able to see God. Other passages, however, refer to the dwelling of God being among the people of Israel, as Exodus states: "I will dwell among the Israelites, and I will be their God" (Exod. 29:45; cf. 1 Kgs. 6:13). The prophets associate the injustices they see around them with the absence of God, and they look to the skies for the intervention of God: "O that you would tear open the heavens and come down" (Isa. 64:1). In prophetic texts, the hope that God will dwell with human beings on Earth becomes an eschatological expectation, as exemplified in the prophecy of Zechariah: "Sing and rejoice, O daughter Zion! For lo, I will come and dwell in your midst, says the LORD" (Zech. 2:10). In prophetic texts, the advent of God on the day of the Lord is described in terms of the darkening of the skies and the falling away of the sun, moon, and stars (Isa. 13:10; Jer. 4:23-28; Joel 2:10; Amos 8:9-10).

The contrast between the skies and the Earth is highlighted in apocalyptic writings in which the Earth is ruled by evil. In texts such as 1 Enoch, seers are taken up to the heavenly world to receive the secrets of the end time. In Mark, an apocalyptic worldview is illustrated at the beginning of the Gospel when Jesus is baptized. The skies are torn apart, the Spirit descends, and a voice from heaven addresses Jesus: "You are my Son, the Beloved; with you I am well pleased" (1:11). In Matthew's Gospel, Jesus proclaims the kingdom of heaven, and he teaches his disciples to pray for the coming of the kingdom: "Our Father in heaven, hallowed be your name. Your kingdom come. Your will be done, on earth as it is in heaven" (6:9-10). Jesus seeks a union of heaven and earth in his desire that God's will might be done on Earth. He seeks an integral spirituality in which there is a unity of the spiritual and material realms.

Today we face an ecological crisis in which pollution poisons the air and global climate change threatens the skies and the Earth. The readings selected for Sky Sunday seek to examine the significance of the skies. To what extent are these texts able to speak to us in relation to current ecological debates? Has our focus on prosperity on Earth led us to ignore the harm being done to the skies? Biblical descriptions of the skies have been regarded as a mere backdrop to divine and human action. This is not the case, however, as we will see. The following reflections focus on the participation of the skies in the biblical drama and aim to interpret the passages from the perspective of the skies. We will identify with the point of view of the skies in our interpretation of these texts, and we will seek to discover new insights from an ecological reading of the passages.

First Reading
JEREMIAH 4:23-28

Our first reading is a prophecy from Jeremiah describing the devastation of the land. The Earth becomes waste and void, and there is no light in the heavens. The mountains quake and the hills move to and fro. There are no human beings to be seen and the birds of the air have fled—indicating the desolation of the scene. The prophet is the sole survivor looking on the destruction. The fruitful land is now a desert, and the cities, which are regarded as the pinnacle of human civilization, have been laid in ruins. The totality of the devastation is emphasized in the references to "all its cities," "the whole land," and "all the birds." Jeremiah's prophecy suggests a return to the situation of the chaos that was present at the beginning of creation. The phrase "waste and void" is reminiscent of the creation account of Genesis, in which the world is described as "a formless void" before God brings creation into being (Gen. 1:2). The absence of light recalls the darkness in Genesis before God creates light on the first day. In Genesis, God looks at each stage of creation, and proclaims it to be good. In Jeremiah, however, the prophet looks at each stage of destruction in horror.

The prophet states that the devastation of the cities has occurred before the fierce anger of the Lord. This verse raises the question of the responsibility of the Lord for the destruction of the Earth. To what extent does the Lord wish to destroy the land and the cities? As noted above, the darkening of the skies is often linked to the judgment of God on the day of the Lord. Isaiah 13:10 includes a prophecy of the darkening of the heavens: "For the stars of the heavens and their constellations will not give their light; the sun will be dark at its rising, and the moon will not shed its light." The prophet speaks of divine retribution for the injustice and idolatry of humanity. God is unwilling to stand back and permit human injustice to continue. From the perspective of the skies, this interpretation portrays the natural world as the innocent victim of the Lord's anger. The destruction, however, may also be interpreted as a result of historical events, since armies from the north have come to conquer Jerusalem and the land of Judea. The battles of human beings have led to the devastation of the land, and human beings are responsible for the destruction of the cities. The warfare of human beings has caused the darkening of the heavens. Smoke obscures the skies, and the pollution of war fills the air, with the result that the birds flee.

Jeremiah prophesies that the Lord will not permit the complete destruction of the Earth: " . . . yet I will not make a full end" (v. 27). The Lord's care for humanity and for the Earth prevents total destruction; nevertheless, there will be a period of mourning. The prophet states that the Earth mourns and the heavens become black. The natural cycle of day and evening is broken. Light is necessary for the emergence and sustenance of life. The silence of the heavens is ominous and the absence of the sound of the birds points to the desolation of the scene. The prophet looks on, powerless to intervene. In this passage, the skies may be interpreted as a subject who mourns the loss of life and the devastation of the land. In Jeremiah, both the Earth and the skies mourn on account of the injustice of human beings. In an ecological perspective, the human and the natural worlds are interconnected. The act of mourning aligns the natural world with the suffering of human beings. A period of mourning is necessary to acknowledge the loss of life and the devastation of creation. A time of mourning is also needed before life can begin again. The land takes time to recover, and crops require time to grow.

Jeremiah's account of the desolation of the Earth may also be interpreted as a rhetorical passage that emphasizes the horror of war and the consequences of human injustice. God's fierce anger is intended to arouse a human response of repentance. Today the warfare of human beings leads to the darkening of the skies and the destruction of the land in many places. Chemical and nuclear weapons threaten the environment, and it is now possible for human beings to cause the complete devastation of Earth. When we read from the perspective of the skies, we see the ways in which the skies and the Earth suffer on account of the destructive actions of human beings. In Jeremiah, the skies and the Earth mourn, while human beings continue to commit idolatry and injustice. The prophet emphasizes the interconnectedness of the human, the animal, and the natural worlds. His prophecy is situated in the midst of a plea for Israel to return to the Lord. The prophet speaks of a God-centered world rather than a world with human beings at the center. Jeremiah cries out for truth, justice, and righteousness, and for the care of orphans and the poor. This passage leaves us with a call to seek peace founded on justice, and to take action to prevent the further destruction of the Earth.

Psalmody
PSALM 19:1-6

Psalm 19 begins with a description of the skies and then celebrates the creative power of God. The skies tell the glory of God, and the firmament proclaims God's handiwork. In ancient cosmology, the firmament refers to a dome-shaped covering placed over the Earth that separates the heavenly waters from the earthly waters (Gen. 1:6-8). In our passage, the glory of God is associated with the power and majesty of God in the heavens. The glory of God is linked with the presence of God in the Temple (Isa. 6:1-5); yet the skies are also depicted as a temple that houses the glory of God (Ps. 11:4). In Psalm 19, the skies chart the progress from the light of day to the darkness of night. For the psalmist, the changing of light and darkness testifies to the power of God. Day turns to day; and the change in the heavens over time is regarded as speech. Similarly, night to night declares the knowledge of God.

In this passage, the skies are depicted as a subject with its own voice. The skies have no need of human speech, since the changing of light and darkness is itself speech. In ancient thought, the movement of the planets and the stars was believed to create music in the skies unheard by human beings. The music pointed to the harmony of the heavenly world. From an ecological perspective, these verses indicate that creation has a voice, and the skies proclaim the glory of God throughout the world. The cycle of light and darkness reaches to the ends of the world and expresses the order and stability of creation. The passage is not centered on human beings, since the skies do not speak in the language of human beings. Nevertheless, human beings are able to learn from the worship carried out by the skies; from this worship, human beings receive knowledge of God's creative power.

The skies are associated with festivity and joy. The sun is compared to a bridegroom who emerges from his wedding canopy and to a strong man who runs his course with joy. The sun is portrayed in masculine terms, as a bridegroom or as a strong man, and its power is given masculine qualities as well. In ancient cosmology, the moon is frequently depicted in feminine terms. Some religions view the sun and the moon as gods. The sun and the moon bring light to the world. In Psalm 19, light is not regarded more positively than darkness. Both light and darkness and their changing cycle bear testimony to God. The positive portrayal of darkness is highlighted in the verse that says, "night to night declares knowledge" (v. 2). The whole created world worships God. The celebration of the skies and the Earth is followed by the description of the law given to humanity. The glory of God is present in creation and the law; and the description of the law is reminiscent of the qualities of the sun, because the law brings joy to the heart—it is clear, and it enlightens the eyes. The psalmist teaches that the ordinances of the Lord are "more to be desired are they than gold . . . sweeter also than honey" (v. 10). The description of fine gold and the sweet honeycomb recalls the golden color of the shining sun. The psalmist builds connections between the glory of the skies and the will of God for humanity; as such, the orderliness of the skies is reflected in the righteousness of human beings.

Second Reading
PHILIPPIANS 2:14-18

Paul's letter to the Philippians focuses on the experience of joy in the midst of suffering. Paul writes from prison, and he does not know whether or not he is about to face death. His faith, however, leads him to regard his own death positively, because he will soon be able to see Christ. Yet he also wishes to live, so that he might continue his work as a missionary. In this situation, Paul exhorts the Philippians to rejoice in the midst of their own persecution and suffering. Paul does not give a description of the location of his prison, but it is possible that he is writing from Rome near the end of his life. He assures the Philippians that his imprisonment on account of his faith in Christ has become known throughout the imperial guard, and this situation has helped others to proclaim the gospel. In our passage, Paul wishes the Philippians to stand firm in their own suffering, and he exhorts them to be blameless and innocent. The Philippians are urged to be "children of God without blemish in the midst of a crooked and perverse generation," and to "shine like stars in the world" (v. 15). In this passage, human beings are taught to imitate the qualities of the natural world. The stars are invincible and unchanging, and they bring light in the midst of darkness. Paul would like the Philippians to hold on to the word of life and thereby to bring light to their opponents.

Paul's statement is reminiscent of a passage from Daniel that also urges human beings to shine like the stars in the skies. Daniel writes: "Those who are wise shall shine like the brightness of the sky, and those who lead many to righteousness like the stars forever and ever" (12:3).

Daniel speaks of a time of great suffering before the end of the age, and he prophesies the deliverance of his people. Those who rise from the dead are compared to the stars that shine in the heavens. In other texts, such as Isaiah 42:6, Israel is instructed to bring light to the Gentiles: "I have given you as a covenant to the people, a light to the nations." This passage also highlights the power of light to overcome opposition, since the light of the people of Israel will attract their former enemies.

In Paul's letter, the stars are portrayed as an image of protest and defiance. The stars continue to shine in the darkness, and the Philippian Christians continue to bear witness to the word of life despite the opposition they encounter. The stars do not hide in the heavens but shine brightly in the darkness, bringing light to the world. The shining stars, however, are also related to the theme of celebration in the letter. Paul is glad and rejoices with all of the Philippians, and he urges them to be glad and rejoice with him during his own suffering. Paul, moreover, believes that the opposition he encounters is a sign that the gospel is spreading and taking effect in the world. The reference to the stars points to the power of God who brought the world into being. Stars can be seen throughout the world and are therefore examples of steadfastness and power. They are images of nonviolent resistance, and they symbolize the determination of the community to stand firm in the midst of persecution, thereby bringing light to the world.

Gospel
MARK 15:33-39

Mark's Gospel gives a bleak and terse account of the crucifixion of Jesus that emphasizes the desolation of the scene. Jesus has been tried before the religious authorities and then condemned by Pilate. He is taken to Golgotha, the place of the skull, and crucified alongside two other men. At noon, darkness descends over the Earth until three o'clock in the afternoon (v. 33). Mark, however, does not give any explanation for the darkening of the skies, and no human being shows any awareness of the darkness. There have been attempts to find natural causes to account for this description of darkness at the crucifixion. The timing of the darkness at noon is unusual, since this hour of day is regarded as the time when the sun shines most brightly. In Luke's Gospel, the descent of darkness at the crucifixion is described as an eclipse (Luke 23:45). In Mark, by contrast, the three hours of darkness indicate a longer period of time than an eclipse, and Mark implies that the darkness at the crucifixion covers a wider area of land. It is probable that Mark intends the account of the three hours of darkness to have theological significance.

In Mark's Gospel, the darkening of the skies has been interpreted as an indication of the anger of God at the rejection of Jesus. As we have noted in our analysis of Jeremiah 4:23-28, the descent of darkness is associated with descriptions of the events that take place on the day of the Lord. God's anger at the rejection of Jesus brings judgment on the Earth; in this interpretation, the Earth becomes the object of God's wrath. When we examine this passage from the perspective of the skies, however, the descent of darkness at the crucifixion may be interpreted as the response of the skies to the death of Jesus. Mark emphasizes the isolation of Jesus by describing the mocking of Jesus on the part of the passersby who challenge him to save himself and come down from the cross. The chief priests taunt him, and even the two men crucified with him revile him (15:29-32). The male disciples have fled at the arrest of Jesus, and they are not present at the crucifixion. The women who followed him from Galilee stand at a distance, and Jesus is unaware of their presence. The three hours of darkness stress the bleakness and cruelty of the crucifixion. The skies are aligned with the suffering and the isolation of Jesus.

Mark alludes to Amos 8:9-10, a passage in which darkness at noon is associated with the mourning of an only son. There, the prophet states the word of the Lord: "I will make the sun go down at noon, and darken the earth in broad daylight. . . . I will make it like the mourning for an only son, and the end of it like a bitter day." Darkness may thus be associated with the mourning of the skies. The skies are not a mere background to human events but an integral part of the web of the human and natural world. This passage expresses the interconnectedness of all human, animal, and natural life, and the skies mourn the death of Jesus. In other texts, darkness is associated with the mourning of a prominent figure. Darkness descends at the death of Enoch (*2 Enoch* 67), and darkness also occurs for a period of seven days at the death of Adam, a period of time that recalls the creation of the world in seven days (*Testament of Adam* 3:6). The skies mourn Jesus' death, and darkness corresponds to the suffering of Jesus. Whereas human beings reject Jesus and fail to support him, the skies empathize with his suffering.

The interpretation of the descent of darkness as the mourning of the skies at the death of Jesus is supported by the account of the tearing of the temple veil from top to bottom (15:38). The action of tearing material is linked to mourning, as shown, for example, in the account of Elisha, who tears his garments at the passing of Elijah (2 Kgs. 2:12). In Mark's Gospel, the high priest tears his robe when Jesus confesses his identity as the Messiah, the Son of the Blessed One (14:63); his action is a sign of mourning, because he believes that Jesus has committed blasphemy. Josephus states that the temple veil was made up of four colors representing the four elements of the universe (*Jewish War* 5.212-215). The tearing of the temple veil thus represents the mourning of the whole creation at the death of Jesus.

In Mark's Gospel, the descent of darkness may also be interpreted as a protest. The darkening of the skies disrupts the cycle of light and darkness necessary to sustain life on Earth. Darkness is linked to death, and light is associated with life. Light is obscured, and the darkness indicates judgment on human actions. In apocalyptic texts, darkness is associated with the end of the world. In Mark's Gospel, Jesus prophesies the events associated with his *parousia*: ". . . the sun will be darkened, and the moon will not gives its light, and the stars will be falling from heaven, and the powers in the heavens will be shaken" (13:24-25). Here, Jesus alludes to the aforementioned prophecies from the Old Testament concerning the day of the Lord. The failure of the sun, moon, and stars is an image of cataclysm. The death of Jesus foreshadows the events associated with the end of the world. Mark 13 refers to wars and rumors of wars, to earthquakes, and to famines. The disruption of the natural world corresponds to the suffering and persecution of the disciples. These events are signs that the present age is being torn apart. In Mark 13, however, these cataclysmic events are followed by the return of Jesus. Hope of new life is also indicated by the parable of the fig tree that begins to bloom (13:28). The darkening of the skies may be interpreted as a protest, since the skies intervene to bring the suffering of Jesus and the injustice in the world to an end. The descent of darkness at noon is unnatural, and crucifixion illustrates the depths of human cruelty. The descent of darkness over the Earth is a protest against human violence.

Darkness lasts throughout the suffering of Jesus until the time of his death, when he cries out, "My God, my God, why have you forsaken me?" (v. 34). Jesus himself appears to be engulfed in darkness. The death of Jesus is depicted as a turning point, and the Roman centurion is the first human being who recognizes him as the Son of God (v. 39). The darkness at the cross recalls the darkness at the beginning of the account of creation in Genesis. In other apocalyptic texts, the old creation returns to darkness before the new age begins (*4 Ezra* 6:39, 7:30; *Life of Adam and Eve* 46:1-2). In Genesis, darkness is an image of chaos, and the first act of God is the creation of light out of darkness. In Mark's Gospel, the death of Jesus is a return to the chaos present at the beginning of creation, and the movement from darkness to light points to the emergence of the new age. The giving of Jesus' life paradoxically brings new life, and his death and resurrection correspond to the movement from darkness to light. The darkness at the crucifixion ends at the death of Jesus, since the power of death is broken by the resurrection of Jesus.

Reflections

These passages focus on the skies, and they depict the ways in which the sun, moon, and stars worship and bear witness to God. In Psalm 19, the skies have a celebratory voice, and the cycle of light and darkness proclaims the goodness of creation. In Jeremiah and in Mark's Gospel, the darkening of the skies occurs as a response to the injustice of humanity. The skies are not presented as the backdrop to human action; on the contrary, they have their own voice. The skies, the Earth, the human and the animal world are all interconnected, and the darkened skies mourn the loss of natural and human life. In Jeremiah, God intervenes to prevent the cataclysmic destruction of the Earth. In Mark's Gospel, there is no indication that anyone is aware of the darkness that covers the land at the crucifixion of Jesus. The skies mourn the suffering of Jesus and protest against human cruelty. The darkening of the skies also suggests a return to the chaos present at the beginning of creation. The light returns after Jesus has died and points to the new creation. The return of light is not a resumption of normal life, because now the power has been broken. God brings light out of darkness, and Jesus has overcome death on the cross.

An ecological reading of these passages raises questions about human responses to current threats to the skies and the environment. In Philippians, the church is exhorted to be blameless and innocent and to shine like stars in the world. Paul's words today urge us to be innocent of any charges of harming the environment. The Philippians are asked to stand firm in the face of opposition. This passage urges us to protest against any harm done to the natural world and to seek ways of enabling the skies and the Earth to flourish. An ecological interpretation of the passages celebrating Sky Sunday thus calls the church to bring light to current ecological debates.

RESOURCES

Dorr, Donal. *Integral Spirituality: Resources for Community, Justice, Peace and the Earth.* Maryknoll, N.Y.: Orbis, 1990.

Grey, Mary C. *Sacred Longings: Ecofeminist Theology and Globalization.* London: SCM, 2003.

Habel, Norman C., and Peter Trudinger, eds. *Exploring Ecological Hermeneutics.* Atlanta: Society of Biblical Literature, 2008.

Habel, Norman C., ed. *Readings from the Perspective of Earth.* Sheffield, UK: Sheffield Academic, 2000.

McDonagh, Sean. *The Greening of the Church.* Maryknoll, N.Y.: Orbis, 1990.

Fourth Sunday in Creation

Mountain Sunday

H. Paul Santmire

Isaiah 65:17-25
Psalm 48:1-11
Romans 8:28-39
Mark 16:14-18

Background

An image of a "cosmic mountain" figures prominently in religious practices throughout the ages and in attendant mythic narratives. Mount Olympus is perhaps the best-known mountain from ancient times. Mount Sinai and Mount Zion figure prominently in the narratives of the Hebrew Bible. In primal cultures, the cosmic mountain was often understood not only as the home of the gods, but also as a kind of cosmic umbilical cord that joined the heavens to the Earth.[1] While much of the mythic aura of the cosmic-mountain theme disappeared in time, especially during periods of modernization, that aura is still detectable in some modernized, even secularized societies.

Thus, in nineteenth-century America, the transcendentalist naturalist and philosopher Henry David Thoreau invested an enormous spiritual currency in the theme "wildness," which he identified with his Massachusetts retreat in Walden, but just as significantly with settings like Maine's mythic mountain Katadyn, about which Thoreau wrote one of his most important essays. Following in Thoreau's footsteps, the American naturalist and advocate for national parks, John Muir, wrote widely about mountains, such as his volume *The Mountains of California*, in which he identified human health, and vitality, and religious meaning with sensitive immersion in mountain wildernesses.[2] The heritage of the cosmic mountain is still evident in the spiritually charged experiences many backpackers and climbers seek, as they attempt to get away from what they perceive to be the superficialities of modern industrial and cybernetic society, and of modern cities in particular, in search of a more authentic engagement with Earth and its vitalities. Even city dwellers, who may know mountain wilderness areas mainly from television or from the paintings of artists such as the Hudson River School, often have a deep spiritual desire to "get away from it all" and to do so in quest of some kind of imagined or even drug-induced "mountaintop experience."

Those who seek to identify and to celebrate the sacredness of mountains need to be aware of ancient mythic meanings of the cosmic mountain and of more modern meanings attached to the "mountaintop experience" in the traditions of Thoreau, Muir, and their more contemporary popularizers. As a matter of course, North American congregations will be heirs to such traditions long before they participate in Mountain Sunday worship in the Season of Creation.

It is critically important for interpreting the meaning of mountains to be aware both of the geographical locations and of the social locations of those who are to hear sermons on the subject. A small-businessman in Ohio who needs electricity from a coal-fired power plant will have a different "social construction" of the mountain theme than residents of a valley village in West Virginia who have been forced to live with poisoned waters and desecrated lands resulting from "mountaintop removal" by a multinational coal company. A college student from Colorado who has traveled to Vail to ski in the Rockies will have yet another take on the meaning of mountains.

More critically, the culture of the mountain theme in the United States has often masked a profoundly destructive social ideology. The American historian Perry Miller refers to America as "nature's nation." And by that, he means that American history has carried within it a kind of schizophrenia, which has pitted the vitalities of the wild mountain areas of the country against the alleged impurities and corruptions of the city. Frequently, the quest for the mountaintop experience in the United States has presupposed an underlying rejection of any interest in justice for the poor or other marginalized groups who have lived mostly in cities.

On the other hand, what might be called an anthropocentric ethos has also been in evidence in Western culture, sometimes with a destructive impact on wilderness areas. Augustine of Hippo gave voice to this kind of sentiment in the late fourth century in his *Confessions*,[3] in which he pilloried those who go out to be amazed by the oceans or the mountains but who fail to turn within themselves to what was for him their true treasure, namely their souls, in order to find meaning in life. The famous fourteenth-century humanist, Petrarch, made that very Augustinian theme his own when, upon descending Mount Ventoux in southern France, he announced that the greatest glory of the world is not such a mountain, but the human soul. In the modern period, such perspectives were picked up and transvalued by the rising tides of industrialism, whose champions, even including radicals like Karl Marx, viewed nature as only "the means of production" and who in our own time do not hesitate, therefore, to move whole mountains in search of coal.

This, then, raises the question: Who will advocate for and celebrate the sacrality of mountains without being caught up in the dynamics of the aforementioned American cultural schizophrenia—on the one hand, to adore mountains at the expense of social justice in the cities or, on the other hand, to celebrate the progress of civilization at the expense of desecrating wild nature, and mountains in particular? Finding a "third way" between these trends will be a huge challenge for any biblical interpreter today.

First Reading
ISAIAH 65:17-25

It is generally agreed that this text is from the testimony of Third Isaiah (TI), chapters 56–66 of the book of Isaiah; the names First Isaiah (FI) and Second Isaiah (SI) refer to the materials collected in chapters 1–39 and chapters 40–55, respectively. The testimonies of TI may have been composed just before and after the restoration of the Temple, following the Babylonian exile (c. 515 B.C.E.). A number of scholars believe that a move away from classical prophecy, as evident in FI and SI, toward a more apocalyptic way of thinking, can be detected in TI. Evidence for this would be the admixture of various themes in our passage, namely, the apocalyptic motif of the new heavens and the new Earth combined with the more prophetic images of the renewal of historical Jerusalem and the land of Israel.

Of the numerous textual and hermeneutical questions this text poses, the issue of apocalypticism is perhaps the most important. An apocalyptic way of thinking is generally thought to mean the annihilation of the old world and the birth of a totally new world. Such a vision, notwithstanding its positive cosmic outcome, seems to suggest a kind of nihilism with regard to the world as we know it and therefore will not foster positive regard for Earth today. This kind of apocalypticism, indeed, has informed the popular "Left Behind" novels in our time. According to this way of thinking, the chosen few are "raptured" up to heaven, while Earth and all its inhabitants are doomed to hellfire and damnation.[4] Call this extreme apocalypticism. Are we encountering this kind of vision, even by implication, in the testimony of TI to the new heavens and the new Earth?

That seems unlikely. To begin with, the text itself is full of allusions to the restoration of prosperity to the land of Israel as it would have been known in the time of TI. The envisioned peace of the new world, centered on Jerusalem, entails mundane blessings like the end of infant mortality; no loss of life due to war or other political causes; indeed, long life for all the people. The land will be fruitful. People will not labor in vain. Violence in nature will be a thing of the past. The wolf and the lamb shall feed together. Such images represent a this-worldly vision. The idea of annihilation of the current world could not be further from the prophet's mind. The image of the world that this prophet expects fits well the classical theological image of the coming of the peaceable kingdom on Earth.

In addition, there appears to be a close relationship between Isaiah 65 and the world-affirming vision of the so-called little apocalypse of Isaiah (chaps. 24–27). TI seems to have drawn on the vision of these prophetic oracles by an unknown prophet, who spoke or wrote in the school of FI and SI. Reference to these materials is helpful, as a matter of fact, not only to underline the this-worldly character of TI's vision, but also more clearly to reveal TI's view of the Jerusalem Temple, Mount Zion, as the center of the renewed Earth and of the renewed human world he envisioned: "On this mountain the LORD of hosts will make for all peoples a feast of rich food. . . . And he will destroy on this mountain the shroud that is cast over all peoples. . . . he will swallow up death forever. . . . [L]et us be glad and rejoice in his salvation. For the hand of the LORD will rest on this mountain" (Isa. 25:6-10).

At the same time, the world-affirming vision of TI expands far beyond Jerusalem and its world to the entire creation. Some would argue that this vision represents expansion to the breaking point and that it is precisely this kind of vision that opens the door to some kind of world-negating apocalypticism. However, such does not appear to be the case here. In continuity with FI, who envisioned the whole Earth full of the divine glory (Isa. 6:3), and SI, who envisioned the God of Israel measuring all the waters of the Earth, weighing the mountains, and stretching out the heavens like a curtain (Isa. 40:12-23), TI sees the God of Israel as the God of the whole creation. This is a God who continuously creates and who, as a glorious extension and consummation of that creativity, will one day, finally, create a new heavens and a new Earth—a cosmos of justice and peace for all creatures, at the center of which a gloriously renewed cosmic mountain, a new Jerusalem, will be a delight for all peoples of Earth.

How is that glorious cosmic future to be realized? And when? Those are questions that TI does not seek to answer in the oracles available to us.

Psalmody
PSALM 48:1-11

This pericope from one of ancient Israel's "Songs of Zion" may have been sung by pilgrims at a temple festival in Jerusalem. It takes us into the heart of the ritual practices of the biblical nation. Psalm 48 can be cautiously dated to a time before the exile, although, as a matter of course, it has been part of Israel's prayer book, and later the church's prayer book, ever since. Indeed, Psalm 48 can be read as a powerful poetic expression of themes we have already encountered in the first reading from Isaiah, particularly the references to the Temple, Mount Zion.

Numbers of Christians, particularly Protestants, have had an uneasy relationship with such texts, mainly because of their cultic orientation. In this psalm, there is a significant focus on the Jerusalem Temple and, by implication, on its regular and seasonal rites. Some Christians have tended to defer to prophetic critiques of the cult, such as those by Amos (for example, Amos 5:20-21). And, if these believers have had some interest in Israel's creation faith, they have viewed that faith mainly through the lens of a prophetic polemic (for example, Amos 4:13). However, this is by no means an error of judgment.

Interpreters of the Songs of Zion, such as Psalm 48, must surely keep that prophetic critique in mind, especially when they encounter the ideology of human kingship in songs that are sometimes being conflated with the theology of Mount Zion. But, as most biblical scholars today assure us, the prophetic critique of the cult (shared by TI and his predecessors in the school of Isaiah) was precisely that, a critique—and by no means a rejection. Our passage, indeed, incorporates a kind of prophetic critique of its own, in testimony to what it envisions as the cosmic power of the one Creator God; that is, the reference to the "far north" in the latter part of verse 1 appears to be pointing to the Canaanite mountain of the gods, which, in the psalmist's eyes, has been replaced by the faith in the Creator God celebrated in the Temple.

What are we to make of what might be called this cultic concentration? To put the answer sharply, from the perspective of this Song of Zion, the strong implication is that the people of Israel have the right kind of creation faith only when they participate in the right kind of temple rituals. Processions of praise, such as walking around God's beautiful and holy mountain on which is located the Temple, shape the people's faith in the Creator God and thus equip them to put the purposes of the Creator God first in everything they do. The psalmist takes this for granted: right cultic acknowledgment of God and righteous living go hand in hand. Importantly for the psalmist, however, the correct cultic acknowledgment of God also brings with it the rejection of idolatry.

Today's interpreters of psalms such as this one may therefore be doubly challenged, not only to identify ways to foster and to shape public, communal rituals that glorify the Creator God, but also to find ways to encourage and embolden the faithful to reject the idolatries that these worshipers will inevitably bring with them as they seek to hold on to both allegiances—to God and to idols, to God and to Mammon.

Second Reading
ROMANS 8:28-39

The eighth chapter of Romans has moved to the center of discussions among Christians in our time. Many have come to understand that Paul's proclamation of the "groaning of the whole creation" (8:22) carries with it a powerful message for a world burdened with fears of our global ecological crisis. This text may be as important for us in our era as Romans 1:17, concerning justification by faith, was for Luther and his followers in the sixteenth century. Given the current popularity of Romans 8, however, church and other scholarly interpreters must exercise all the more care in their studies of this text.

In saying this much, we have already touched on what may be, for some, a new platform on which to build our interpretations of Paul. Until very recently, Luther's approach to Paul's theology, and to Romans in particular, had carried the day, at least as far as his theological heirs were concerned, numbers of whom were leading biblical scholars in their respective eras. Luther's approach involved the idea that the central construct of Romans is justification by faith. No scholar worth his or her salt today will deny the validity of Luther's approach to Paul in response to the crises of Luther's own time. But many scholarly interpreters of Paul's theology have taught us to see that Paul's concerns in Romans are much broader than were Luther's.

Paul, it appears, took the whole narrative of faith bequeathed to him by the Hebrew Scriptures with utmost seriousness, from the Genesis creation narratives, through the calling of Abraham and the people of Israel to be a light to the nations, to God's sending Jesus in order to inaugurate the consummation of that creation and bring salvation history to its consummation at the end of time. And Paul assumed, too, that those to whom he wrote in Rome also took that grand narrative of faith for granted. Paul did wrestle passionately with particular issues, such as the inclusion of the Gentiles as well as Jews, in this grand narrative of creation and salvation history, but he always thought and taught on the basis of that comprehensive biblical narrative. This was particularly the case when Paul worked on issues such as "the righteousness of faith," issues that were later to preoccupy Luther in his time.

Paul believed further that, with the coming of Jesus, especially in the cross and resurrection, the grand narrative of faith had taken a dramatic and final step forward. In this sense, Paul thought of himself in world-historical terms. As the apostle to the Gentiles, it was his calling, he was convinced, to establish Christian communities throughout the ancient Mediterranean world, communities that themselves would in turn reach out to and include the Gentile world as members of the ancient people of God. In Paul's view, once that inclusion had been accomplished, then the Creator God of Israel would inaugurate the last days of creation and of salvation history—and the consummation of the whole creation would take place.

We can, in this respect, regard Paul as an apocalyptic thinker, as long as we use that term with care. Paul was not an extreme, hellfire-and-damnation apocalypticist. He felt no need to celebrate the annihilation of the creation. Rather, in the tradition of the school of Isaiah (one scholar has argued that Paul drew on the little apocalypse of Isaiah when Paul shaped his discourse in Romans 8), he looked forward to the next and consummating chapter of the grand narrative of biblical faith—God's establishment of a new heaven and a new Earth in which God's righteousness would everywhere be finally vindicated and established.

It was in the context of this grand narrative that Paul announced that the whole creation was groaning in travail, waiting for its own liberation, as soon as the heirs of Adam and Eve would themselves finally be liberated from sin and death. On the one hand, Paul held that the whole world of creation—except for humans, who had fallen—was, under the majestic power of God, heading for its final consummation. On the other hand, Paul also believed that all the nonhuman creatures had been subjected to "vanity." Here Paul picked up the Genesis theme that God cursed the Earth because of the sin of Adam and Eve. However, Paul stressed that this subjection was done by God "in hope," that is, with a view to the day when all creatures would finally be consummated by God, once human-kind had been liberated through the unfolding history of human salvation that began with Abraham.

Presupposing all this, Paul then spoke pastorally and passionately to the members of the Roman church to whom he was writing (vv. 28-37). In doing so, he assumed, as a matter of course, that those early Christians were under severe duress—strife in their church and in their families, hardships of life as a scorned minority living under ruthless Roman power, and many other discouragements, above all the prospect of death. In response, Paul did not just speak to troubled individual souls, assuring them of God's love for them, although Paul's discourse in many ways was profoundly personal. Rather, Paul called to mind the grand narrative of faith that he knew he shared with those to whom he was writing. The word of individual comfort he speaks is predicated on his vision of the works of God in a creation that is groaning in travail: "We know that all things work together for good for those who love God, who are called according to his purpose" (v. 28). Then Paul reminds the faithful at Rome that they had been called by God to be conformed to Christ Jesus, the very one who has inaugurated the last chapter of the grand narrative of faith by his death and resurrection.

Building on this theology of God's history with the whole creation, Paul then uttered one of the most striking proclamations of the mercy and power of God in the whole Bible: "For I am convinced that neither death, nor life, nor angels, nor rulers, nor things present, nor things to come, nor powers, nor height, nor depth, nor anything else in all creation, will be able to separate us from the love of God in Christ Jesus our Lord" (v. 38). He emphatically returned to this universalizing theme later, too, after he had celebrated the inclusion of the Gentiles along with the Jews in salvation history: "O the depth of the riches and wisdom and knowledge of God! . . . For from him and through him and to him are all things" (Rom. 11:33-36).

Is it possible for interpreters in today's postmodern world—so rife with religious violence, global poverty, warfare among peoples, and rampant desecration of Earth itself—to find a way to comfort the afflicted by announcing the grand narrative of faith that Paul took for granted? And can they then proclaim that, by and in the love of God in Christ, the era of the groaning of the whole creation, and with that every human ill, is now coming to an end, because the day of the consummation of all things is at hand? That is the profound interpretive challenge that Paul's universalizing theology places alluringly before us.

Gospel
MARK 16:14-18

This text is an invitation for Christians today to hear anew the Gospel promise for the whole creation, as it was understood by the apostolic church, not only from the perspective of this Markan pericope but also from Matthew's angle of vision and that of other New Testament writers as well. It is generally agreed that Mark 16:9-20 does not belong to the original Gospel of Mark, but that it was created by an unknown author, who, facing the conundrum of the abrupt ending of Mark's original Gospel,[5] pulled together materials from other Gospels, especially from the ending of Matthew's Gospel, in order to provide what was for that author a fitting ending for Mark's Gospel.

What does the post-Markan author (PMA) mean to suggest when he has Jesus say, "Go into all the world and proclaim the good news to the whole creation" (v. 15)? Is this some injunction to preach, let us say, to the birds, as well as to downtrodden humans, in a way that St. Francis was later to do? Probably not. We have no solid evidence to allow us to conclude that PMA and the early Christian community with which he was associated understood Jesus' command that way. Alternatively, should not this text be read as another case of poetic license, as PMA's way of saying that Jesus intended the good news to be preached to all humans—to male and female, rich and poor, slave and free, Jew and Greek—and not just to the powerful and to Jews alone? That interpretation seems plausible and, indeed, it appears to be the option chosen by most scholars who have examined this text.

If we invoke two traditional interpretive principles, however, we can discover a more fruitful approach. If we "let Scripture interpret Scripture," rather than supplying our own meanings to a somewhat obscure text, and if we interpret that opaque text in terms of a text or texts that have clearer meanings, then it is possible to uncover a clear and even illuminating meaning of this obscure and opaque PMA text.

Enter the ancient biblical theological theme of the cosmic mountain, in particular the image of Mount Zion. That theme, which we saw adumbrated in the prophetic traditions of Isaiah and also in the world of Psalm 48 (perhaps it informed Romans 8 also, if we read that text in terms of the little apocalypse of Isaiah), was a commonplace in Jewish thinking during the first century. The vision of all peoples coming in peace to a restored New Jerusalem, in the midst of a renewed creation, may even have shaped the consciousness of Jesus as he rode into Jerusalem on a donkey as the Prince of Peace. Jesus' own "parables of growth," moreover, such as the story of the mustard seed, show that he understood the relatively isolated work that he was undertaking himself (or, more appropriately, that God was undertaking through him and his followers) to be but the beginning of a huge, perhaps cosmic, transformation of the whole creation. The seer of the book of Revelation also presupposed this kind of thinking, as when he envisioned himself being carried away to a high mountain (21:10) where he witnessed the New Jerusalem coming down out of heaven to be settled in the midst of a new heaven and a new Earth (21:1, 2).

Matthew took the ancient biblical cosmic mountain theme for granted and indeed integrated it into his own telling of the Gospel story (here following the findings of Terence L. Donaldson's careful study; see below). As Matthew worked with the Gospel of Mark and other sources, he used the theme of the cosmic mountain, Mount Zion, as one of his primary narrative motifs. Matthew made a radical adaptation, however. No longer would the Jerusalem Temple be identified as Mount Zion. Rather, Matthew saw Jesus, on the mountain, as the one who fulfilled the ancient promises of God for salvation flowing to the whole world from Mount Zion. Thus, Matthew shows us Jesus in the following dramatic mountain settings: (1) the mountain of temptation (4:8-10); (2) the mountain of teaching (5:1—8:1); (3) the mountain of feeding (15:29-31); (4) the mountain of transfiguration (17:1-9); (5) the Mount of Olives (21:1, 24:3); and (6) the mountain of commissioning (28:16-20).

Our attention must be limited here to that concluding setting, the mountain of commissioning, since a scenario like this also appears in PMA's concluding picture of Jesus in Mark. In carefully crafting that concluding mountain scene, Matthew seems to have drawn on materials available to him in the traditions of the apostolic church. Many of the particular details of the story evidently were not originally of his making. Narratives about postresurrection appearances of Jesus on mountaintops were apparently quite common. These traditions, in turn, were shaped by a commonplace in Jewish expectations that the end times would begin from Mount Zion. And a number of these traditions accented Isaiah's theme of the inclusion of the Gentiles in the last days of salvation history.

Strikingly, in contrast to the primary missionary use of this Matthean text throughout the centuries, Matthew's accent seems to have been—again, within the parameters of the Mount Zion theology—on the *ingathering* of the nations, represented at the core by the disciples, with no suggestion that any of them departed on mission journeys. In sum, says Donaldson, for Matthew: "As one who is greater than the temple, Jesus replaces Zion as the center of eschatological fulfillment. He is the one around whom the people are to gather and to whom the Gentiles will make procession. The journey of the Magi to Jesus at the beginning of the Gospel is but an anticipation of [all the nations] commanded at the end."[6] In this sense, for Matthew, Jesus is a cosmic figure on whom the turning of the ages depends.

There is no explicit statement in Matthew's mountain narratives, to be sure, that announces the dawning of the new heavens and the new Earth, images that are very much part of the Mount Zion tradition and that are familiar to us from the traditions of the school of Isaiah and elsewhere. Nor do we meet any statement in Matthew about the groaning of the whole creation, as we do in Paul. But we have seen enough here to be able to state with some confidence that such themes may well have been taken for granted by Matthew and that they therefore implicitly may frame the image of the foregrounded figure whom Matthew seeks to celebrate, namely, Jesus now portrayed as the new temple on Mount Zion.

If this was the case, as it appears to have been, then is it any surprise that another apostolic author, our post-Markan author, who was cognizant of the kinds of traditions that Matthew shaped when Matthew concluded his Gospel, should as a matter of course report that Jesus sent the disciples at the end not just to preach to all nations but indeed to preach to the whole creation? To be sure, interpreters of the words that PMA puts on the lips of the resurrected Lord at the end of Mark's Gospel may choose to be cautious about identifying the words "the whole creation" with the Mount Zion theology as Matthew carefully adapted and radically revised it. This proposed interpretation of our passage is by no means a matter of historical certainty. But it does seem plausible, and in that respect it is suggestive.

Minimally, the words of PMA will give interpreters occasion to explore a range of meanings in the "Great Commission" narrative and other mountain scenes in Matthew's Gospel where references to the eschatological Mount Zion theology are clearly present. And such a theology can then be read as resonating with meanings of a whole range of biblical texts, such as those we have already met in the traditions of Isaiah, in Psalm 48, and in Romans 8.

With such texts in view, and particularly with the Matthean vision of Jesus as the new temple on the new Mount Zion before us, other interpretive questions will inevitably emerge. Must not the Matthean materials, in particular, prompt further questions about the Christ figure portrayed by Matthew and perhaps also by PMA? Does the grand biblical narrative that they see coming to completion in Jesus also imply what can be called a "cosmic Christology"? If so, interpreters would then be well advised to turn to other New Testament texts, such as Colossians 1:15ff., where Christ is proclaimed precisely in such cosmic terms.

Reflections

In what respect, if at all, is the "cosmic-mountain" motif alive in the minds and hearts of your congregation? Do your congregants harbor the idea of "getting away from it all" in order to enjoy some "mountaintop experience"? If so, how can you address such aspirations so as to transform them, by bringing the biblical vision of a grand narrative of faith, from creation to consummation, to the forefront of your congregation's consciousness, and then by helping them to see Jesus Christ as the center of it all? "Mountaintop experiences," and indeed the mythic reality of mountains themselves, are taken for granted by biblical faith, but not as a thing in themselves. All such meanings are swept up into the vision of God's history with the whole creation, whose concluding stage is inaugurated by the coming of Jesus Christ.

How can you help your hearers to understand the difference between "the negative apocalypticism" of some popular interpretations of the Bible and "the positive apocalypticism" of the traditions of Isaiah and Paul? Perhaps it would be helpful to address explicitly the claims of the immensely popular "Left Behind" novels, which are profoundly negative. Contrast those ideas with the creation-affirming ideas of Isaiah and the psalmist, of Matthew and Paul.[7]

What role does ritual or liturgy play in holding together and fostering the grand biblical narrative of cosmic renewal?[8] Many Protestants, in particular, need to be reintroduced to liturgy as a creative, identity-forming agency that helps us to contemplate God's universal purposes and God's all-embracing love for all things, as distinct from worship that is focused on the needs of individual worshipers alone. Maybe the time has come to make "the Songs of Zion," the processions around Zion, and their witness to cosmic renewal also the hymns and processions and witness of every Christian congregation.

Can today's worshipers hear "the groaning" of the whole creation? Can today's preachers help worshipers develop this new kind of hearing, to discover the sense that St. Francis had of being *kin* with all other creatures and thereby having empathy with them? Can Christians today so identify with otherkind, not only with a will to care for them but also to care *about* them in appropriate ways?[9] One could readily think, in this respect, of Christian communities dedicating themselves to the protection of wilderness areas, where mountains sometimes stand forth in awesome splendor.

On the other hand, can we learn to so bond with otherkind that we are also free to step back, in wonder or even in fear, and let other creatures of nature be, and indeed thrive, on their own terms? Can we be willing to encounter the wild beasts and the tsunamis and the droughts and the mountain avalanches of the greater world of nature and to do so in faith, knowing that our own understanding of the ways of God is profoundly limited? And at the same time, can we still engage all things in hope, as Paul did, including the wild and threatening elements, while we await the coming day of the new heavens and the new Earth?

Can today's preachers proclaim the gospel of Jesus Christ in cosmic terms? Much popular piety today focuses on Christ's benefits *for us*. Those preachers who point to Christ, in addition, as "the Lord of *history*," have a point. But can preachers also find the imagination to proclaim the cosmic lordship of Jesus Christ—the one who stands on the mountain of God's creation and beckons his followers to bring all nations to him—even as we await the dawning of the day of the new heavens and the new Earth?

RESOURCES

Adams, Edward. *Constructing the World: A Study in Paul's Cosmological Language.* Edinburgh: T & T Clark, 2000.

Braaten, Laurie J., "All Creation Groans: Romans 8:22 in Light of the Biblical Sources." *Horizons in Biblical Theology* 28, no. 1 (2006): 131–59.

Brown, William P. "'I Am about to Do a New Thing': Yahweh's Victory Garden in Second Isaiah," in *The Ethos of the Cosmos: The Genesis of Moral Imagination in the Bible*, 229–70. Grand Rapids: Eerdmans, 1999.

Donaldson, Terence L. *Jesus on the Mountain: A Study in Matthean Theology.* Sheffield: JSOT, 1985.

Habel, Norman C., and Peter Trudinger. *Exploring Ecological Hermeneutics.* Atlanta: Society of Biblical Literature, 2008.

Horrell, David G., Cherryl Hunt, and Christopher Southgate. *Greening Paul: Rereading the Apostle in a Time of Ecological Crisis.* Waco: Baylor University Press, 2010.

Levenson, Jon D. *Sinai and Zion: An Entry into the Jewish Bible.* San Francisco: Harper & Row, 1985.

Santmire, H. Paul, "A New Option in Biblical Interpretation: An Ecological Reading of the Bible," chap. 10 in *The Travail of Nature: The Ambiguous Ecological Promise of Christian Theology.* Minneapolis: Fortress Press, 1985.

—————. *Ritualizing Nature: Renewing Christian Liturgy in a Time of Crisis.* Theology and the Sciences. Minneapolis: Fortress Press, 2008.

NOTES

1. See Mircea Eliade, *The Sacred and the Profane: The Nature of Religion,* trans. Willard R. Trask (New York: Harcourt, Brace & World, 1959), 37–41.

2. John Muir, *The Mountains of California* (Boston: Houghton Mifflin, 1916).

3. Augustine, *The Confessions,* book 10, chapter 8.

4. For a thoughtful review of this "Left Behind" kind of thinking, see Barbara Rossing, *The Rapture Exposed: The Message of Hope in the Book of Revelation* (Boulder: Westview Press, 2004).

5. For a discussion of this point, see a standard study resource such as *The Access Bible,* (New York: Oxford University Press, 1999).

6. Terence L. Donaldson, *Jesus on the Mountain: A Study in Matthean Theology* (Sheffield: JSOT, 1985), 185–86.

7. See Rossing, *The Rapture Exposed.*

8. On liturgy as identity forming, see H. Paul Santmire, *Ritualizing Nature: Renewing Christian Liturgy in a Time of Crisis,* Theology and the Sciences (Minneapolis: Fortress Press, 2008).

9. As ethicist James Nash invites us to do in his book *Loving Nature: Ecological Integrity and Christian Responsibility* (Nashville: Abingdon, 1991).

YEAR C

THE WISDOM SERIES

First Sunday in Creation

Ocean Sunday

Jione Havea

Job 38:1-18
Psalm 104:1-9,
24-26
Ephesians 1:3-10
Luke 5:1-11

Background: Ocean Views

The first biblical creation story (Gen. 1:9-10) portrays G*d as calling ocean into being in order for earth/land to be. The existence of ocean was necessary for the creation of Earth. As one psalm puts it, G*d "founded the world upon the seas and established it upon the floods" (Ps. 24:1-2). In other words, without ocean, earth would not have been possible.

On day one of creation, G*d called light out of darkness, then named light "day" and darkness "night," with evening and morning setting them apart (Gen. 1:3-5). On day two, G*d called forth a dome (or "expanse," as in the NJPS) to separate the waters above from the waters below, and G*d called the dome "sky." Then, on day three, G*d called the waters under the sky to gather at one place so that dry land might appear. G*d called the waters under the sky "seas," which gather in the ocean (I use *sea* and *ocean* interchangeably here), out of which came "earth" (which I use to refer to dry land).

One may rightly conceive the events of day three as the birthing of Earth.[1] Out of the waters of the mighty ocean, baby Earth was born. This is a powerful image, in which G*d functions as a midwife who announces the parting of the waters so that a new creature may begin life. And the life of baby Earth began immediately upon birth, with vegetation of all sorts (Gen. 1:11f.).

I extend this understanding by viewing ocean and earth/land as bodies that share the same beginning, as if they were twins. And as twins, both ocean and earth were productive, with swarms of living creatures of different kinds (Gen. 1:20f., 1:24f.). Ocean and earth connect in their shared beginning, in their cycles of living, and in the processes of aging and dying, such that their fates entangle, as one would expect of twins. Of course, what one expects from this relationship depends on one's understanding of and experience with twins. Twins share (sometimes inexplicably) vibes and connections. They can understand each other, and each can be the best companion, sustainer, and keeper of the other. But twins are not always kind to one another, as we see in the story of Cain and Abel, whom the text invites us to see as twins since they were born one after the other (see esp. Gen. 4:2a: "Then *she continued to birth* his brother Abel"), and in the story of Esau and Jacob (cf. Gen. 2:23-26). Stories of twins raise critical questions about what it means to be "keeper" (watcher, protector, confiner) of one's brother or sister. Along this line, earth and ocean are "keepers" of one another.

To imagine the connection between ocean and earth as between twins invites us to entertain a complex relationship. Oceans cover 71 percent of the planet's surface, over half of these waters being more than 3,000 meters (9,800 feet) in depth. The deepest part of the ocean is in the Mariana Trench (10,923 meters/35,837 feet deep) near the Northern Mariana Islands in the Pacific Ocean. The ocean spreads over more surface space than the combination of all the dry lands; therefore, it is the larger twin, making it astonishing, humbling, and menacing to us. These effects are especially experienced throughout the sea of islands in the Pacific Ocean, also known as the "liquid continent" or Oceania, where dry lands are small in size and the distances between them are far and wide.

The threat that ocean poses to earth has become more frightening as a result of two recent events: the Boxing Day tsunami in Asia in 2004, which reached the shores of Africa; the September tsunami in Oceania in 2009, and the tsunami in 2011 that devastated Japan. Mindful of these tsunamis, this chapter offers an oceanic invitation: let us relate to ocean with the care that we owe earth, and let us extend to earth the respect that we have for ocean. This chapter will consequently make complex what the phrase "ocean views" means: this phrase refers to our views of the ocean, perspectives with humbling care and respect; and it also invites us to imagine how "ocean" might view things. Ocean is more than just the object of the human gaze; ocean is also an agent with views and perspectives of its own. Hence, in speaking of ocean views, I imagine ocean to have senses and feelings. The following sections will engage complex ocean views on selected passages, without pretending that I have the only feel for ocean views, because, even though I have felt the flow of some of the seawater springs, I have not "walked in the recesses of the deep" (Job 38:16).

First Reading
JOB 38:1-18: OCEAN LIMITS

The story of Job is astonishing and humbling—and menacing. Job was upright and blameless, a rich family man, qualities that may seem contradictory. After all, Scripture rarely depicts the rich as upright and blameless, and we are accustomed to their being portrayed in far less flattering, even evil, terms, fairly or not.

Job was the key victim in a two-part wager between YHWH and Satan, resulting in the destruction of Job's wealth and household, the rejection of his wife, and the infliction of loathsome sores on his body. Following this are three cycles of debates between Job and three counselor friends on religious and cultural teachings about human suffering; behavior and destiny; divine justice and retribution (Job 4–31), into which the younger Elihu inserts himself (Job 32–37). Then YHWH answers Job from a whirlwind (Job 38–41). A whirlwind is a fitting medium for YHWH's rhetorical response (in Oceania, a whirlwind is seen as a blind man who knocks into and digs things up), swirling with a series of confronting queries that sounds like a harsh lesson in biblical ecology.

In the passage for this reflection, YHWH calls on Job to explain, if he can, what Earth is like (vv. 1-3), based first on the image of Earth as a constructed structure (vv. 4-7) and then on the imagery of birthing (vv. 8-11). The second image is crucial for this reflection insofar as it relates to ocean. There are thus two key subjects in our passage: earth (vv. 4-7 and 12-15) and ocean (vv. 8-11 and 16-18). The interconnections between the twins (see the background section above) are emphasized in the structure of our passage, with the focus alternating between earth and ocean. Here is the pattern: earth (vv. 4-7); ocean (vv. 8-11); earth (vv. 12-15); ocean (vv. 16-18).

The two passages relating to earth bring home two points. First, Job did not witness the laying of the foundations or the formation of the earth; therefore, he does not know its makeup and purpose. And, second, Job has neither directed the paths of nor influenced the happenings on earth since his birth. Job knows zilch about earth! But ocean, on the other hand, would know something about the creation of earth, which would intertwine with its own being and purpose. We get a glimpse of that in the two passages relating to ocean.

Job 38:8 can be ambiguous for English readers because two referents are possible for the second clause: "And who shut in the sea with doors when *it* burst out of the womb?" What was the "it" that burst out of the womb? Is Job 38:8 about the birthing of earth (subject of v. 4), requiring the sea to be shut behind doors so that it (sea) does not threaten earth, or is it about the birthing of sea? The ambiguous "it" can be clarified by consulting the Hebrew text, in which the pronoun reference is a third-person masculine singular pronominal suffix. Since the word for earth is feminine in Hebrew, "it" must refer to sea (which is masculine in Hebrew). Job 38:8-11 is thus about the birthing of the ocean.

At birth, with the impression that it is a favored child, the ocean is clothed with clouds and swaddled with deep darkness (v. 9). Clouds and darkness are fluid and wilting, so they can easily associate with ocean. Their fluidity means that they can creep into places, which explains the need to "shut in" (v. 8), to prescribe "bounds," and to "set bars and doors" (v. 10). Their fluidity requires the establishment of ocean limits.

I use "ocean limits" in a double sense, reflecting the complexity of ocean views. First, Job 38:11 stresses the need to put limits on the ocean, because the bounds, bars, and doors are set in order to say, "Thus far shall you come, and no farther, and here shall your proud waves be stopped" (v. 11). This first view portrays the ocean as wild but tameable. The second ocean view invites us to see the ocean itself as the limit. Ocean is both the subject that needs to be limited as well as the agent that limits. This second view invites an alternative response, since we are dealing with a fluid limit, a limit that is flexible, ebbing and filling. In this regard, ocean is a limit that is as deep as darkness and as present as wisdom. The ocean is deep enough for G*d to dwell there—which is not a foreign thought to me, because our ancestors believed that *Pulotu*, the place where dieties live, is in the ocean, the place where the sun returns at the end of each day. Also, it is in *Pulotu* that the spirits of our ancestors gather.

I propose to go further than my ancestors, drawing upon the story of Job in order to argue that ocean is divine in the sense that, like earth (vv. 4-5), ocean is beyond knowledge (v. 16). It is ironic that in the book of Job, this "beyond knowledge" quality can no longer be said to belong fully to G*d. In speaking from the whirlwind, G*d reveals something about G*dself that overwhelms Job into responding,

> I had heard You with my ears,
> But now I see You with my eyes;
> Therefore, I recant and relent,
> Being but dust and ashes. (Job 42:5-6; NJPS)

Of what does Job recant and relent in 42:6a? One possibility is that Job recants and relents G*d, who is the object of the verbs in 42:5. In this regard, Job feels regret toward G*d but could not do the same toward earth and ocean, which are beyond his understanding. According to this ocean view, the narrator depicts Job as having more reverence for earth and ocean than for G*d. The upshot of reading the story of Job with ocean views, in this way, is that it invites us seriously and critically to respect earth and ocean in their own rights.

Psalmody

PSALM 104:1-9, 24-26: TROUBLING WATERS

If creation testifies to the wisdom of its Creator, then Psalm 104 presents a "very great" Creator (v. 1) who is clothed with light (v. 2) and who rides the clouds upon the wings of the winds (v. 3). The winds are the messengers of this majestic Creator, for whom fire and flame minister (v. 4). The interweaving of the awesome features of the Creator and the soundness of the creation in the verses of Psalm 104 invites wonder from its readers. The Creator and its creation are astonishing and humbling.

Earth is anchored to a firm foundation (vv. 5-9), and it is watered (vv. 10-13), cultivated, and cultured with animals and humans (vv. 14-23)—with ocean surrounding it (vv. 24-26). Moreover, earth and ocean and their multitudes look to the Creator for sustenance (vv. 27-30). Given the soundness of the creation, who can but sing praise and rejoice in the Creator (vv. 31-35)? Could the creation be any better?

This psalmist is confident that the creation represents its Creator, YHWH the Lord. Without entering the debate on the "politics of representation," how do we as readers of Psalm 104 experience the Creator being present in the creation? When we admire the creation as reflecting the creativity of the Creator, do we also see the Creator as being present in the creation? This is a rhetorical question, and at once a theological question. How one responds will depend on one's view about this Creator, YHWH the Lord. Ones who perceive YHWH as truly distant and transcendent will most likely lean toward saying that the Creator is beyond, and more than, the creation. On the one hand, to see the Creator as present in the creation is to trap the ungraspable in transient forms, which is the temptation of idolatry and an adversary of monotheism. On the other hand, those who perceive YHWH as immanent and ever-present, already at hand, will be able to imagine well the Creator as being present in the creation. They would not go to the extent of seeing the creation as divine, but they would not have any trouble encountering the Creator in and through the creation. Both views are supportable on biblical and doctrinal grounds, but they are not always held in a healthy tension when thinking of the relationship between the creation and the Creator, YHWH the LORD.

I quickly add that there are damaging consequences of both views. On the one hand, biblical teachings against idolatry (cf. Exod. 20:4-6), for instance, refute the expectation that YHWH was created and can be manifested in material forms. YHWH G*d cannot be contained. On the other hand, the view of a completely transcendent G*d is destructive when it permits people to have no respect for the creation, which then becomes an unending store of resources in their eyes. This has resulted in the abuse of the environment and of natural resources. In light of these damaging consequences, it is better to hold the two views in healthy tension. I offer this twinlike suggestion based on the ocean views in Psalm 104.

The Tongan saying *tāau pē lei mo e tofuaʻa* ("a whale-tooth befits a whale") echoes how the psalmist holds the healthy tension in Psalm 104. A whale tooth is called *lei* in Tongan, and the gist of the saying is that a *lei* says something about the whale, seen as a majestic and noble fish. The *lei* is awesome (expressed most clearly in the Fijian *tabua*), and the only fish that befits such an expression is a whale. This has to do with the size and shape of the tooth, when compared to a tooth from other sea creatures such as sharks, tunas, and turtles. As a *lei* reveals the majesty of a whale, a special mammal of the ocean, so does creation manifest the majesty of its Creator. Insofar as the *lei* that Tongans access comes from a dead whale, the *lei* itself is the point where the "healthy tension" stands, because the *lei* also manifests that which is no longer present. The challenge herewith is whether we as readers of Psalm 104 can encounter the Creator (which the psalm makes at once present and at a distance) in the creation in the same way Tongans hallow a whale through the *lei*.

As a seawater person, I cannot help but notice that the emphasis of the psalmist falls on earth. Earth is solid, and the psalmist is worried because of the waters that cover the earth, which have the capacity to stand above the mountains (v. 6). These are troubling waters that the Creator rebuked

(v. 7) and "set a boundary that they may not pass, so that they might not again cover the earth" (v. 9). According to this view, the ocean is a threat to earth. Ocean therefore needs to be controlled, to be kept back from earth.

A position that favors waters and ocean will invite a different reaction. Psalm 104:25-26 gives a different ocean view. Ocean is not seen as a threat; rather, it is portrayed as great and wide with innumerable creeping things, small and great. This is not a scary place, for ships cross it and Leviathan sports in it. The Hebrew word for "sport" (*śhq*) occurs most of the time in Wisdom literature (whereas its synonym *shq* occurs mainly in Genesis) and suggests a "joyous event." The NJPS translation complements this ocean view: "There go the ships, and Leviathan that You formed to sport with." Leviathan is like a bathtub toy with whom YHWH sports, formed to provide a "joyous event" for YHWH. In verses 25-26, therefore, is the view that ocean is a place both of safety (for ships cross it) and of pleasure (for YHWH plays with Leviathan in it). In this view, ocean does not need to be controlled.

In Psalm 104, the psalmist holds both ocean views—that ocean needs to be controlled and that it is also a place of safety and pleasure—in healthy tension. This tension challenges readers to find ways to hold both earth and ocean in a healthy relationship. It is also an invitation for readers and worshipers who are on the shores of stability to step into the sea, into the place of travel and of joyous sporting.

Second Reading

EPHESIANS 1:3-10: GATHERING BELOVEDS

Though Ephesians 1:3-10 does not say anything about ocean, one may still reflect on it with ocean views. Indeed, when it comes to the Bible, this is my preferred line of navigation, because I am not always convinced by what it says about the ocean, bearing in mind that the Bible came together in dry-land-based and freshwater cultures. I prefer this path also because it is interesting to ponder how ocean views might help us to reflect on and to engage biblical texts in a different way. Ocean Sunday is therefore not just an opportunity to explore how the Bible understands or misunderstands the ocean; it is also an invitation to see Earth and human-centered texts from the point of view of the ocean.

Ephesians 1:3-10 is human centered, with a strong expectation of a time in the future, the "fullness of time," when Earth and heaven will gather in Christ (v. 10) the Beloved (v. 6). That will be an eschatological time of gathering, at which time horizons will fuse. Heavenly and earthly horizons will overlap with the good pleasure of G*d's will (v. 5). The purpose for which G*d chose humans before the foundation of the world will intersect with the spiritual blessings that await in heavenly places (vv. 3-4). The mystery of G*d's will, revealed to humans through wisdom and understanding (vv. 8-9), will interweave with the redemption and forgiveness that testify to the riches of Christ's grace (v. 7). The epistle then continues on to portray the "fullness of time" as having to do with heritage and inheritance (vv. 11f.); as such, time and space also merge.

The fusion of horizons anticipated in Ephesians 1:3-10, nonetheless, is yonder, on the "other side of the river," figuratively speaking. This view would comfort and inspire "the saints who are [in Ephesus and are] faithful in Christ Jesus," to whom this epistle is addressed (v. 1). But what might it do for readers with ocean views? What might this passage *say* and *do* to readers who, like me, are not wholly "holy and blameless before G*d in love" (cf. v. 4)?

The forward-looking orientation of the fullness-of-time view is dislocating, in the sense that it gives the impression that Earth, earthly places and things, are dispensable. True, the fullness of time is about the fusion of horizons. But no event of fusion is free of costs, without exclusions and frictions, and it is the costs to Earth that concern us here. If we were to take the fullness of time seriously, then "the here and now" will be part of the costs. I will see Earth as expendable and transient. The fullness-of-time view is thus costly to Earth and Earth-lovers who might not be holy and blameless in the eyes of the saints and faithful.

The fullness-of-time view is dislocating also in the way it does not fuse heaven and Earth with ocean. One can rightly argue that ocean is inherent to Earth, but it is not clear to me that the epistle writer Paul had that understanding in mind. There are no traces of ocean in Ephesians 1:3-10 other than the reference to the foundation of the cosmos (v. 4), if one reads with an eye to the first biblical story of creation (see the background section above). This possibility invites one to see a trace of ocean in the reference to heaven, the Greek word for which (*ouranos*) also translates as sky. The same Greek word is used in the Greek version of Genesis 1:8 as the name for the dome that G*d called into being in order to separate the waters below from the waters above. In this regard, the heaven/sky that will fuse with Earth at the fullness of time is a reminder of the ocean/seas. Noting this is one of the benefits of viewing Ephesians 1:3-10 with ocean views.

It is worth noting here also that, in the first creation story, G*d did *not* announce sky/heaven as good, as one would expect, in light of the repeated storytelling pattern at the end of each day of creation. Sky/heaven is in the same category as darkness, which also is *not* announced as good. The implication here is that sky/heaven may not always separate the waters above from the waters below. The upshot of interpreting Ephesians 1:3-10 with ocean views is that it may enable one to see the "fullness of time" in a more holistic manner, with the fusion of Earth and sky/heaven and ocean. In this connection, the fullness of time represents a point of gathering beloveds and of a Beloved One who does the gathering. Surely, it will be a joyous occasion for the "saints who are faithful in Christ Jesus."

Gospel
LUKE 5:1-11: SINKING BOATS

Luke 5:1-11 is a complex fishing story. Different kinds of fishing, reflecting the meaningfulness of the term *fishing*, with twists and turns, take place in this story. There is a curious shift of purpose from fishing for fish to fishing for followers, inviting one to connect fishing, teaching, preaching, discipleship, mission, and conversion. There is also an interesting transformation of subjectivity, with some of the fishers (Simon and his fellows) becoming the fished, only to be released (or disciplined? Or discipled?) so that they become fishers of people, using the fisher (Jesus) who fished them, so to speak, as bait. The spiral of twists and turns in this story are inspiring and humbling.

In this fishing story (I would have preferred a fishing story from the open ocean, being a seawater person myself, but I can cope with this lake story!), Jesus steps away from shore and from the pressing of the crowd into a boat. He steps away from pressure and people, so that he might speak to them about the word of G*d (v. 1). But the narrator seems not to be too concerned with precisely what the content of the word of G*d is in this particular instance, for the narrative does not reveal what Jesus taught the crowd from the boat (v. 3)—because this is a fishing story. The narrator is attentive to the vessels and the gear of fishing. The boat was empty, for the fishermen had gone to wash their nets (v. 2). I am not sure what the rituals were for washing nets during the time of Jesus; however, in Oceania, the washing of nets suggests that there will be a time-out from fishing. Washing takes place when it is time to stop and rest, as in Sunday rest, and to repair the nets, as well as the fishermen.

The fishermen step out of the pressure to catch and provide, having just worked all night without catching anything (v. 5). The time of the event is not given, but it was the day after a bad night for Peter and his fellow fishermen. They stepped out of the pressure of failure and disappointment in order to wash and rest, whereas Jesus steps out of the pressing of the crowd in order to teach them. The boat is the meeting point between Jesus and the fishermen, as well as between Jesus and the crowd.

The narrator does not say if Jesus went out of the boat after teaching the crowd; so he might have remained in the boat when he instructed Peter, "Put out into the deep water and let down your nets for a catch" (v. 4). When Peter falls down at the knees of Jesus and says, "Go away from me, Lord, for I am a sinful man" (v. 8), it seems to suggest that Jesus was in the boat with the fishing party. So instead of returning to shore, Jesus moved farther away from the crowd.

The narrator is so eager to get to the catch that time speeds up in the narrative, and he fails to mention how the nets were carried back to the boat, who was in the boat, how far into the deep they put out the boat, and what happened to the crowd. Were they satisfied with what Jesus taught them? Did the crowd disperse? Or did they wait to see if the fishing party would succeed? Who went out with Peter? The subjects in verses 6 and 7 are plural, "they" (cf. v. 9, "he and all who were with him"), which points to Peter and others. The sons of Zebedee, James and John, were partners with Peter (v. 10), but they do not have a speaking role in this story and it is not clear if they are in the same boat with Peter. They may have been among "the partners in the other boat" (v. 7). This narrator does not give many details, because the focus is on the huge catch of fish.

The catch testifies to the wealth in the waters. There is deep water in the lake, where they caught so many fish that their nets were beginning to break (v. 6). They filled their boat and the boat of their partners, and both boats began to sink (v. 7). That is how great the catch was, and how rich the waters were—there were enough fish to sink the boats!

The catch was great; and it appears greater because of the failure in the previous night. None got away in this fishing story (except maybe the crowd). Peter did want Jesus to go away, but Jesus assured him: "Do not be afraid; from now on you will be catching people" (v. 10). Peter did so upon their return to shore, for he and his fellows left everything and followed Jesus (v. 11). The swiftness and finality of their response suggest that these fishers were driven by the allure of dragging in a huge catch. Who among devoted fishers would not pursue the chance to catch "the big one"?

I am troubled by what appears to be greed on the part of the fishers. Did they have to haul all the catch onto the boat? Could they not have released some of the fish? The wealth of the waters is not endless, and failure to question actions that abuse it is irresponsible. Based on ocean views, it is not so much the waters/ocean that we need to control, but those who abuse its resources. The sinking boats are evidence of this abuse, especially since the text states that they dropped everything and followed Jesus—with no mention of whether they washed the nets or donated the nets or the fish to their partners. I will, of course, change my mind if the catch in the sinking boats was distributed among the crowd, which is probably what happened; but the narrator is guilty of emphasizing the fishing story instead of taking responsibility for the resources of the waters/sea. The latter is important in ocean views, inviting us to bear in mind the effects of fishing activities on aquatic and marine worlds.

Reflections: Remembering Ocean

The ocean views presented in this chapter remember ocean in several texts that make reference to ocean as well as in one text that does not. To remember ocean is not to seek to make it static and rigid, as if it were possible to tame it, but to honor its fluidity and richness. It also involves remembering ocean as home to many creatures, including people from South and North, and all over the world. Ocean is not an uninhabitable wilderness, but a hive buzzing with life and mysteries.

I have imagined and shared ocean views as an invitation for worshipers and readers to be more conscious of the presence of ocean and its capacity to influence and affect Earth. This invitation cannot be more urgent than at the present, as we struggle to cope with and survive the devastating "tsunamis" of garbage and of refugees caused by our carbon civilization.

I am troubled by how the discussion about the "politics of global warming"[2] prefers to speak of ocean as a "carbon sink" that can no longer inhale our carbon waste. In so doing, the politics of global warming shifts the blame to ocean for not doing its cleanup job and thereby avoids the need to confront the destructive human tendencies and abusive actions. Ocean and earth will survive human destruction, albeit with scars and fractures; however, humanity might not survive if we stay on the current course. I hope that Ocean Sunday will be an opportunity for us to transform the way we relate to ocean and earth, and for us to come clean about our responsibilities to our contexts and our world.

Ocean is home to many of us, and it is home to the memories of our ancestors. One of the words used in Oceania for the deep sea is *moana*, which connotes depth and mystery, as well as plenty and endurance. *Pulotu*, where spirits gather with the dieties, is in the *moana*. As *moana*, ocean is wisdomlike: "Wisdom is a deep impulse within all parts of creation, designing their mysteries, guiding their purposes, and mentoring their functions."[3]

RESOURCES

Habel, Norman C., and Peter Trudinger, eds. *Water: A Matter of Life and Death*. Adelaide: ATF, 2009.

Lacocque, André. "The Deconstruction of Job's Fundamentalism." *Journal of Biblical Literature* 126, no. 1 (2007): 83–97.

Ntreh, Abotchie. "The Survival of Earth: An African Reading of Psalm 104," in *The Earth Story in the Psalms and the Prophets*, ed. Norman C. Habel, The Earth Bible, vol. 4, 98–108. Cleveland: Pilgrim, 2001.

Sugirtharajah, R. S. "Tsunami, Text and Trauma: Hermeneutics after the Asian Tsunami." *Biblical Interpretation* 15 (2007): 117–34.

Walker-Jones, Arthur. "Psalm 104: A Celebration of the Vanua," in *The Earth Story in the Psalms and the Prophets*, ed. Norman C. Habel, The Earth Bible, vol. 4, 84–97. Cleveland: Pilgrim, 2001.

NOTES

1. See Norman C. Habel and Peter Trudinger, eds., *Water: A Matter of Life and Death* (Adelaide: ATF, 2009).

2. I have borrowed this term from George Zachariah.

3. See The Season of Creation Web site, http://seasonofcreation.com/worship-resources/readings/series-c-the-wisdom-series/, accessed April 11, 2011.

Second Sunday in Creation

Fauna Sunday

Dianne Bergant

Job 39:1-8,
26-30
Psalm 104:14-23
1 Corinthians 1:10-23
Luke 12:22-31

Background

According to the first creation narrative, God initially established the structure of the universe (Gen. 1:1-19). Once Earth was fashioned and made habitable, animals were brought forth to fill the waters and the air and the land. The last life form created was a human couple, a man and a woman who lived on the land amidst "the fish of the sea, the birds of the air, and all the living creatures that move on the earth" (Gen. 1:28). Preoccupied with genuine human needs, sometimes driven by exaggerated human desires, the descendants of this first couple often lost sight of their place in the Earth community. As they moved away from fear of the animals that lived around them, they often lost respect for them as well. As they grew in their understanding and manipulation of the forces in nature, they came to see themselves as the pinnacle of the natural world, as the standard for judging the value of other instances of natural creation. If something was perceived as primarily serving human ambition, it was considered valuable and was preserved; if it was not, it was deemed worthless and often was discarded.

The deficiencies of this distorted anthropocentric point of view are becoming clear today. We experience them in the tragic consequences of ecological insensitivity prevalent for centuries in many of the societies of the world. As we become environmentally aware, we come to realize the need not only for a more sensitive way of living in our world, but also for an entirely different worldview, one that is both God centered and Earth centered. On this Sunday, Fauna Sunday or Animal Sunday, we focus on one facet of this new worldview: our relationship with other living creatures of Earth.

First Reading
JOB 39:1-8, 26-30

Job has been crying out to God for an explanation for his suffering. He has insisted that while he may be a weak human being, he certainly does not deserve the tribulations that he is being forced to endure. He has demanded that God appear and provide an explanation for his predicament (Job 31:37). God does appear, but God does not address matters of human suffering or justice. Some might say that God completely ignores Job's predicament. That is not really so. Instead, God directs Job's attention to the wonders of creation, first to the magnificence of the universe and then to some of the fascinating animals that are part of Earth itself. By asking questions, as good teachers always do, God leads Job to an insight that helps him come to grips with the dilemma in which he finds himself.

Through the use of very simple questions, God parades a variety of animals before Job just as, at the time of creation, the animals had been paraded before Adam (Gen. 2:19-20). The Genesis passage recounts how Adam named each animal, suggesting that he grasped something of their nature. Here Job is questioned about animals, but is unable to explain aspects of their behavior. This passage describes four different species; two of them are ground animals (vv. 1-8) and two of them are birds of prey (vv. 26-30).

Mountain goats dwell amid high, inaccessible cliffs. Far from human habitation, their normal behavior would be unknown to Job, to say nothing of the manner in which the female gives birth. Job would be both ignorant of the habits of the mountain goat and lacking in resources to care for or protect it. There was actually no need for human care, because these new offspring begin to fend for themselves almost immediately. The nature of God's questioning made all of this clear to Job. He neither understands nor does he control this elusive creature.

The wild ass is best characterized by its freedom. It has not been confined and subsequently domesticated by human beings. It thrives in the wilderness, far from human habitation, where it can roam unrestrained, without danger of being ensnared by human hunters. Like the mountain goat, this animal is outside the realm of human control. Once again, God's questioning exposes Job's limitations.

The hawk is noted for its ability to soar into the upper regions of the sky as well as for its innate sense of migration. In its soaring, it is carried by air currents that it can detect and utilize. As if it reads the disposition of the winds, at seasonal changes it spreads its wings for a journey that will take it to a climate more to its liking. This bird is not dependent on human ingenuity. It has no need of human guidance, and so Job has no control over it.

The eagle rules the skies just as the lion rules the forest. It, like the hawk, soars high above the surface of Earth, and it builds its nest in secluded rocky crags without the aid of any other creature. From there, with its keen eye it can observe its prey and then swoop down upon it without warning. This bird dwells so far above the sphere occupied by human beings that it is beyond the reach of human control. Job can only gaze in amazement at its undisputed majesty.

By questioning Job about the nature and habits of animals, is God avoiding Job's demands for an explanation of his suffering? Not at all. Rather, God's questions challenge Job to consider some of the marvels that God has brought forth from Earth. They open Job's eyes to the fact that the animals follow patterns of behavior that he cannot even begin to comprehend and over which he exercises absolutely no authority. This depiction of animals that exist and thrive far from the realm of human influence seems to contradict the directive that God gave to the first human couple as found in Genesis 1. There they are told to ". . . have dominion over the fish of the sea and over the birds of the air, and over every living thing that moves upon the earth" (Gen. 1:28). But does it *really* contradict that directive?

The influence that humans are meant to exercise over Earth's creatures is not absolute or tyrannical. The Genesis story tells us that the first couple was created in the "image of God," not as autonomous gods. As "image of God," they represented God, stood in God's place, responsible for the created world and accountable to the Creator who made it. God's questions do indirectly address Job's struggle with suffering. They lead him to see that there is much that he cannot understand and is not able to control. They can also act as a corrective for us whenever we, like Job, forget that Earth is not ours to do with as we please. Rather, "The earth is the LORD's and all that is in it" (Ps. 24:1).

By means of questioning, Job is led to realize that, just as God holds tenderly these mysterious animals, so God holds tenderly the mystery of Job's own existence, suffering and all. The real unspoken question that God poses is a challenge to Job, and to us: Can Job (or we) accept his place in this world as the animals accept theirs, and can he trust in the God in whose hands everything is held?

Psalmody
PSALM 104:14-23

This psalm is a hymn of praise of God (vv. 31-35) as creator (vv. 5-9, 24-26), as sovereign ruler (vv. 1-4), and as divine caretaker of the entire world (vv. 10-23, 27-30). This passage exalts both God's creative power in fashioning a rich and many-faceted world and God's ingenuity in the way various aspects of this world work in harmony to provide what is necessary for survival, growth, and enrichment.

The world functions as one, like a body whose parts share in the building up and growth of one another. While the various life forms are distinct from each other, they are all essential parts of the whole. The grass and plants are made not only for themselves but also as food for animals. As the cattle and beasts of burden feed on the produce of the land, the plant growth reproduces itself so that it continues to flourish and the animals continue to be nourished by it. One form of life sustains another in a wondrous manifestation of synergy.

Human beings, too, enjoy the fruits of the land. Earth is prodigal in bringing forth the wheat that will be transformed into bread that sustains life, the grape that will be crushed into wine that will delight the heart, and the olive that will be ground into oil that will soothe and strengthen. No official contract of production has been made with Earth; no binding terms regarding quantity of yield have been set. Earth simply produces a cornucopia of harvest, asking nothing in return other than that the natural laws that govern growth be respected. Along with the cattle and the beasts of burden, human beings depend upon Earth's generosity for their lives. Like a self-emptying mother, Earth simply gives and gives and gives.

Harmony within creation is also evident in the unselfishness of the water that flows through the land. It is there, unprotected, giving of itself without reserve so that the trees in the forests might be replenished and the cycle of life might move forward. For their part, the trees open their branches like welcoming arms, eager to embrace the birds of the air who find shelter there. Branches, twigs, and leaves, which had been shed as life within the trees grew outward, are now brought back to the trees by the birds as they build their nests in the boughs. In the world of nature, nothing is wasted; everything is recycled, contributing to the development and enrichment of the whole. The high mountains and rocky cliffs, so inhospitable to human beings, provide a protective dwelling for mountain goats and badgers and animals of various species. The fauna of the world find free lodging wherever they choose to establish their residence.

Night, which often strikes terror in the human heart, is natural and inviting for many creatures. The shadows that emerge as the sun sets, the delicate sounds and imperceptible movements that are lost to creatures who have succumbed to sleep, call out to the nocturnal animals. In the darkness of night, creatures too many to count are free to roam about in search of food and drink. Then slowly, as the horizon prepares for the sun's display of radiance, these animals creep back into their dens or burrows or caves, making room for the morning birds and the daylight animals. There is an unspoken agreement among the creatures of Earth. Daytime and nocturnal animals take turns sharing Earth's cordial protection, its open comfort, and its generous bounty. Though independent of human management, these animals live interdependently with each other.

The psalmist sings out in praise of God, whose creativity has not only burst forth in an unimaginable array of life forms, but has also placed deep within the heart of creation itself the sense of being one, despite its diversity. What mistakenly appears to some people as a hostile world is really a panoply of life and beauty and mystery.

Second Reading
1 CORINTHIANS 1:10-23

This short passage from Paul's first letter to the Corinthians can be divided into two separate yet related sections. In the first section (vv. 10-17), Paul appeals to the members of the community to end the boasting that is threatening to cause a rift among them. In the second (vv. 18-23), he discusses his theology of the cross. This latter theme—the role of the cross in the lives of believers—is the linchpin that unites the two sections.

The divisions within the community of which Paul speaks are not caused by disagreements over membership or doctrine or worldview. It is not a case of Jew versus Gentile or Gnostic versus Enthusiast. Rather, the rivalries grew out of the loyalties that existed between the new believers and those who baptized them. It appears that those involved in such rivalry presume that the authority or status of those who baptized them somehow rubbed off onto them, thus providing them comparable standing within the community.

Paul seeks to correct this rivalry in two ways. He first reminds the Corinthian Christians of the union that is theirs ever since they have been baptized in Christ. He insists that if each is united to Christ through baptism, then those united to Christ are united to each other. If, despite their union with Christ, they are separated from each other, then Christ is divided. Paul then returns to the apparent source of the rivalry, namely, loyalty to those who baptized them. Using himself and the allegiance that some might have toward him, he argues that those who baptized them were not crucified for them. It was Christ who was crucified. Nor was it in the names of the baptizers that the Christians were baptized. They were baptized in Christ's name. Those who baptized them were merely ministers of the mystery of Christ.

As for Paul himself, he insists that he was called by God to preach the gospel, not to baptize. Although Paul did baptize some, that was not his primary ministerial responsibility. According to him, the heart of the gospel message that he preached is the cross of Christ. As he develops this theme, he makes a rather strange statement. He claims that the use of human eloquence might empty the wisdom of the cross of its meaning. How can this be? He explains this by contrasting wisdom and foolishness in a way that is similar to the teaching found in the Jewish wisdom tradition. Providing several examples of antithesis, he compares the effects of the cross on those who accept it with the situation of those who do not. He first claims that the wise who open themselves to the power of the cross will be saved, while the fools who reject the cross will perish. He then argues that what, according to human standards, appears to be the weakness of the cross, is in reality the power of God. Quoting the prophet Isaiah (29:14), he describes this antithesis yet again by declaring that the wisdom of the wise will be turned upside down.

Paul is really contrasting the wisdom of the world with the wisdom of the cross. This is why he states that human eloquence might empty the meaning of his preaching about the cross. The cross is a mystery beyond human comprehension. The Greeks, with their fondness for clear philosophical reasoning, would not have been able to comprehend the meaning of the cross. The Jews, on the other hand, looked for signs, extraordinary occurrences that would give their wisdom authenticity. Their religious traditions could not provide insight into the meaning of the cross.

In other words, everyone seemed to want some kind of proof before they would accept this mystery—and there was none. Nonetheless, even in the face of such obstacles, Paul continued to preach Christ crucified.

Paul dismisses the Corinthian Christians' squabble over trivial matters by reminding them of the central issue of their faith, as well as the opposition they might have to face because of their commitment to this faith. He maintains that their loyalty must be to Christ and his cross and to no one and nothing else.

Gospel
LUKE 12:22-31

In this reading from Luke's Gospel, some form of the verb *merimnao* (to be concerned/worried/anxious) appears three times in the first five verses (vv. 22, 25-26), thus underscoring the prominent theme of the passage, namely, the need for the disciples to have confidence in God. The reasons offered for such confidence are grounded in examples taken from the natural world.

In this account, Jesus first addresses human preoccupation with having basic human needs met. Whether the word *psyche* is translated "soul" or "life," the fundamental meaning is the same: there is no need to worry about our well-being. Both our inner needs (food) and our external needs (clothing) will be supplied by God. Jesus then reaches into the natural world for examples that will illustrate this point. He chooses the raven, a bird that feeds on carrion, a bird that in Israel was considered unclean. Though despised by human beings, this bird's nourishment is provided by God. It neither sows nor reaps nor gathers its surplus into barns. Yet God has planned that Earth will provide it with the food it needs. Jesus argues that if God cares for the insignificant raven, certainly God will care for human beings. The raven has no worries in this regard; neither should human beings.

Next, Jesus points to the field flowers that grow wild. Their charm, delicacy, and beauty captivate the human imagination and fill the human spirit with awe. The flowers do nothing to guarantee their exquisite attire. They neither spin the fabric of their covering nor sew it together as a cloak. Yet there they are more resplendent than the king in his official royal garb! If God can clothe the fragile flowers in such grandeur, certainly God will care for human beings.

Consideration moves immediately from this flower image to the grass that carpets the ground with fresh-smelling green growth. As luxurious as it sometimes is, the comfort that it brings is not lasting. Grass eventually withers and dies and is then thrown into an oven as fuel for the fire. If God can cause the grass to grow and thrive, regardless of how fleeting the time of its life might be, then surely God will care for human beings.

Luke employs an *a fortiori* form of argument to make the case that God's care for "lesser" beings assures us that God also will care for "higher" creatures. However, that form of argument can be understood in a way that does not imply inferiority/superiority. Rather, it maintains that God's providential concern pours out to all creatures: to those whose beauty is appreciated by all, like the flowers of the field; to those who are despised by some and thought to be unclean, like the raven; and to those whose moment of life is brief, like the grass. In other words, there is no discrimination when it comes to God's care for creation. The discrimination is ours, not God's. If this is the case, why should human beings be anxious about how they will be clothed or how they will be fed or how long a life span they might enjoy? God's providential concern pours out to all creatures.

The reading closes with a final exhortation: Seek the reign of God! Just what is this reign of God? Is it an eschatological reality that will be brought to birth only in the future? Or might that future burst open in the present whenever we live according to the plan of God? And what is God's plan for us? Does it not call us to live faithfully the life we have been given as children of God and children of Earth? Does it not include the entire world and all of its creatures who live interdependently as part of it? Surely if we do everything in our power to bring this reign to birth, we will receive all that we need in life.

Reflections

Several distinct yet interrelated creation themes are found in the readings for today. The first is the interdependent nature of the world of which we are a part. Both the reading from Job and the portion of Psalm 104 develop this theme. With rich poetic imagery, they sketch the care with which one aspect of creation is open to and provides for another aspect of creation. They give examples of the mutuality that governs the creatures of Earth. These examples demonstrate a very important fact: the natural world is not under human control. It does not need human beings in order to survive and thrive. Such teaching should give us pause. We human beings are part of this world, not outside of it. While it is not dependent on us, we are dependent on it for every aspect of our being. Earth's fruits nourish our bodies; its waters keep us alive; its beauty excites our imaginations. And what do we contribute to its health and well-being? Do our recent "green" interests stem from genuine concern for Earth, or merely from concern for our own human survival in an environment that is now being threatened by our mistakes?

Related to the theme of eco-interdependence is the question of human responsibility/accountability. If the world is an integrated, inter-dependent, synergistic reality, then how are we to understand the directive to "subdue . . . and have dominion" found in Genesis 1:28? In the ancient world which produced that creation narrative, the expression "subdue . . . and have dominion" suggested monarchic rule. A further suggestion of monarchy is the phrase "image of god." In that ancient world, it was quite common for people to set up some kind of an image, symbol, or represen-tation to signify the locale of their god's jurisdiction. Since ancient mon-archs were often thought to be divine, they could be considered images of the god. Israel would certainly reject any thought that its monarchs were divine. Therefore, the man and the woman in the creation account could be depicted as royalty with responsibility for the rest of the created world. However, they would not be considered divine. The world was not theirs to do with as they pleased. They were accountable to God, as the story of the first sin demonstrates (Genesis 3).

We can say, then, that while human beings are totally dependent on Earth for their life, they have a special duty to exercise responsibility for the created world, and they are accountable to God for this responsibility. Today we speak of this responsibility in terms of stewardship. The second creation account says it in very simple words. It directs us "to serve and guard it" (Gen. 2:15; my translation).

The message of the Gospel text redirects our attention from awesome aspects of the natural world in their own right to human attitudes regard-ing our well-being in that world. It describes a kind of carefree attitude that is present in various life forms. Animals are not anxious about their next meal, and yet they seem to survive; flowers do not worry about their covering, yet they are enfolded in beauty; grass is not disturbed by the brevity of its life, yet it continues to grow. Why do we human beings seem unable to trust nature in a comparable way? Why do we fail to see that, through the mysterious workings of Earth, God provides our basic needs? Might it be that we human beings are not satisfied with the way we have been created? We want more than we need, so we exploit and we hoard at the expense of Earth itself, of other human beings, and of other forms of life? God has called us forth from Earth and has sustained us as part of the Earth community. Why are we anxious? Where is our confidence?

Of all the gifts we have received from our Creator, the greatest gift is to have been given the opportunity to be a part of this great mystery of life. The most profound prayer—perhaps the only appropriate prayer—is "Thank you!"

RESOURCES

Allen, Leslie C. *Psalms*. Word Biblical Commentary. Waco: Word Books, 1983.

Edwards, Denis. "Kinship with Creation-Cultivation of Creation," in *Ecology at the Heart of Faith: The Change of Heart That Leads to a New Way of Living on Earth*, 18–26. Maryknoll, N.Y.: Orbis, 2006.

Habel, Norman C. "Is the Wild Ox Willing to Serve You? Challenging the Mandate to Dominate," in *The Earth Story in Wisdom Traditions,* ed. Norman C. Habel, The Earth Bible, vol. 3, 179–89. Cleveland: Pilgrim, 2001.

Hays, Richard B. *First Corinthians. Interpretation: A Bible Commentary for Teaching and Preaching*. Louisville: John Knox, 1997.

Jenzen, J. Gerald. *Job. Interpretation: A Bible Commentary for Teaching and Preaching*. Atlanta: John Knox, 1985.

Olley, John W. "'The Wolf, the Lamb, and a Little Child': Transforming the Diverse Earth Community in Isaiah," in *The Earth Story in the Psalms and the Prophets*, ed. Norman C. Habel and Shirley Wurst, The Earth Bible, vol. 4, 219–29. Cleveland: Pilgrim, 2001.

Ringe, Sharon H. *Luke*. Westminster Bible Companion. Louisville: Westminster John Knox, 1995.

Walker-Jones, Arthur. *The Green Psalter: Resources for an Ecological Spirituality*. Minneapolis: Fortress Press, 2009.

Third Sunday in Creation

Storm Sunday

Monica Joytsna Melanchthon

Job 28:20-27
Psalm 29
1 Corinthians 1:21-31
Luke 8:22-25

Background

> Did you know?
> That time stood still
> At that precise moment,
> That exact second,
>
> When the earth opened its mouth and roared,
> And the oceans wept,
> Such deadly tears it poured,
> As the unknowing world slept,
>
> How many did one tear kill
> In that precise moment,
> That exact second,
> When God's teardrop exploded,
> And time stood still.[1]
> —Sarfraz Ahmed

Poets often respond to the imaginations of a community that has experienced a catastrophe. They put collective experience into words, shaping the communal memory. The poem quoted above perceives a storm as God's teardrop that exploded. Thunder, raging winds, lightning, hail, and pelting rain are natural phenomena that trigger reactions of fear or awe and wonder. Before this violent natural phenomenon could be scientifically explained, cultures around the world attempted to make sense of storms by perceiving a counterintuitive agent, invisible but powerful, behind and responsible for the storm. They put forward conscious explanations as to the special, counterintuitive nature of this agent, resulting in personified natural phenomena. Special deities were formed for the phenomenon of thunderstorm and its accompanying manifestations, the thunderclap and the lightning, which agitate most powerfully the feelings of humankind. While some agents behind these natural phenomena were deified (Adad, Baal, Thor, Zeus, Indra, and so on), others were demonized, such as Rudra, the malignant storm god who brought death in the mythology of early Hinduism. A serious belief in these agents met the social/religious and emotional needs of the community. Rituals, chants, and devices (bells) were developed to appease these gods or demons and thereby to dispel the storm. I believe that reference to God within natural phenomena also enabled people to revere these phenomena and to accept to them as holy.

A survey of storm gods in the cultures of the world would reveal that they were mostly male deities. Powerful and full of energy, they were also thought to bring fertility to the land despite their violent streak. We would recognize this from the Old Testament, where Baal, the god of the Canaanites, although male, was also a god of fertility. The ancients believed that the rain was the seed of the male god that fertilized the female earth. The energy of the gods was usually expressed by thunder, which was said to be produced by various means: for example, the Nordics believed that thunder was the sound of Thor's chariot wheels, while others believed that thunder was the sound of storm gods drumming on tree trunks or roaring like powerful beasts. These storm gods were believed to hurl lightning down on Earth in the shape of thunderbolts.

There are numerous traditional beliefs and significations attached to thunder and lightning. Some believed that if a thunderstorm occurred during a marriage ceremony, the couple would have no children. Nursing mothers should never suckle their babies during a thunderstorm, as their milk would be tainted with brimstone and sulphur. Among the Christians in India, rain at the time of a wedding is considered a sign of blessing, although it is not clear how a full-blown thunderstorm and lightning might be conceived. Some among the fisher folk believe that a thunderstorm, when one is out at sea, is a sign of an erring spouse! It is a notion that has negative consequences, primarily for women, who are held responsible for the lives of their spouses.

The ancient Hebrew people believed that God, without any detriment to God's majesty, makes God's presence known even through forces of nature. Unlike cultures that deified the stars and the moon, the Israelites envisioned God as one who reveals God's self through the sudden and the unexpected, the terrifying and awesome forces of nature, namely the thunderstorm and the lightning. God delivers judgment ("retributive theodicy") and offers assistance through the thunderstorm. Exodus 19 and Psalm 18 reveal this image of God as one who causes God's voice to resound in thunder, a God who uses lightning as arrows. Bolts of lightning are God's burning breath or tongues of flame; in anger, God may send lashing rain and the smiting hail. The thunderstorm acquired the most favored medium of a theophany, a vehicle of divine presence. It is a spectacle that involves the senses, both the eyes and the ears, evokes fear, and makes a mockery of human defenses.

"Storm" therefore gives definitive expression to many themes: fertility, blessing, anger, theodicy, wrath, and destruction. In India, storms, typhoons, and cyclones are annual experiences. After months of hot, dry weather, the monsoon is eagerly anticipated, prayers are offered, and *poojas* are performed—strange rituals such as marrying two donkeys, which was meant to ensure that the monsoon arrives on time. These monsoons are invited, despite the widespread flooding that results in many areas of South Asia.

Storms are also metaphorically understood as the injustice meted out against the poor and the weak—metaphors, for example, about the ways in which the beauties of nature are needlessly destroyed by humanity or the innocent purity of young love is so often crushed underfoot by society. The storm is used as a metaphor for unrest and coming change. There is, as it were, an inextricable connection between the disharmony in society (absence of community) and the disorder in nature and environment. On the one hand, this has been expressed in the Hindu belief that if there is justice and harmony in society, then there will be rainfall—so that nature will flourish and bear abundant fruits. On the other hand, conflict in society and the lack of righteousness will bring about disasters and cataclysms in nature. Despite the presence of such beliefs, issues of social injustice are never addressed when the country or a region is facing drought!

The thunderstorm is commonly seen only from an anthropocentric perspective. Even when it is destructive, the thunderstorm is attributed to God's purposeful action, often as a response to human disobedience. While I believe it is entirely appropriate for reflective people of faith to be deeply troubled by the destruction caused by storms and to ask how it squares with their belief in a loving Creator, we still need to develop a perspective regarding storms and their function.

From an Earth perspective, storms are a natural and necessary consequence of physical forces acting on the Earth; for example, the atmospheric circulation driven by differences in the amount of solar energy received and absorbed at the Earth's surface, and the effects of Earth's circular movement. Storms are nature's way of refreshing and renewing Earth. Ecosystems are nourished and sustained by storms and floods and cyclones. But storms are seen negatively because they are potentially destructive to human life and property. When human beings engage in profit-driven developmental projects in areas reclaimed through the use of modern technology for economic gain, particularly on shorelines, the surrounding area is controlled and its natural system is altered. The consequences are then destructive, not only for Earth but for human life as well. Inappropriate technological intervention is employed to save human life, but it does not provide for Earth. And the results, namely the protection of human life, are never satisfactory. Most ordinary people are unaware of the interlinkages that exist among storms, development projects, and the after-effects of storms. Storms are not meant to be seen as punishments or judgments of God but as natural processes integral for and to the refreshment and renewal of Earth. As created beings, we are part and parcel of the ecosystem. And while we acknowledge the interconnectedness between humanity and the rest of the created order, we need to be discerning and wise in regard to the ways we live out our relationship to Earth and in regard to our attempts to make Earth habitable for humanity. Thunderstorms are divine in that they are agents/instruments employed by God for and on behalf of Earth and the cosmos—for Earth's continued survival and regeneration.

First Reading
JOB 28:20-27

The first set of dialogues between Job and his friends (chapters 4–27) is followed by this famous chapter that celebrates wisdom. Markedly different in tone, it is a hymn of praise to wisdom, a treatise on the nature of wisdom. Much attention has been given to the relationship of this chapter to those that precede it (4–27) and those that follow (29–31). Opinions vary, and while some interpreters see this chapter as a continuation of that first set of dialogues, others see it as an independent, self-contained unit that looks back to what precedes and that points forward to what follows. The poem is a response to questions concerning the location of wisdom, the source of wisdom, who the possessor of wisdom is, and how one acquires it. The poem consists of three strophes of approximately equal length interspersed with the refrain, "But where does wisdom come from? Where is the place of understanding?" (28:12, 20). In the first strophe, Job celebrates and takes pride in the human capability to bring to the surface the treasures of the Earth. And yet human beings are impotent when contrasted with God, since they are not capable of finding wisdom. In the second strophe, Job speaks of the fact that wisdom is not a commodity that can be purchased, found, dug up, or exchanged, even for the most precious of stones. Wisdom is inaccessible to human beings, to other living creatures, and to the ruler of the underworld.

Finally, in verses 23-27, Job gives a positive answer. Only God knows the way and the place where wisdom can be found. All created beings and God search for wisdom, but only God finds it and knows how to acquire it. This knowledge that God obtains is acquired through God's skill and creative activity, manifest in the superterrestrial phenomena. Job identifies four specific creative activities of God, namely, the weight of the wind, the measure of the primordial waters, the seasons and locations of rain, and the way of lightning. It is in the creation of these phenomena that God "saw" wisdom and experienced it. It is not completely clear as to whether God finds wisdom by accident or through a deliberate search, but God finds it in God's creation of the Earth. There is something quite human about this search for wisdom by God. What is stunning is that God finds this wisdom in the Earth and in the cosmos. Some argue that this wisdom is not something God employs in God's creative activity but something that God actually discovers during the process of creation. Wisdom dwells in the Earth and is discovered by God, not in the depths or the heights of creation, but in the totality of creation. This does not mean that God is not wise. God's wisdom is apparent in God's capacity to create according to a plan or design. But the wisdom that God discovers, God considers and validates. This wisdom is perhaps beyond complete human comprehension. This insight also implies that the wisdom inherent in God extends beyond the wisdom that is found in nature, beyond the wisdom found in the Earth that God has created.

In affirming this wisdom that God finds in the Earth, in the meteorological phenomena that God has created, God exhibits an awareness of the world as being and having value and worth. Any violation of Earth is therefore tantamount to insulting God's holiness. We are invited to celebrate this wisdom along with God and to conduct ourselves as those who have been given stewardship, a custodianship that is characterized by justice and care, by resistance to all that hurts and harms the Earth, and by a passion to maintain the intrinsic worth of the Earth and our connectedness to her. The wisdom that is inherent in the storms might escape us; nevertheless, it is hallowed and cherished by God, who has created the storm for the recovery and the revitalization of Earth.

Psalmody
PSALM 29

Psalm 29 is a Hebrew doxology in praise of YHWH, sovereign of the universe, who is manifested in the mighty acts of nature. The psalm is comprised of three main movements: invitation to praise, description of theophany, and a concluding acclamation (vv. 10-11). It is quite obvious that the psalm has been influenced by Canaanite religion, a religion in which Baal was worshiped as the storm deity and the rider of the storm clouds. There is extant literary evidence where Baal is referred to as thunder, lightning, and rain. Drought was understood to be the effect of Baal's absence; and when he comes, he brings rain and thunder. It has been suggested that this psalm might actually be an ancient Canaanite hymn composed originally in honor of Baal. In case anyone wonders how such a psalm made it into the canon, Charles Fensham responds that the "Hebrews may have used this hymn as part of a missionary effort; by using the psalm, zealous Israelites may have sought to reach the Canaanites and even those other Israelites who had fallen away from the true faith."[2] Or it might be a deliberate imitation or adaptation of a Canaanite hymn for the purposes of Israel's faith, since ancient Israel was often detracted from its worship of YHWH by the fertility cults of Baal.

In its present form, the psalm is definitely a polemic against the idols of Canaan, particularly Baal. It calls for the praise of YHWH as the Lord over nature; and it uniquely affirms ancient Israel's faith in the one God, YHWH. The psalmist wanted to convey to his audience that YHWH was the Lord of history, the one who led Israel out of bondage in Egypt, to Sinai and beyond, but that this Lord of history is also the Lord of nature. In the context of ancient Israel, where it was popularly believed that the domain of nature belonged to Baal, the psalm boldly and categorically sings out its praise to YHWH.

The hymn is composed for use in the Temple, an enthronement psalm that leads the community to imagine YHWH as sovereign Lord of the universe, seated on the throne in YHWH's palace above the cosmic waters that surround the Earth. YHWH is surrounded by the heavenly host (heavenly council/court), which is summoned to give praise and glory. The human community assembled in the Temple is called to join this heavenly chorus and glorify God in similar fashion. The doxologies on Earth are to be equated with the doxologies in heaven.

The psalm begins with three occurrences of the command to "ascribe to the Lord" appropriate "glory," which is the organizing motif of the psalm. Glory is used in two ways. The "glory" of YHWH refers to the attributes of YHWH—power, majesty, strength, and holy grandeur. But the "glory" is also a reference to the manifestation of YHWH, the manner in which YHWH reveals YHWH's sovereignty and dominion over the Earth. The psalm then describes "the voice of the LORD" to show that God has exercised great power for the community; and this powerful voice is therefore a convincing reason to praise YHWH. In verses 3-10, the psalm employs the description of a thunderstorm—thunder, lightning, and wind—to evoke praise for the power and might of YHWH. Thunder, which is presented as the voice of God, is referred to seven times. This voice is more a sound than speech. It is thunder, it is powerful, and it is full of majesty. In very militaristic language that stresses the idea of YHWH as warrior, the psalm describes the acts of the voice of YHWH as powerful enough to break the cedars of Lebanon and Sirion (Canaanite symbols of stability) and to shake the wilderness of Kadesh. The voice of thunder flashes forth fire (lightning), causes the deer to calve early, and strips bare the forests. Thunder is therefore an active agent that is seen and heard and stirs awe among the people, causing them to shout "Glory!" God's voice as thunder commands praise—not for the thunderstorm but for YHWH, who is sovereign over nature. The thunderstorm is an established and popular medium of divine presence and a literary and theological strategy designed as a doxology. The proclamation reaches its climax in a declaration that YHWH is enthroned over the flood as king forever (v. 10). The declaration states the meaning of the proclamation; the thunderstorm is the glory, the display of the powerful rule of YHWH.

As human beings, we are inclined to view the world as a complex entity that needs to be rationally explained and plundered. We employ science and technology, and we shrink the world to the dimensions of our reason and needs. Our perceptions are influenced by economics and research, thus reducing the "poetic and mythological." Accepting some of the mystery regarding the functioning of Earth and its wisdom might enable us to appreciate her more and thereby increase our respect for her.

Second Reading

I CORINTHIANS 1:21-31

We have a tale in India about a weary traveler who, after walking for miles, sat under a banyan tree to rest. While he cooled down in the shade of the large tree, he noticed a watermelon vine nearby with several large melons. He scoffed at what he considered to be foolishness on God's part. Such a frail-looking vine with large and heavy fruit, and a huge and strong tree with fruit the size of berries! Cynical and amused, he fell asleep and was awakened by the banyan berry that fell on his head! He then understood the wisdom behind God's creation of the watermelon vine and the banyan tree and the size of their fruit. In some ways, this is what the text here in Corinthians is speaking about. We judge God by our standards of wisdom!

Paul speaks knowingly of this divine wisdom and its peculiar functioning in the world. The Corinthian church was squabbling over who had the right gospel and the right interpretation of the cross. Leaders within the church were boasting to each other about being the custodians of the truth, competing with one another and accusing one another of holding flawed interpretations. Paul reminds the church that they were evaluating each other with human wisdom. This boasting on the part of the leadership was in contradiction to their identity as Christians, for the cross (gospel), Paul stresses, does not gain superiority by the addition of human wisdom. Divine wisdom is something that stands in complete, uncompromising contradistinction to human wisdom. The true gospel is about the power of Christ and the wisdom of God, which may seem like folly, absurdity, and foolishness from the point of view of human wisdom.

Paul uses the Greek term for "foolishness" or "folly" six times, and he claims that this foolishness of God is wiser and more powerful than human wisdom. It is a wisdom that is unnerving, unsettling, and upsetting. He predicates this point by calling attention to the fact that the ones whom God chose to make God's new people are the lowly, the weak, the poor, and the noninfluential, like the members of the Corinthian church, who are a visible confirmation of this foolishness of God. Therefore, they had no grounds for boasting; for if they were to apply the same human wisdom to themselves, it would show how insignificant they really were.

"God chose what is low and despised in the world, things that are not, to reduce to nothing things that are, so that no one might boast in the presence of God" (vv. 28-29). The choice of such people reveals the ultimate divine will to obliterate all human grounds for boasting. They were chosen in order to shame the world, to upset its rationality and its conceptions of power and influence. By choosing a crucified man to reveal God's self, God challenges all ideas of what it means to be "divine." By becoming weak, by emptying God's self of all power, and by becoming a victim to death, God makes foolish the wisdom of this world, which understands power to be the ability to impose suffering and pain, to subjugate. And God makes foolish all human conceptions of superiority, strength, and might. Through the work of Christ, whom God made as the true "wisdom," God made possible the redemption of all humanity by putting us in right relationship with God. This is the gracious character and wisdom of God, possibly beyond human understanding. We as the church are called not to identify God or God's people with power and pomp.

What might this text be saying to Earth and our relationship to Earth? How do we deal with and respond to the increasing number and intensity of storms due to global warming, storms that disrupt our lives? Everything has its way, including the storms. And this, for me, even if I am not able to comprehend it fully, indicates that Earth is governed by systems and principles based on some wisdom. There is a natural wisdom in the manner and functioning of Earth. The storms are governed by this same natural wisdom. In my limited capacity as a human being, I might understand this wisdom as foolish. What good are storms when all they bring is havoc and panic? For human beings, perhaps, yes! But this is not so for Earth. Wisdom therefore resides in the Earth and in the principles and the forces that regulate her and order her. We as human beings would grow in wisdom if only we would observe and explore the creation and respect it and have reverence for the God who brought her into being. The God who reconciles human beings through the death of Jesus Christ will also equip us to reconcile with Earth and all natural forces.

Gospel
LUKE 8:22-25

The calming of the storm is a miracle story that may serve as a preface to three stories of healing, namely, the healing of the demoniac the healing of the hemorrhaging woman, and the raising of the daughter of Jairus. These episodes are followed by the commissioning of the Twelve, and hence it has been suggested that these four "miracles" (power over nature; exorcism; physical healing; raising of the dead) could be considered as illustrative of Jesus' ministry as he prepared the Twelve. Through these four miracles that take place before the commissioning of the twelve disciples, Jesus is presented and recognized as Lord of nature and Lord of history, as Lord of the sea and Lord of the land. Jesus is in a boat on the Sea of Galilee (actually a lake), and the miracles are performed on either side of this sea. The sea is seldom gentle, but always a thing of treachery and greed, ship-shattering and angry, where those who venture are fearful, trembling, and overly bold. Seas, wind, and rivers all provide violent metaphors. As frequently depicted in the psalms, however, these parts of nature are also under the power of God. To still the storm and save those in danger is possible through the power of God (cf. Ps. 107:23-32).

Whether Jesus is on the sea or by the sea, the sea is central to the spatial orientation of Jesus' ministry of healing. Hence, one needs to discern the significance of the sea and its crossing by Jesus. The boat ride and the storm give the disciples the opportunity to experience Jesus' power, its nature and source. And once they are back on the shore, they see that very same power employed to bring healing to people whom Jesus encounters. By virtue of being on the sea and in a boat, Jesus has the complete and undivided attention of the disciples, and the disciples have private time with Jesus.

Jesus is tired. He sleeps and is rudely awakened by his disciples calling for help because of the storm that was rocking the boat and filling it up with water. In language very similar to the words used to heal the demoniac, Jesus rebukes the wind and the raging waves. And immediately the waters of the sea become calm. Was Jesus scolding the waters? Or was he rebuking the evil spirits that were stirring the waters, spirits that were commonly believed to reside in the waters? The miracle is reminiscent of other such instances in ancient mythology, such as Neptune stilling the storm to save the fleet of Aeneas. Jesus manifests power over the sea. And later, Jesus uses the harmful power of the sea to drown the swine now possessed by Legion. So, the destructive power of the sea can be used against those who have the potential to obstruct faith. It is this devastating power of the sea over which Jesus exerts control; and it is the same power that he uses to heal and provide succor.

Yet the question remains: When a miracle story claims that a god or hero controls nature, what set of meanings is available to the ordinary person—whether in antiquity or in the present—to make sense of it? For those who believed or believe now that there were gods controlling the sea and the evil spirits that churned the waters of the sea, the miracle clearly affirms that Jesus is Lord of nature. Jesus is familiar and, hence, in tune with the wisdom of nature and its logic and thereby is able to command its attention. Even though God separated the land from the waters and provided human beings with the land to "till and to keep" (Gen. 2:15), the waters remain under the sovereignty of God. The chaotic and threatening power of the sea and of the storm is manifest and frightening to the disciples; but the power in the word spoken by Jesus is stronger. The sea is controlled and the storm is obstructed from manifesting its destructive power by the power of the spoken word of Jesus.

This narrative records one of the few instances when Jesus actually ministers to his own disciples, since most of the time they are spectators to Jesus ministering to others. The incident that is recorded at the head of this cluster of miracle stories provides occasion for Jesus to manifest his power, test the faith of the disciples, and make them reflect on the person of Jesus. Who is Jesus? Jesus is wisdom—the wisdom of God that works in harmony with the wisdom of nature.

Reflections

As I complete this task, I am aware that it has been raining incessantly for three days here in Chennai. Much of our seminary campus is flooded, and students are having to eat their meals in a dining room filled with at least six inches of water. Looking at the pictures of the campus, a friend asked, "Is God trying to tell us something, Monica?" Act of God or not, it is certainly the case that elements of nature—whether floods, tsunamis, volcanic eruptions, or earthquakes—evoke fear of devastation, and for logical reasons. We need to be cognizant of the questions that such experiences raise, but also we need to be equally aware of our choices/actions and their effects that might contribute to the devastation caused by such eruptions/expressions of nature. Recognition of our fragility as human beings, of our of dependence for life on these very same forces of nature (the elements of earth, air, water, and fire), and of their destructive potential—all these strike at our consciousness, often only after a devastation. We have to come to terms with the fact that the Earth and all its elements transcend us; the Earth is not derived from us. Instead of attempting to "subdue" the Earth, we need urgently to recognize that we are not separate from the Earth; rather, our lives are inextricably linked with it and dependent on it: "We inhabit it, on loan."[3] We are called to be sensitive toward and to live in tune with the wisdom of the Earth—be grounded in it and discern within such life the wisdom of God. In such a relationship with the Earth, and in our daily actions with one another and with the Earth, we will encounter the divine. May the God of the Storm continue to bless us and equip us to be mindful of the Earth and all its inhabitants.

RESOURCES

Craddock, Fred B. *Luke. Interpretation: A Bible Commentary for Teaching and Preaching.* Louisville: John Knox, 1990.

Craigie, Peter C. *Ugarit and the Old Testament: The Story of a Remarkable Discovery and Its Impact on Old Testament Studies.* Grand Rapids: Eerdmans, 1983.

Deane-Drummond, Celia. *Eco-Theology.* Winona, Minn.: St. Mary's, 2008.

Habel, Norman C. "Wisdom Cosmology and Climate Change," in *God, Creation, and Climate Change: Spiritual and Ethical Perspectives*, ed. Karen L. Bloomquist, 115–26. Geneva: Lutheran World Federation, 2009.

Spivak, Gayatri Chakravorty. *Death of a Discipline.* New York: Columbia University Press, 2003.

Whybray, Norman. *Job. Readings: A New Testament Commentary.* Sheffield: Sheffield Academic, 1998.

Van Wolde, Ellen. *Mr. and Mrs. Job.* Trans. John Bowden. London: SCM, 1997.

NOTES

1. Sarfraz Ahmed, "God's Teardrop Exploded," *Kala Kahni* (2011) http://www.kalakahani.co.uk/32534.html (accessed March 7, 2011).

2. Charles Fensham, as cited by Peter C. Craigie, in *Ugarit and the Old Testament: The Story of a Remarkable Discovery and Its Impact on Old Testament Studies* (Grand Rapids: Eerdmans, 1983), 68–71.

3. Gayatri Chakravorty Spivak, *Death of a Discipline* (New York: Columbia University Press, 2003), 73.

Fourth Sunday in Creation

Cosmos Sunday

Vicky Balabanski with Shirley Joh Wurst

Proverbs 8:22-31
Psalm 148
Colossians 1:15-20
John 6:41-51

Background

In this final Sunday of the Wisdom series, we turn our attention to the cosmos as a whole. As we widen our horizon to glimpse the great expanse of creation, a prior question arises: Why have we chosen to use the term *cosmos* to refer to "all things," and not the word *universe*? One reason is that the term *universe* may be too small. Many cosmologists are shifting toward the concept of a "multiverse," with our known universe just a component in a far vaster cosmos. What we think of as our "universe" may not ultimately be "universal."

The word *cosmos* comes directly from the Greek *kosmos* and has the primary meaning of "order." We see order all around us—we glimpse order on a macroscale as we gaze through a telescope at the heavens, and we glimpse ordered reality on a microscale through a microscope. Contemporary cosmologists are also looking for order. They seek to account for the way cosmic reality is ordered.

In our Scriptures, *kosmos* has a range of additional meanings. It often refers to adornment or ornament (from which we get our term *cosmetics*). In later writers, such as Wisdom and 2 Maccabees, the orderliness and beauty of creation become more prominent. So in the Prayer of Manasseh (v. 2), God is described as the one "who made heaven and earth with all their order" (*kosmos*). In the Gospel of John, the word *kosmos* has a range of meanings, including the totality of creation and the world of human affairs; it can have a negative connotation as well, referring to "this world" as contrasted with the world above.

How we understand cosmos reflects something about ourselves, too, and about what we hold to be the underlying attitude of God toward the creation. Though many of us have learned to see the world dualistically, the Season of Creation has been challenging us to see the cosmos holistically. Wisdom takes its stand on the holistic side, as set out in this affirmation in the Wisdom of Solomon 1:14: "For God created all things so that they might exist; the generative forces of the world [*kosmos*] are wholesome, and there is no destructive poison in them, and the dominion of Hades is not on earth." The cosmos as we know it, both through revelation and through science, is characterized by an *impulse to life*. One of the great scientific puzzles of our time is the way in which the very nature of the cosmos seems to be intrinsically shaped—even fine-tuned—by the fundamental forces through which the particles of matter interact to make the emergence of life possible. For example, if the weak nuclear force that controls disintegration processes in atomic nuclei were only very slightly weaker or stronger, then supernova explosions would not occur and the stardust of heavy elements essential to life would not have been available to form Earthlike planets. Or, if the strong nuclear force between the proton and the neutron were only slightly weaker or stronger, the sun's processes would have been different from what they are, such that life on Earth could not have developed.

Scientists have discovered self-organizing systems with a remarkable tendency toward increasing order (*kosmos*!). These systems exist in a state between rigid stability and chaos—that condition of exquisite sensitivity to the initial conditions that makes the future condition unpredictable, as in the so-called butterfly effect. It is near the edge of chaos where order, complexity, and lifelike behaviors occur. Very diverse fields such as biology, seismology, history, and economics are studying this phenomenon, which appears to be fundamental to the nature of the cosmos. Perhaps life appears as an emergent possibility of sufficiently complex systems.

Scientists recognize that there is more to reality than can be deduced from ever-greater study of its constituent parts. We live in a cosmos where order continues to emerge, revealing an underlying impulse to life. For those of us open to the transcendent, we see in this impulse the "invisible hand of God" at work—not in an interventionist sense, but wove into the very fabric of reality.

The order of the cosmos reveals an impulse to life. We might use another term for this reality, namely, "grace." We most frequently think of grace in relation to God's acts of salvation and redemption, but the fact that we exist at all, in a cosmos imbued with life, is itself a demonstration of grace. God's grace is the reason that there is a world instead of nothing at all or only a swirl of random matter.

Wisdom is glimpsed in seeing God's acts of creation and redemption not as separate, but as a unified act of self-bestowing love. The problem of keeping these two theologies separate is that it seems that one relates to all of creation, and the other only to humanity. Yet creation and re-creation are both expressions of God's grace. The impulse to life and the invitation to new life are both part of the order through which God is pleased to offer grace to us and to all creation.

First Reading
PROVERBS 8:22-31

This passage from Proverbs is one of several texts in the Hebrew Scriptures focusing on Wisdom.[1] Together with the passages from Job that are explored during this series, Proverbs 8 outlines some of the mysteries and marvelous aspects of God's creation of Earth.

The passage opens with a reference to God's "way"[2] or "work"[3] (v. 22). The Hebrew concept of *derek* has the sense of "characteristic way of being," "integrity," "means of flourishing," or "most expeditious path," and is intimately connected with the Hebrew biblical concept of wisdom. Being wise is a matter of knowing and pursuing your *derek,* that is, being true to who you are. All creatures have their distinctive *derek*, their characteristic way of being; human beings need to choose the way of righteousness to be true to the inbuilt order of the cosmos.

Proverbs 8:22-31 establishes Wisdom's credentials as a teacher of God's ways for all living things, including human beings. She acknowledges that she is a creation:[4] God made her, too. In contrast to other creations, however, she is primary—the first creation: "the first of God's works of old" (v. 22b). The use of the term *derek*, especially when read in conjunction with Job 28:23-27, suggests that God generates or gives birth to Wisdom in order to create Earth and all Earth's ways.

In Proverbs 8, Wisdom's extreme old age is underlined by the multiple use of terms that allude to beginnings, precedence, and being old: "at the beginning" (repeated), "works of old," "in the distant past," "at the origin of Earth," and "before" (repeated). Wisdom also confirms that she was "before" and that she preceded those aspects of Earth that are foundational, namely, the "big-picture" items characteristic of the way our world is: the "deep," "springs," "foundations of the mountains," "hills," "earth and fields," "lumps of clay," the "heavens," the "seas," the "horizon," "fountains of the deep," and the "foundations of the Earth."

In the same way, she reiterates her beginnings: "I was fashioned," "I was brought forth," and "I was born." In this sequence, the ordering is instructive. It demonstrates that she is conceived (constructed/shaped/formed), that she develops and emerges from, that she is differentiated, and that she is born and becomes an individual being independent of her creator. Each of these processes is passive: they happen *to* her. Wisdom is born; she does not generate or give birth to herself.

Perhaps the most unexpected and challenging implication is that God is her birth mother. There is nothing except God; and God makes her and gives her independent being before creating or giving life to anything else. In verse 30 we glimpse a delightful depiction of a paradigmatic parent-child relationship. The Hebrew term *amon*, translated on the basis of the Septuagint and Vulgate as "master craftsman," can also be translated as "darling," "cherished one," "intimate," "nursing child," and "confidant" (JSB), focusing on the *relationship* between God and Wisdom rather than on the *task* of crafting the cosmos.

Wisdom is seen as an exuberant source of joy: "a source of delight every day, rejoicing before God at all times" (v. 30bc). This is a compelling picture of an innocent, chuckling child and her doting parent sharing the pleasures of an intimate, trusting, and loving companionship. In Proverbs 8, Wisdom is depicted as a playful, laughing child, who works closely with God in their creation project: together with her father-mother, she creates an Earth full of living beings that delight both the laughing child and her doting parent. In addition to the mutual and reciprocal pleasure is the fascination and enthusiastic joy at what they have made together: Earth, a world filled with beautiful, diverse, and intriguing living things, including human beings. This is another perspective on the garden of Eden, where God and humans delight in each other's companionship, chatting together in the cool of the evening, sharing the pleasures of the day.

This picture of God as fundamentally relational, as God in community, requires us to see ourselves that way as well. Our world is a community, and the way of Wisdom is to learn how we can live interdependently and symbiotically for the well-being of the whole. As with God and Wisdom, who together generate life (cf. John 1:3, NKJV), so also for us who participate in the way of wisdom, generating life is a collaborative project.

An integral aspect of this creative project—the *way* it works—is that it is interactive and interdependent. Nothing is made without an *other*, a close companion. God's "way" in creation is collaborative; God's creation is collaborative. Without an *other*, nothing can flourish. And this "way" is also how Earth flourishes. In collaboration, in mutual and reciprocal interdependence, lies the "integrity," the wholeness of all creation. No created thing is an island unto itself. The interconnectedness of the web of life is a constant reminder that we are not alone—as individuals, as a species, or as Earth. We are all part of Earth, part of Earth's well-being. We are made from its "lumps of clay." We are earthlings. We are constructed from Earth and we return to Earth.

Contemporary Earth sciences, especially those focusing on the cosmos—the "world" of which our Earth is a part—have revealed the immensity of a cosmos in which our Earth is a mere speck. Our Earth is made from the cosmos. Just as we are made from "the dust of the Earth," so our world is "the dust of the cosmos." As physicist Edward Zganjar (pronounced "Skyner") asserted, "We are . . . stardust."[6] According to the big bang theory, our cosmos exploded into being, and will ultimately return to nonbeing, swallowed by a black hole. We are a part of something that is bigger than we can imagine, yet we participate in the essence of how this immensity has being and how it flourishes. In recognizing our interconnectedness with the cosmos, we can participate in the joy that God and Wisdom share.

Psalmody
PSALM 148

Many readers see Psalm 148 as metaphorical, especially the verses that invite sea monsters, ocean depths and waters above the heavens, sun, moon, and stars, fire and hail, snow and smoke, storm winds, mountains and hills, fruit trees and cedars, wild and tamed beasts, creeping things and winged birds to praise God. From a Western perspective, physical aspects of our Earth, the elements, animals, and trees, cannot praise God. We are comfortable with people of all ages and statuses praising God; we can perhaps more easily imagine angels and the inhabitants of heaven praising God—a common conception of heaven includes angels, harps, and choirs! We can even imagine birdsongs as praising God—unless the singers are crows or buzzards!

For us, praise is beautiful, delightful, pleasing to our sensibilities: there will be no wrong or flat notes in the heavenly choirs!

However, when we are reminded of our initial responses to Eastern music and throat singing, the ululations of Arabic women, the throbbing of the didgeridoo, the recordings of whale songs, we realize that our senses are capable of appreciating diverse sounds. And what we "like" is often a "taste" we have developed or a preference we have been enculturated to recognize as the highest form of art. For some listeners, heavy metal is sublime. And there are those for whom Mozart is an acquired taste!

Psalm 148 is one of the final psalms in the Hebrew Scriptures' songbook. It is the middle psalm of the final group of five psalms—the Hallelujah psalms—each beginning and ending with the exclamation "Hallelujah!" This group of psalms of praise is a fitting final element in a book that is about praising God. Together, these five psalms provide a resounding accolade to the God who creates, nurtures, comforts, and saves. They are the apotheosis of the book of Psalms—a "concluding doxology" (JSB, 1443) and part of the "daily Hallel" (JSB, 1442) in the Jewish daily morning service.

Structurally, Psalm 148 moves from the expected to the unexpected in a series of waves; at the end of each, there is a rationale for the invitation—for the command—to praise God. In effect, the psalm demonstrates that praise is a requirement and a response: once you know what God has done, you will automatically respond with hallelujahs!

In the first wave, it is the heavens that are exhorted to praise—angels, hosts, sun and moon, and stars. These beings are, in the Hebrew cosmological scheme, closest to God; they are immortal creations, unchanging. They are, in a sense, made for celebration. They are at the top of the world; and they therefore establish a pattern for those beneath (vv. 5-6).

In the next set, the invitation is extended to "all you who are on Earth" (v. 7b). Surprisingly, our anthropocentrism is subtly admonished: human beings are only included at the end of the set in verses 11-12.

And, in another unexpected and ironic reversal, the first of Earth's inhabitants mentioned are sea monsters and ocean depths! With the next group, "fire and hail, snow and smoke, storm wind" (v. 8), a critique of humans is implicit. These elements "execute God's command." And the listing of "kings," "princes," and "judges" in verse 11 implicitly reminds the discerning reader that the "peoples of the Earth" do not always execute God's work and are sometimes blind, deaf, and dumb to their Creator God.

The second invitation to "praise the name of the LORD" contrasts with the first. This set (vv. 7-13)—including disparate creations ranging from sea monsters, climatic elements, mountains, hills, fruit trees, cedars, and wild and tame beasts, creeping things, and human beings—is to praise "the name," because God's "name . . . alone, is sublime," and because God's "splendor covers heaven and Earth." Initially, the praise is to be a response to being created; then, it is to be a response to God's being!

The imagery provides a common thread. God, whose being is light, is splendid. God's light shines on everything God created. And God's "faithful ones," the people "close" to God, will be glorified—implying that God's glorious light will shine through and from them, too.

The Hebrew term *sagab* describes God's name and is variously translated as "sublime," "exalted," and "worthy of praise." The use of this term demonstrates that the name of God exemplifies God's being as eternal: without beginning and without end. God is. And because God is, everything else praises, can praise, will praise. God's existence requires—indeed, demands—praise and exaltation.

The focus on creation in Psalm 148 suggests that this psalm is part of the wisdom tradition. The final verses demonstrate the idiosyncratic aspect of God that makes God sublime: this Creator shares divinity with mundane creation. Indeed, God's splendor—God's light, life, being— "covers" everything. In the wisdom tradition, this means that everything exemplifies God's greatness. Created in collaboration with Wisdom, everything that exists demonstrates that the "way" can be "fruitful and multiply" and can exemplify how it is to be.

For the psalmist, this is exemplified in the gracious choosing, preserving, and exalting of God's people—the people whose history of relationship with their God is expounded in the Hebrew Scriptures. Unlike the other gods—often depicted as sun, moon, trees, mountains, wind, or fire—the deity celebrated in Psalm 148 is an Earth-friendly God who comes close to and exists in intimate contact with the world and its inhabitants. This God is committed to the chosen people; as God's book demonstrates, God's choice is forever.

In the words of Proverbs 8, God and Wisdom—God's close collaborative co-creator—"rejoice" in the "inhabited world" and "find delight" in their creations. This "delight" is exhilaration; it is the highest level of pleasure and celebration: sublime ecstasy.

And, in Psalm 148, heaven and Earth—the whole cosmos—reflect back God's delight. God's delight in creation is infectious. Being covered by God's splendor, creation's very existence celebrates God.

There is a sense in which this psalm advocates that hallelujah is our essential being. In response to our Maker, we are helplessly and endlessly, involved in praise. Just as the form of the psalm demonstrates, we begin and end in exaltation! Like every created thing, we are born for exaltation! It is *who* we are and *how* we are to be. And Psalm 148 advocates that we let ourselves be how we are created to be, so that we will inevitably join with the endless exaltation of the whole cosmos!

Second Reading

COLOSSIANS 1:15-20

Our hymns of praise distill those things that we hold to be especially worth remembering and celebrating in our relationship with God. In Colossians 3:16, the recipients are encouraged to sing as a way of letting the word of Christ dwell in them: "Let the word of Christ dwell in you richly; teach and admonish one another in all wisdom; and with gratitude in your hearts sing psalms, hymns, and spiritual songs to God." Colossians 1:15-20 is widely held to be just such a hymn. As such, according to Colossians 3:16, these verses would have had a dual function: they would have served not only to express the praise that the believers at Colossae wanted to offer Christ, but they also would have offered a way of teaching and admonishing one another in the faith. The teaching and admonishing/instructing were to be "in all wisdom"; hence, for the Colossians, such a hymn was closely connected with wisdom.

With regard to the question of authorship, Colossians is likely to have been written by someone other than Paul himself, a conclusion based on substantial differences in style and theology evident to scholars across a theological spectrum. Nevertheless, the world we encounter in the letter itself is Pauline. Whether the actual author was Timothy, who is named as co-sender; Epaphras, the founder of the community of believers at Colossae (1:7, 4:12-13); or another unknown follower of Paul, the letter foregrounds Paul's authorial presence and so we will refer to the author as "Paul."

The first thing to notice about this hymn is its focus on "all things," *ta panta*. All things are named twice in verse 16, twice in verse 17, and once in verse 20, and other forms of "all" appear in verses 15, 18, and 19. That makes eight times in this one passage! The whole of reality—the whole of the cosmos—is in view here, both visible and invisible. As such, this passage affirms and celebrates a holistic vision of the connection of all things to Christ and through Christ to every other part of creation.

When we think of the scope of "all things," we might begin by thinking of Earth and all living things, all the geological formations that are a record of the planet's history, the winds and ocean currents, all the stars in our galaxy—perhaps a hundred billion in number—all the other galaxies in the visible universe, and any life that may exist on distant planets. We might think of the beauty of mathematics that describes the world in its amazing complexity. We might think of art or music or the intangible reality of love. Nothing in the whole of the cosmos is outside the scope of *ta panta*.

The hymn has a logical structure. Verses 15-17 focus on Christ's connection with creation. Creation is named in verse 15, and then the verb "create" is used twice in verse 16. Verse 18a is transitional, specifying the church as a key example and locus of how all things cohere in Christ. Verses 19-20 focus on Christ's reconciliation and peacemaking through the blood of his cross. So we might set out the structure of the hymn this way:

Vv. 15-17 Creation	Christ as God's image; "firstborn" of all creation: the source and goal of creation, preeminent and the means of coherence of all things.
V. 18a	The body of the church also expresses Christ's preeminence.
Vv. 18b-20 Reconciliation (new creation)	Christ as the origin, "firstborn" from the dead: revealing his preeminence, the whole fullness (of God), reconciling all things, having made peace through the blood of his cross.

This hymn is immensely Christocentric. The invisible God is named in verse 15, and the reference in verse 19 to the whole "fullness" refers to God; yet each affirmation focuses on the centrality of Christ as the key to the cosmos. Elsewhere in Colossians, "Paul" writes of Christ as God's mystery (2:2), and of Christ among you (or in you) as the rich and glorious mystery that God has revealed among the nations (1:26-27). It would be insufficient to see these lines as references to salvation alone. Christ permeates creation, gives it coherence, in addition to being the means of reconciliation.

Both parts of the hymn refer to Christ as "firstborn" (*prototokos*). A study of this word suggests that the sense of being set apart for God's purposes (Exod. 13:2) is prominent, more so than chronology or birthing. In Psalm 89:27 (LXX 88:28), David is appointed firstborn (although he is not literally firstborn) as a way of naming his preeminence. Christ is firstborn of all creation, which affirms both his connection with creation and his preeminence over it. Christ is also firstborn from the dead, which connects him across time and space with all who have participated in life, whether they were human or whether they were creatures now extinct. In the mystery of Christ, all things are present to God.

A striking feature of this hymn is the use of prepositions to articulate the mystery of Christ: *in* him all things were created (v. 16); *through* him and *for* him all things have been created (v. 16); he is *before* all things (v. 17); *in* him all things hold *together* (v. 17); *in* him the whole fullness was pleased to dwell (v. 19); and *through* him and *to* him (v. 20) all things are reconciled. Here we have a "prepositional metaphysics" showing just how connected Christ is with all things. A theology of "heavenism," a view that this world serves only as a staging post on the journey to the next, is simply not able to be true to the breadth and depth of Christ expressed in this hymn. While the Christology that we find expressed here is one of the highest in all the Scriptures, it does not push us into dualistic thinking, a perspective that separates Christ from creation. Wisdom is found in recognizing that in Christ, matter and spirit, creation and new creation, present and future, visible and invisible cohere; *all things* are precious to God and *all things* can reveal the grace that comes to us in Christ's death, offering us life.

Gospel
JOHN 6:41-51

This passage evokes the formative experience of God's care in the wilderness during the exodus. The exodus was central to the identity of the Hebrew people and to their relationship with God. And at this point in John's Gospel, we are prompted to recall that key event and see what parallels might be at work. The link is made explicit in various ways, first by the word used in verses 41 and 43 for complaining or murmuring: *goggidso*. It is a very evocative, even onomatopoeic word in Greek, referring to and making a throaty, grumbling sound. It is what the Hebrew people did in the wilderness (LXX; Exod. 15:24, 16:2, 7, 12), and it showed their inability to trust in what God was teaching them. The same reluctance is evoked here by the use of this word. Second, the reference in verse 41 to the bread from heaven makes the connection between this event and the exodus event more explicit (cf. Exod. 16:4; Ps. 78:24, 105:40). And in verse 49, Jesus names the connection explicitly.

It is clear that another formative experience of God's care is unfolding here. Jesus is offering "manna" that is more than the miraculous sustenance of old. The life and death that is at stake here is not just survival in the wilderness, wonderful though that was. The life offered here is participation in the life of God. The one who offers this life is also the one who embodies it. There is no dualism between spirit and flesh in the person of Jesus.

Jesus speaks as incarnate, embodied, enfleshed Wisdom here—the one who comes from God, seeking a home and looking for a welcome among those who are God's people (cf. John 1:10-11), and offering life-giving sustenance (cf. Sir. 24:19-22). In order to recognize this moment as a moment of divine visitation, however, the people have to be attuned and open to hearing the resonances of God. They have to risk receiving the grace being offered.

The central image of John 6 is bread. The chapter begins with the concrete action of feeding five thousand people and moves into a discourse that becomes increasingly symbolic of the life-giving sustenance that the relationship with the Giver offers to the cosmos. It remains true that the insight required to perceive the symbolic truth of the feeding is an insight that is given by God alone. It is a fact that you do not learn by experience; you learn by *reflecting* on experience. It is God who teaches us to perceive God at work (John 6:44-45). The passage challenges us to learn new ways of perceiving, so that we move beyond thinking that our way of being and thinking is the only way. The word for "teach" is also the word for "disciple"; this reminds us that discipleship is a matter of learning to see the cosmos as God sees it.

If we do not find this passage difficult to grasp, perhaps we are missing something. Just as the original murmurers in the wilderness found it difficult to move beyond the categories shaped and imprinted by their life in Egypt, we, too, carry with us the impulse, shaped by our own cultural context, to pare God's revelation back to what may be comfortable for us to receive. So it is convenient to explain this passage simply as a reference to eating the sacrament of Christ's body and blood with reverence and thanksgiving. Or we might take it primarily as a promise of life after death. But there is more to it than that.

In the background reflection, we noted that the impulse to life is evident in the cosmos and that it is at the edge of chaos, moving beyond the rigidity of the known, that we find this life. In this passage of John, eternal life is in view. We know that eternal life is not simply a future promise; life in God is available to us now (v. 47). Perhaps we need to expand our understanding of eternal life even further. This may be possible if we look carefully at John 6:51c: ". . . the bread that I will give for [*hyper*] the life of the world is my flesh."

The term *hyper* in that verse means "on behalf of" and "for the sake of." This verse invites us to recall a parallel verse, namely, our earliest account of the eucharistic words in 1 Corinthians 11:23-26. There we learn that Jesus took, blessed, and broke the bread; in that symbolic action, Jesus named the bread his body (*soma*) "for your sake." In John 6:51, the verb is future, and invites us to see the giving as the giving that will be effected on the cross. In John, Jesus' immediate actions do not demonstrate the breaking; nevertheless, the breaking of his body is implicit in the verb, as set out below. If Jesus' death on the cross is in view in both passages, as I think it is, Jesus is stating in this passage in John that his death is for the life not just of those disciples present or for those disciples who will come afterward but also for the life of the cosmos.

1 Corinthians 11:24 b, c	John 6:51c
"This is my body that is for [*hyper*] you. Do this in remembrance of me."	". . . the bread that I will give for [*hyper*] the life of the world [*kosmos*] is my flesh."

The life of the cosmos, the orderly, beautiful creation, is the object of the gracious gift of Christ's flesh. This comparison also shows us something very close to what is being said in Colossians 1:20: "all things, whether on earth or in heaven," are touched by the reconciliation and peace that Jesus makes through the blood of his cross.

Reflections

We humans are an important subset of the cosmos, but we are not the ultimate recipients or the end point of that grace. We are those who have the privilege and responsibility to recognize and receive the grace of God offered to the cosmos. And in doing so, we also have the privilege and responsibility to embody and pass on this grace to the rest of Earth community.

In the gracious paradox of the incarnation, Jesus changed the way of God's being eternally. Jesus shared our material being, by becoming flesh, so that the material reality, God's creation, could share God's being. And, as Paul asserts, "the whole creation has been groaning" (Rom. 8:22), thirsting for the promised re-creation that the incarnation assures. We are not only Earth dust, stardust, cosmic dust; we are now God dust. As such, we are capable of delighting in, exuberantly enjoying, each other and every other way of being. Sharing God's being, Wisdom's way of being, we, too, have the God-given capacity to be "a source of [God's] delight every day." We can "rejoice" in Earth's fullness, in every created aspect of God's creation. We can delight exuberantly in Earth and cosmos—everything in God's presence.

RESOURCES

Balabanski, Vicky S. "Critiquing Anthropocentric Cosmology: Retrieving a Stoic 'Permeation Cosmology' in Colossians 1:15-20," in *Exploring Ecological Hermeneutics*, ed. Norman C. Habel and Peter Trudinger, 151–59. SBL Symposium Series 46. Atlanta: Society of Biblical Literature, 2008.

———. "Hellenistic Cosmology and the Letter to the Colossians: Towards an Ecological Hermeneutic," in *Ecological Hermeneutics: Biblical, Historical, and Theological Perspectives*, ed. David G. Horrell, Cherryl Hunt, Christopher Southgate, and Francesca Stavrakopoulou, 94–107. New York: Continuum, 2010.

Edwards, Denis. *Ecology at the Heart of Faith: The Change of Heart That Leads to a New Way of Living on Earth*. Maryknoll, N.Y.: Orbis, 2006.

———. *How God Acts: Creation, Redemption, and Special Divine Action*. Theology and the Sciences. Minneapolis: Fortress Press, 2010.

Horrell, David G. "A New Perspective on Paul? Rereading Paul in a Time of Ecological Crisis." *Journal for the Study of the New Testament* 33 (2010): 3–30.

Turner, Marie. *God's Wisdom or the Devil's Envy: Death and Creation Deconstructing in the Wisdom of Solomon*. Adelaide: ATF, 2009.

NOTES

1 When Wisdom in capitalized, it refers to the personified figure of wisdom in the Hebrew Scriptures, depicted as Woman Wisdom.

2. Translations in this section on Proverbs 8 come predominantly from the *Jewish Study Bible* (JSB) (New York: Oxford University Press, 2004). The JSB translation is "course"; other translations use "way" (e.g., KJV, NAS, ERV, NKJV).

3. NRSV; some translations use the plural "works" (e.g., NIV, NJB, NET, JSB, NKJV).

4. Hebrew *qanah* means "created" or "acquired;" "acquired" includes creation as a means of acquiring something (JSB, 1461).

5. "Deep" is the primordial sea in the Israelite worldview; see JSB, 1461.

6. See "Physicist Finds Out Why 'We Are Stardust," *Science Daily* (1999) http://www
.sciencedaily.com/releases/1999/06/990625080416.htm (accessed March 7, 2011).

7. JSB, 1445, notes that God's name is God's essence.

Blessing the Animals
A Sermon
David Rhoads

And God said, "Let the waters bring forth swarms of living creatures, and let birds fly above the earth across the dome of the sky." So God created the great sea monsters and every living creature that moves, of every kind, with which the waters swarm and every winged bird of every kind. And God saw that it was good. And God blessed them, saying, "Be fruitful and multiply and fill the waters in the sea, and let birds multiply on the earth. . . ." And God said, "Let the earth bring forth creatures of every kind: cattle and creeping things and wild animals of the earth of every kind." And it was so. God made the wild animals of the earth of every kind, and the cattle of every kind and everything that creeps upon the ground of every kind. And God saw that it was good. (Gen. 1:20-22, 24-25)

And Jesus said to them, "Go into all the world, and proclaim the good news to the whole creation." (Mark 16:15, from the longer ending)

Through him [Jesus] God was pleased to reconcile to himself all things, whether on earth or in heaven, by making peace through the blood of his cross. (Col. 1:20)

First, I want to address you varieties of dogs and cats and other creatures who are here today. And I want to speak with you fish and ferrets and hamsters and parakeets and snakes brought here today by your human companions. You are here for your own sake, and you also represent all those who are not here today, animals of every kind—cattle and goats and horses and elephants and bees and cougars and crocodiles and puffer fish and eels and insects—so many we cannot begin to name them all.

I want to announce the good news to all you creatures. I want you to know that God loves you. God loves you for your own sake—and not because of what you can do for humans.

You are good in yourselves. The Good Book tells us that when God created you—fish of the sea and birds of the air and creatures of the land—God looked at all God had created, and God saw that "Indeed, it was very good!" (Gen. 1:12, 18, 21, 25, 31).

When God created you, God blessed you. God told you to "Be fruitful and multiply and fill the waters of the seas, and let birds multiply on the earth" (Gen. 1:28). God created you in huge swarms and in great diversity. God wants all of you to survive and to thrive on the Earth.

God created the world for you, so that you have what you need to live. The psalmist tells us that God made the rain to water the trees, the trees for you birds to nest, the grass for you cattle to graze, and the crags as a refuge for you mountain goats (Ps. 104:14-24). God wants you to receive your "food in due season" and to be "filled with good things" (Ps. 104:27-28).

The Bible tells us that when the flood came, God rescued each of your species through Noah in the ark. And God made a covenant with you fish of the sea and birds of the air and domestic animals and all animals on Earth to protect you for the future (Gen. 9:8-17). God made the first "endangered species act."

Just like us, you are called to worship God. The hills are to clap their hands. The fields are to exalt (Psalm 148). You cattle and dogs and cats are to praise God by being who you are and exalting in it. John the seer had a vision in which he heard the entire creation—everything in heaven, on the earth, under the earth, and in the sea—cry out in praise: "Blessing and honor, glory and might, be to the one who sits upon the throne and to the Lamb forever and ever" (Rev. 5:13; my trans.).

We human animals need to confess to you that we have systematically mistreated you, depleted your numbers, destroyed you, slaughtered you, crowded you out, neglected you, treated you as commodities in our quest for comfort and ease. We have not seen you as God's creatures. We have not shown proper reverence or respect. Against God's will, we have not set limits upon ourselves so that you might live and thrive. What we have done! We are sorry!

You who are here today are so fortunate because you have human companions who care for you. But so many of your cousins are threatened with extinction—snow leopards and timber wolves and green sea turtles and condors and paddlefish and fin whales, among so many others.

We humans may so crowd out or deplete these kin of yours such that not a single one of them will ever again exist on Earth.

When we destroy you and diminish you in these ways, we not only compromise your ability to survive, we also stifle your capacity to praise God. Along with all creation, you are groaning in labor pains, waiting for the revelation of children of God who will care for creation and make provisions for you to thrive (Rom. 8:19-23).

Now I want to address you human creatures. I want to announce the good news to you also. God loves you. God loves you for your own sake and wants you to thrive. When God made you, God saw that this, too, was good.

God said also to you: "Be fruitful and multiply and fill the Earth" (Gen. 1:28). Yet we have already done this! So we need to find ways to limit the impact of our species, because God did not mean for us to crowd out the rights of other creatures to be fruitful and multiply also. In developed countries, we have become like an infestation—taking over land and destroying habitats and devouring species and infiltrating homes and migratory routes of so many other animals—and we need to learn our limits and exercise restraint.

God even created us humans with a special responsibility—to exercise dominion (Gen. 1:28). This does not mean that we are to exercise domination over other creatures or to exploit them for human misuse. Rather, we are to delight in other creatures, as God does, and respect and care for them. Our love for creation is the only basis for our right use of creation. We are to exercise dominion as servants of creation. As Jesus has said, we are not to lord over anyone, but be as slaves to all (Mark 10:42-45). We are to take responsibility for all creatures, to serve their needs, and to work to preserve them (Gen. 2:15).

And we are to do this not with a sense of superiority but in solidarity with all other creatures. We were created to be together, to be companions to one another, to thrive all together. All animals are our cousins, our kin. And God made a covenant with us and with all other animals together. Admit it, we humans are also animals, primate mammals.

And Jesus was a mammal. Jesus was born and lived in solidarity with all of life. Jesus lived to care about all who were oppressed and made vulnerable and marginalized by society; and right now that includes most creatures, not just humans. Jesus died in order that God might reconcile to God's self *all things* in creation (Col. 1:20).

In response to God's love, we are freed to behave in ways that enable all of life to thrive together. We do not need to prove anything. We can set limits on ourselves. We can simplify our lifestyles so that others may survive and thrive. We can become aware of our actions toward other creatures and curtail our activity. We can act to establish safe homes and habitats for those animals that are endangered.

Now I want to address all of you creatures together. I had this vision in a dream while I was sleeping one night. I was in the front row of a cathedral looking at the scene before me during a service of communion. I saw the priest passing bread to the first person kneeling at the communion railing. As I looked, the next figure at the railing was a snake! It was curled at the bottom with its back arching up over the rail and with head straining forward to receive the grace of Christ. The next figure was another person. Next was a raccoon with paws up on the communion rail leaning forward to receive the grace of Christ. Then I saw a bird perched on the corner of the railing eating bread crumbs.

As I finished surveying this scene in my dream, suddenly the side walls of the cathedral fell away and outside was thick foliage of forest and jungle on each side, with all manner of wild animals roaming around. In this moment, it seemed as if the walls of separation had been removed and there was a seamless web of all creation praising God and exalting in the grace of Christ.

From the time I awoke from that dream until this day, I have never been able to think of worship in the same way again. I see all of Earth as the sanctuary in which we worship, and I see myself invoking and confessing and giving thanks and praising God and offering myself in solidarity with *all of life*. May that vision also be our common vision.

You who are here today are very fortunate because you have a relationship of love and care and loyalty between yourself and your human or your pet companion. You model how all relationships between humans and other animals should be. We wish to project this relationship as the model for our relationship with all animals. May we care about all animals as we care for our companions at home.

I invite you to come forward for a blessing. Sometimes when we have a service for the Blessing of the Animals, we bless only the nonhuman animals, as if we ourselves are not also animals. Therefore, as an expression of solidarity with each other, I invite all of you—nonhuman animals and human animals alike—to come for a blessing. We will bless you as companions together and we will bless your relationship:

"May God bless each of you with health and safety and well-being and long life. And may God bless your relationship together so that it may be filled with love and joy."

For services of the "Blessing of Animals," visit *Season of Creation*, http://www.seasonofcreation. com, and the worship section at *Web of Creation*, http://www.webofcreation.org (accessed February 2011).

Contributors

Norman C. Habel is professorial fellow at Flinders University, Adelaide, Australia. Since 1996 he has been actively involved in developing materials linking faith and ecology. Together with the Uniting Church of Australia he initiated The Season of Creation. He also initiated The Earth Bible series and its forthcoming sequel, The Earth Bible Commentary. His other related publications include *Seven Songs of Creation* (2004), *Exploring Ecological Hermeneutics* (2008, with Peter Trudinger) and *An Inconvenient Text* (2009). A pastor in the Lutheran Church, he is actively involved in promoting worship with creation in a wide range of denominations across Australia and beyond, as well as mission to Earth as a part of the church's ministry.

David Rhoads is emeritus professor of New Testament at the Lutheran School of Theology at Chicago. He has published books and articles on many areas of New Testament study. In environmental studies, he edited and contributed to *Earth and Word: Classic Sermons on Saving the Planet* (2007) and has written two articles: "Who Will Speak for the Sparrow? Reading the New Testament in an Environmental Age," and "A Beloved Earth Community: Christian Mission in an Ecological Age" (with Barbara Rossing). He is director of the Green Congregation Program and author of *The Green Congregation Training Manual* (2011 edition). He supervises three Web sites that provide ecological resources for faith communities: http://www.webofcreation.org; http://www.lutheransrestoringcreation.org; and http://www.racinegreencongregations.org.

H. Paul Santmire has been a founder and leading voice of ecological theology for more than forty-five years. His 1966 Harvard doctoral dissertation explored Karl Barth's theology of creation. He is the author of *Brother Earth: Nature, God, and Ecology in a Time of Crisis* (1970), *The Travail of Nature: The Ambiguous Ecological Promise of Christian Theology* (1985), *Nature Reborn: The Ecological and Cosmic Promise of Christian Theology* (2000), and *Ritualizing Nature: Renewing Christian Liturgy in a Time of Crisis* (2008). He is now working on a new book, *Blessedly Obsessed with Nature: A Christian Spirituality*. A retired pastor of the Evangelical Lutheran Church in America, he now lives and writes in the Boston area.

Vicky Balabanski is senior lecturer in New Testament at Flinders University, South Australia, at the Adelaide College of Divinity, and at the Uniting College of Leadership and Theology. She is a writer and editor in the international Earth Bible Project, and is now working on an ecological commentary on Colossians.

Dianne Bergant, CSA, is professor of biblical studies at Catholic Theological Union in Chicago. Her many publications include *Preaching the New Lectionary*, vols. A, B, & C (Liturgical), and *A Word for Every Season,* Years A, B & C (Paulist). She is presently working in the areas of biblical interpretation and biblical theology, particularly issues of peace, ecology, and feminism.

Jione Havea, a native of Tonga, in the South Seas, is currently senior lecturer in biblical studies at United Theological College and School of Theology, Charles Stuart University, Australia. Ordained in the Methodist Church of Tonga, he has published "The Politics of Climate Change, a *Talanoa* from Oceania" in *International Journal of Public Theology* (2010).

Theodore Hiebert is Francis A. McGaw Professor of Old Testament at McCormick Theological Seminary in Chicago. He is author of *The Yahwist's Landscape: Nature and Religion in Early Israel* (1996). A member of the Mennonite Church, he has been a director of the Chicago Theological Initiative in Eco-Justice Ministry.

Monica Jyotsna Melanchthon teaches Old Testament/Hebrew Bible at the Gurukul Lutheran Theological College, Chennai, India. She is the secretary of the Society of Asian Biblical Studies and co-edits *International Voices in Biblical Studies*, an online open-access series of the Society of Biblical Literature.

Susan Miller teaches New Testament Studies in the Centre for Lifelong Learning at the University of Aberdeen. She is author of "The Descent of Darkness over the Land: Listening to the Voice of Earth in Mark 15:33," in *Exploring Ecological Hermeneutics* (2008), *Women in Mark's Gospel* (2004), and is currently writing *Women in the Fourth Gospel*.

Ched Myers is an activist theologian and cofounder of the Sabbath Economics Collaborative (http://www.sabbatheconomics.org), and of Bartimaeus Cooperative Ministries (www.bcm-net.org). His most recent book is *Ambassadors of Reconciliation: A New Testament Theology: Diverse Christian Practices of Restorative Justice and Peacemaking* (with Elaine Enns, 2009).

Barbara R. Rossing is professor of New Testament at the Lutheran School of Theology at Chicago, where she also directs the Environmental Ministry Emphasis. She is author of *The Rapture Exposed: The Message of Hope in the Book of Revelation* (2004) and of numerous book chapters, sermons, and articles on the Bible and ecology.

Alice M. Sinnott hails from Ireland and has lived in New Zealand for several years. She lectured in biblical studies at the University of Auckland (1990–2009) and is based at the Catholic Institute of Theology in Auckland. Her publications include *The Personification of Wisdom* (2005) and numerous articles in journals and books dealing with care for creation and the Bible.

Gerald West is professor of Old Testament and biblical hermeneutics and director of the Ujamaa Centre in the School of Religion and Theology at the University of KwaZulu-Natal, South Africa. He has published extensively on African biblical hermeneutics as it has grappled with a range of contextual features, including land issues and the environment.

Shirley Joh Wurst is senior lecturer in the School of Humanities at the Tabor Adelaide Christian Education Centre in South Australia.